Piers
Courage

Piers Courage

LAST OF THE GENTLEMAN RACERS

ADAM COOPER Foreword by SIR FRANK WILLIAMS

DEDICATION
For Tinneke

First published in July 2003

A catalogue record for this book is available from the British Library

ISBN 1 85960 663 6

Library of Congress catalog card no 99-80192

Haynes North America Inc.,
861 Lawrence Drive, Newbury Park,
California 91320, USA.

Published by Haynes Publishing, Sparkford,
Yeovil, Somerset BA22 7JJ, UK.
Tel: 01963 442030 Fax: 01963 440001
Int. tel: +44 1963 442030 Int. fax: +44 1963 440001
E-mail: sales@haynes-manuals.co.uk
Website: www.haynes.co.uk

Styling: Simon Larkin. Page-build: James Robertson

Printed and bound in Great Britain
by J. H. Haynes & Co. Ltd, Sparkford

CONTENTS

ACKNOWLEDGEMENTS

This book would not have been possible without the support and help of Piers Courage's friends and family, many of whom have gone out of their way to provide me with assistance.

It goes without saying that I owe a huge debt to Lady Sarah Aspinall, the former Sally Courage, who not only shared her memories of life with Piers, but also allowed a complete stranger to borrow her collection of irreplaceable scrapbooks and other memorabilia. And hang on to it for rather longer than she probably envisaged!

Her son Jason Courage has been an enthusiastic supporter from the very start, and kept faith in me when other commitments made my progress slow. Although I didn't make contact with Amos Courage until fairly late in the day, he too has been very supportive. Piers's brothers Charlie and Andrew provided priceless insight into their family background, and consistent encouragement.

Piers's closest friends are the real backbone of the story. I would like to thank Charles Lucas, Jonathan Williams, Sheridan Thynne and Bubbles Horsley, all of whom put up with endless phone calls and questions about obscure events that happened more than four decades ago. They also found the time to read and offer advice on the final manuscript. I wasn't brave enough to bother Sir Frank Williams on such a regular basis, but he invited me to his house so that we could talk about Piers away from the hustle and bustle of a Grand Prix meeting. I'm also extremely grateful that he agreed to contribute the Foreword. Roy Pike was perhaps not a full-time member of the 'inner circle,' but he was close to the action and his detailed recollections have been extremely useful.

Sadly, I had only one lengthy telephone conversation with Charlie Crichton-Stuart, for he died before I got to the stage of checking facts and filling in gaps in the narrative. I'm sure he would figure even more prominently if I had been able to speak to him again, but I'm grateful for the input he gave me. At this point I would also like to acknowledge two other people who are no longer with us, Roy 'Tom the Weld' Thomas and Barrie Gill, for their help in the early stages of my research.

I would like to thank the following, who shared their memories of Piers or otherwise helped me with the story: Chris Amon, Arabella Amory (formerly von Westenholz), Richard Attwood, Jean-Pierre and Jacqueline Beltoise, Herbie Blash, Sir Jack Brabham, John Cardwell, Stan Collier, John Coombs, Pierluigi Corbari, Hermione Courage, Monny Curzon, Andrea de Adamich, Justin de Villeneuve, Gianpaulo Dallara, Chris Davis, Sylvia Davis, Frances Denman, Bernie Ecclestone, John Fowler, Howden Ganley, Frank Gardner, Peter Gethin, Selwyn Hayward, Robin Herd, Toine Hezemans, Bette Hill, Roger Hill, Loti Irwin, Roland Law, Joanna Lumley, Andrew Marriott, Pat McLaren, Paddy McNally, John Miles, Max Mosley, John Muller, Doug Nye, Tim O'Rorke, Jackie Oliver, Steve Ouvaroff, Tim Parnell, Rob Petersen, John Peterson, John Pettit, Heinz Pruller, Brian Redman, John Rhodes, Tony Rudd, Martin Ryan, Les Sheppard, Louis T Stanley, Jackie and Helen Stewart, Ed and Sally Swart, Peggy Taylor, Dewar Thomas, Diana Thomas, John Thompson, Daphne Thorne, David Wansbrough and Eoin Young. I must save a special mention for Nina Rindt, who gave me some very personal insights into life with Jochen in the months after Piers's death.

In 1970 Piers was working on an autobiography, and at the time of his death he had taken the story up to March 1968. Co-author Patrick Macnaghten filled in the rest, and after some debate with the family, a book was published privately by Mrs Jean Courage, in an edition of only 100 copies. The story has a somewhat jumbled chronology, and many details are hazy, but it has been an invaluable source of anecdotes. Unless otherwise credited, all Piers's quotes have come from this book. Others have been taken from surviving letters to his parents, and interviews conducted by Peter Garnier, Richard Garrett, Barrie Gill, Anthony Marsh and Eoin Young. A bibliography is contained elsewhere.

A large number of the illustrations and documents have been loaned by Lady Sarah Aspinall and Jason Courage. Charlie Courage, Charles Lucas, Roy Pike, Jonathan Williams and Les Sheppard also raided their personal collections. The majority of the rest, including the fabulous front cover shot, are courtesy of LAT, owners of the archives of *Autosport*, *Autocar*, *Motor*, *Motor Sport* and *Motoring News*. I would like to thank Peter Higham and Kevin Wood for their assistance and allowing me to trawl through the LAT files. Other pictures have been kindly provided by Michael Cooper, Nick Loudon, United Photos de Boer and the BARC. I would also like to thank Patrick Lichfield for allowing me to use some of his work, and for providing a new print of a superb and previously unpublished picture of the family.

Courage Breweries archivist Ken Thomas provided valuable assistance, as did the Eton College Library. Duncan Rabagliati and Paul Sheldon of the Formula One Register helped me to clarify some of the more obscure F3 statistics. I must acknowledge *Autosport* as the key source of information on Piers's racing career. It was and continues to be the definitive weekly record of the sport at all levels, while *Motor Sport* was also very useful.

Finally I would like to thank all at Haynes Publishing for their patience and faith in a project that turned out to be a late developer, especially Mark Hughes, Flora Myer, Darryl Reach, Patrick Stephens and James Robertson. I hope it was worth the wait.

A signed picture of Piers at the wheel of the BRM P126 in 1968.

FOREWORD
Sir Frank Williams

Piers Courage lived in an era which does not exist today. I only knew him in the adult years of his life but was instantly bowled over by his youthful spirit, energy and charm. Furthermore, coming from a more humble background than his, I was fascinated by his mannerisms, his outlook on the world around him and the way in which he dealt with the routines of daily life.

To me as an aspiring young racing driver, I could well identify with Piers in his quest for success and fame in Formula 1. The mountain seemed to be unscaleable, but Piers set off with admirable self-confidence. In truth, to the best of my knowledge he received only modest support of a financial nature, despite his formidable family background. He achieved much success, fought his way into Formula 1 and stayed there until his untimely and most regrettable death. How he did it is well documented later in this book, but I also recommend the account therein as a peep back into how an interesting individual from the young England of that time spoke, thought, socialised, raced and lived.

The Williams organisation shows its stuff at a chilly Goodwood in November 1968. Piers sits in the newly completed Tasman BT24W while Frank poses with F2, F3 and FF1600 machinery. And answers his driver's request for a better retainer…

Allowing myself the fewest words possible to explain how I saw Piers, I say that he had a sense of style and humour that I no longer see around me today. It seemed almost everything had an amusing side, and when it inevitably did not, he created one. He did this with unique charm, choice of words and selection of phrase that died with him.

His racing exploits may not be well-known now, but are well catalogued here. In my opinion he was about to step into the ranks of the truly great drivers and was certainly one of the best British Formula 1 drivers with whom I have been involved. Indeed, of all the drivers who have driven for me throughout the various times of my private Formula 1 career, and more recently during my successful association with Patrick Head, he was as gifted with as much car control as anyone I've seen – except perhaps Jochen Rindt!

He was an adoring husband and doting father. I have often thought that his death robbed him of one of life's greatest gifts: his family. He had so little time in which to enjoy them.

He was a great man, highly popular, and I remember clearly that when he died a nation grieved, as did all of us in Formula 1 at that time.

Grove, Oxfordshire, May 2003

INTRODUCTION

I was only five years old when Piers Courage died at Zandvoort and grew up with the generation who supported James Hunt. Thus the seventies is 'my' time as far as motor racing is concerned. When in 1999 *Motor Sport* magazine asked me to write a feature about Piers, I knew relatively little about the man, apart from the bare details of his Grand Prix career. That made finding out about him even more of a challenge.

I spoke to a couple of his friends and tracked down his brothers Charlie and Andrew. I soon learned that there was much more to Piers than the statistics that showed he started 28 Grands Prix and finished second in two of them. Those who knew him began to paint an intriguing picture and made me want to know more about the man.

When Piers's son Jason told me that both he and his mother Sally had enjoyed my *Motor Sport* story, the concept of this book began to take shape. The first time I went to meet Sally in London, I sat on a bench at the local railway station. Directly opposite me was a poster advertising Courage beer. I took that as a sign…

The project took on another dimension when Sally made available a cache of memorabilia that had been sitting in boxes on top of a wardrobe. It included

documents that literally spanned Piers's life, from a colourful embossed baptism certificate dated 1942, to a solemn typed document issued by the coroner of the city of Zandvoort 28 years later. The collection included all his school reports from the age of six to eighteen, bills for tuition fees and equipment, and dozens of letters that Piers wrote to his parents, charting his youthful development almost on a weekly basis.

That same day I also came across several scrapbooks that had been in Jason's custody and that Piers had himself put together early in his racing career. There were shots that would have been impossible to find elsewhere, captioned in his own words. With this material, and the input of those who knew him, I felt I could really do justice to his story.

But why write a book about a man who didn't actually win a Grand Prix, when there are drivers with far better records whose careers have gone unrecorded?

Firstly, he lived through an interesting era. The years 1962–70 have a special significance to many folk, for they represent the duration of the official recording

Left Frank Williams with Piers in the paddock at Spa in 1970.

Below V for victory? Jonathan Williams, Charlie Crichton-Stuart, Charles Lucas, Frank Williams and Piers Courage preparing for a race at Brands Hatch circa 1963.

career of The Beatles. By coincidence, those dates also bookend Piers's career.

As he made his first tentative steps in a Lotus Seven in early 1962, with little clue as to what he was doing, a provincial record shop manager called Brian Epstein was hustling his unknown group around the London recording companies. Some eight years later, in April 1970, it was announced by Paul McCartney that The Beatles were breaking up. Just a couple of months after that, with the group's epitaph *Let It Be* topping charts around the world, Piers was killed at Zandvoort.

Over those eight years, the world changed. Popular music developed beyond recognition from the innocent mop top era of *Love Me Do*, and the sport of motor racing changed almost as rapidly. When Piers started out, it was still very much the era of British racing green and pale blue Dunlop overalls. He saw the dawn of big wings, big tyres, and big commercial sponsorship. In other words, the start of Grand Prix racing as we still know it today.

Secondly, this is as much a story of lost potential as success achieved. At the time of his death the sport was dominated by his friends Jackie Stewart and Jochen Rindt. Piers was one of perhaps two or three drivers they truly

Below Piers stands in front of the family Land Rover on a holiday in France in the summer of 1959, as brother Charlie stokes the campfire. Youngest sibling Andrew is in the background.

Opposite Piers, Jackie Stewart and Jochen Rindt were close friends off the track.

respected, and who in effect led the pursuit. He never drove a competitive works Grand Prix car, but his performances on the more level playing field of Formula 2, where he ran with the best, are testimony to his pure speed.

"He wasn't as good as Jackie or Jochen and that was going to be a problem," says Sir Frank Williams. "But he would have been as good, or was as good as anybody else. He was acquiring more maturity, and he was becoming a top driver in his day."

Most observers still rank Stewart in the top half dozen of all time, and while Rindt is often overlooked in such polls of all-round achievement, contemporaries swear that he was the fastest driver they ever saw. That says a great deal about how good Piers Courage was by 1970.

Sadly, the statistics don't really reflect what might have been. But what could Piers have achieved had he not perished at Zandvoort? It's difficult to make such a judgement of a man who in most people's minds is forever trapped in the monochrome sixties. Although he was in some ways out of his time – he could have fitted in well a decade or three earlier – Piers himself was by no means rooted in the past, as his pioneering Carnaby Street fashion sense showed.

Had he lived, he could have raced well into the seventies and would have adapted to the changing motorsport culture with ease. Don't forget that he was actually six weeks younger than his 1968 Temporada F2 team-mate

Carlos Reutemann who competed at the top level until 1982, and two years younger than Mario Andretti, who was still trying to win the Le Mans 24 Hours in 2000, and even practised at Indianapolis in 2003.

At the start of 1974, the first season after Stewart's retirement, Piers would have been only 31 and, arguably, at the peak of his game. If things hadn't worked out with Frank Williams, perhaps he would have finally agreed terms with Colin Chapman or Enzo Ferrari, both of whom had previously offered him drives. In the right environment he would surely have been a World Championship contender. As Frank suggests in Chapter 12, he could also have become one of Britain's premier sportsmen. He might even have caught the wave of public support that carried James Hunt to success.

Piers was a far more intriguing character than the average racing driver, thanks to his family background and a lively personality that would have stood out whatever type of life he chose. It's no coincidence that I have been able to draw upon the recollections of so many people who loved and admired him. Several count Piers – fondly nicknamed Porridge or Porge – as the best friend they ever had, and such testimony says a lot about any human being. At least two of his closest friends readily admit that a light went out in their lives on 21 June 1970. Over three decades later, his death still weighs heavily on their shoulders.

Monny Curzon, a cousin of Sally's with no motor racing connections, sums him up superbly: "Piers did have a magical quality, be it part charm, part the nature of his spirit, that made his loss deeply and lastingly felt. It acted as a magnet to people so that they remember the period when he was around as being, in different ways, centred on him. Perhaps it was the quality of loving life, and showing friends how to live accordingly."

A photograph from Piers's own scrapbook appears at the start of this section, and it says everything about why there's a book about Piers Courage. It shows him with four of his closest chums – Willums, Charlie Stu, Luke and Wanker Williams – at a race meeting at Brands Hatch in around 1964. In another life, two decades earlier, they could have been at Biggin Hill, awaiting the next sortie over the English Channel.

This is the story of the five guys in that picture, of the others who remained close to Piers until he died, and of Sally. Their priceless memories brought Porridge and his times to life for me, and I hope they do the same for you.

"Piers was almost like an epitome of a golden age," says Loti Irwin, the former wife of arch rival Chris Irwin. "There were wonderful people about, real characters as opposed to now, when they all seem a bit like cardboard cut-outs. They were all recognisable individuals. Piers fitted in wonderfully as the last of the gentleman racers."

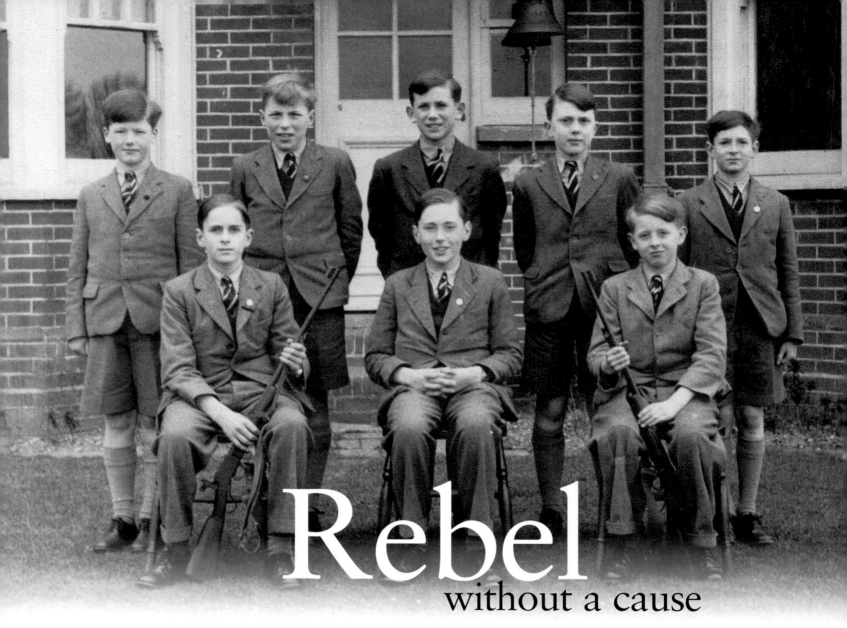

Rebel
without a cause

Lent term, 1955. Shooting was one of many pursuits that Piers (front row right) enjoyed at St Peter's School.

Richard Courage never really understood quite what his son saw in motor racing. At some point in the sixties, while standing in the hall of the family home, he actually asked Piers why he enjoyed it so much. "Well dad," he replied. "You had the war…"

When Piers decided that a life in the family business was not for him, it was no surprise that his family was a little disappointed. It is well known that his father was the chairman of Courage Brewery – this fact accompanied just about every article concerning his motor racing activities – but what perhaps isn't so widely appreciated is just how dramatic a step he took when he veered off the career path he had seemed destined to follow. Six generations of Courages had followed their fathers not only into the beer business, but eventually into the role of chairman. The succession ended with Piers.

In 1932 one G.N. Hardinge, a former Courage executive, wrote a fascinating little history of the brewery. He revealed the French origins of the family:

"After the Revocation of the Edict of Nantes in 1683 France became an uncomfortable country for Protestants, and among the 200,000 who preferred to place a distance between themselves and Louis the Fourteenth were members of a family named Courage."

They ended up in Northern Scotland, and there's evidence in a 1696 poll book of the taxes paid by a John Courage. During the 18th century the family became well established in Aberdeen, although bad luck was something of a trademark: "Violent deaths were the notable fate of one branch of the family," wrote Hardinge. "A member of this branch was drowned in a well in Aberdeen, which is known as Courage's well. Others were drowned at sea, were blown up, or disappeared in foreign countries… These early Courages appear to have been men and women of ability and character and, like other persevering and vigorous families, did things which bordered on the eccentric."

The man who established the business that made the family famous across the nation was John Courage, the great-nephew of the John Courage mentioned above. He married a Harriot Stewart, and came to London from Aberdeen in 1780, working initially as a shipping agent. It's thought that his interest in brewing developed as a result of his Thameside activities, and in 1787 he bought an established 'berehouse' for the princely sum of £615 13s 11d. It was located opposite the Tower of London in Horseleydown; indeed today the southern approach road to Tower Bridge goes right through the original Courage site.

The founder didn't have much time to enjoy the fruits of his labours, as Hardinge noted: "John Courage the first did not live long to develop his new business. He must have had a stout heart in the metaphorical, but not in the physical sense, for in the excitement following an Election in 1793, being an ardent Reformer, he died suddenly – a man in the prime of life."

His only son, yet another John, was only three at the time, but he joined the firm at 14, and eventually took charge. And so it carried on, through the generations.

The 20th century line began with Raymond Courage, who was made chairman in 1904. He had six children; Audrey, Edward, Pamela, Rachel, Richard and Bridget. They grew up at Shenfield Place, the Courage family estate in Essex, and later at Edgecot in Northamptonshire.

Born in January 1915, Richard followed Edward to Eton as the first step towards the family business. However, initially it wasn't that clear cut for the younger brother; he had a passion for railways, and after leaving school undertook an engineering apprenticeship at Darlington with the LNER. He also spent some time in Rhodesia, where one of his sisters lived.

With war clouds on the horizon, Richard joined the 2nd Northamptonshire Yeomanry as a Lieutenant in 1938. In March 1941 he married Jean Elizabeth Agnes Watson, daughter of the late Sir Charles Cunningham Watson, a former secretary to the Viceroy of India. There was a nice symmetry in his choice of bride; the family tree reveals that in 1726 yet another John Courage, uncle of the brewery founder, had also married a Jean Watson. Until her father's illness led them to return to England, the 20th century Jean had enjoyed an enviable colonial lifestyle.

"I know my mother thoroughly enjoyed India," says her middle son Charlie. "They were living at a fairly high class level, let's put it that way, wined and dined by all the nabobs and maharajahs. I think life was good there."

Toddler Piers, already showing the grin that would become his trademark.

Richard and Jean's first child was born on 27 May 1942, in Colchester, and the boy was christened Piers Raymond. Jean took the name from Piers Plowman, Chaucer aside, the most celebrated author in English literature of the Middle Ages. The hostilities ensured that Richard didn't get to enjoy the boy's early years, for he was busy as a tank commander.

"He was in Canada and the States up until 1944," says Charlie: "then at something like D-Day plus six he was landed in northern France. He had a terrible time at the Falaise Gap, where God knows how many tanks got nobbled. He went on to help at Le Havre when that was relieved, and then went up into Germany. He didn't talk about it much, unless you really wound him up."

"He was the kind of person who saw it as his duty to do what he was told," says youngest son Andrew Courage. "They went into battle with these terrible Cromwell tanks, against Tigers. They were in the turret and I think the turret blew off, but he got the driver out and ran across a potato field and jumped through a hedge, followed by machine gun bullets. He got a splinter in his backside which he had to his dying day…"

This incident occurred during 'Operation Goodwood,' but there was another odd co-incidence, for injured driver John Godfrey recovered and became a successful amateur racer. "Their tank was hit on John's 21st birthday," says Doug Nye, who knew Godfrey. "Those blokes really drew the short straw. He was very badly injured, and his memory was of crawling away from the burning tank, grasping the corn stalks to drag himself along to get clear of it. He was in hospital for two years after that and married the woman who was nursing him. He then became a very successful jeweller and he owned and raced an Aston DB3S, a Ferrari Dino 196, a Testarossa and D-Type Jaguar. He always told me that his commander was Piers's pop."

Mentioned in dispatches, Richard was demobbed at the rank of Major in 1946. Any thoughts of designing trains were put aside, and he followed older brother Edward into the family firm. On 1 January 1947 he began work as manager of Courage's Windsor branch, on an initial salary of £600. In May 1948, at the age of just 33, he was appointed a director of the main company. There were two more sons; Charles Hubert was born in 1946, and Andrew John in 1949.

At six Piers was sent to the Upton School in Windsor, until in about 1950 the family moved into Fitzwalters, a much-loved house on the Shenfield estate. Life changed for Piers when in September 1950 he was dispatched to prep school. From the age of eight to 13 St Peter's in Seaford in Sussex was to be his home for some nine months of each year, broken only by holidays and the odd visit home during term time. For a lad so clearly devoted to his parents it could have been a miserable time, but luckily the Courages made a wise choice. Under benign headmaster Patrick Knox-Shaw, St Peter's was a happy place.

"It was a bloody good school," recalls Charlie, who would overlap with Piers for two terms in 1955. "It was on the Sussex coast, not far from Newhaven. It was an area where there was a mass of prep schools. I think there were eight or 10 – the next door school was just a hop over a flint wall. We were just allowed to run riot over the South Downs. It was wonderful, because there was no one about. It was a passably good academic school. Piers could never run, so he didn't have a great interest in sport. But I think he enjoyed himself."

Three weeks into his first term Knox-Shaw sent Mrs Courage an informal report on her son's progress. Although the headmaster admitted that he'd only known the boy for a short time, his initial analysis was remarkably perceptive – and in retrospect shows that at eight, Piers's personality was already fully formed:

"He has adapted himself to the ways of the school very well, considering his tender age, and I love his gay, cheerful attitude to things. He has been well taught, and I think he is probably quite intelligent, but he is not exactly a world's worker yet. He exerts himself by fits and starts and he needs periodic prods and digs to keep him up to the mark. I think it is probably true to say that he has ability and is by nature lazy – a criticism which applies to many of my friends. In English his reading is fairly good and likewise his spelling, but he has careless lapses, and can write quite neatly when he is not in a slap-dash frame of mind. He knows a little French already and is always bright and eager in form.

"I like his general attitude to school life. He is a most friendly soul, entering into everything with much zest and popular with his fellow creatures. So far he has not proved himself a nuisance in any way, but I expect he is keeping something up his sleeve for us."

Piers wrote to his parents every week, and the surviving letters paint a picture of an idyllic, Enid Blytonesque existence. While he always looked forward to his visits home, missed his brothers, and was constantly requesting sweets, he clearly had a great time. There was no shortage of things to do between the odd bout of 'flu or German measles.

Life seemed to revolve around sporting activities, with frequent matches against neighbouring schools with names like Chesterton, Holmwood, Ladycross and Kingsmead. Despite what his brother says Piers was keen on cricket, and was a good bowler. In football he certainly preferred the less strenuous role of goalkeeper, although he was small for his age and judging by the scores he reports, he doesn't appear to have been very

effective. He enjoyed rugby, but not after he was put into the scrum for the first time, and his ears took a battering. The fact that a team-mate broke an arm in that match wasn't very encouraging.

He was not too keen on boxing, but grew to like it after "I gave someone a cut lip." There was squash, tennis, swimming, cycling, shooting and, for the older boys, even billiards. Unofficial activities included roller skating, and Piers was soon beating his pals in races. He also took part in plays, caught butterflies on the downs, and even nurtured a patch of the school garden, where he grew radishes. He played with model planes, trains and boats. Cars don't seem to be much of a passion, but one November Sunday his parents paid a visit and took him to see the finish of the London to Brighton veteran car run.

Highlight of the week was the Saturday night film show. It wasn't all Lassie or Disney nature documentaries; the boys were exposed to all kinds of war movies and action adventures like *The Overlanders* and *The Way Ahead*. They even got to see the Marx Brothers. There's no doubt that Piers developed his lifelong love of the cinema and wacky humour while at St Peter's.

Knox-Shaw seems to have been a thoroughly good egg, treating his charges to ice cream on his birthday, donating his old clothes for the bonfire night guy, and even taking Piers and a small group of boys to the donkey races in Seaford – and giving them 2/- each for bets! In only one letter does Piers speak of getting into any kind trouble – on 'Buttonhole Day' he made the mistake of nicking one of Mrs Knox-Shaw's much prized daffodils...

Piers's letters very rarely stray into academic territory, but that is pretty well covered in his reports, which show that he had a way of getting the staff on his side. In his first year the maths master recorded that Piers "...has relied on a charming manner to get himself out of trouble." Two years on Knox-Shaw said: "I think he's a bit of a rascal, but I have a very warm spot for him all the same."

In his last years at St Peter's there were signs of progress, at least in English, where he hovered around the top of the class. But he continued to exasperate his maths and French masters: "He needs constant supervision and driving," wrote the latter, Mr Collins. "Otherwise he is at once playing with something, dropping something, or just gazing out of the window."

But when it really mattered, Piers knuckled down. On 20 June 1955 he took the common entrance exam, and it won him a place at Eton, where his father and many other Courages had been before. It was not as straightforward as it might seem; company records show that at the time Richard Courage earned a basic salary of £3,250, and the annual Eton fees of £360 made a big hole in whatever the taxman left him. While he would earn rather more in the future as he was promoted through the ranks, Richard certainly wasn't as wealthy as many of the fathers whose sons Piers would come across. Contemporaries included Prince Michael of Kent, future Tory MP Jonathan Aitken, and, ironically a member of the rival Whitbread family.

It was quite a step from laid-back St Peter's to Eton, with its unique uniform, endless traditions and special language (a term is known as a half, and classes are divisions). Piers at least had the advantage of knowing Windsor a little, having spent his formative years there, but at first he was a bit at sea. Although 13 and three months when he arrived, he was physically immature for his age, and stood only 4ft 10ins tall. He would soon shoot up.

Life at Eton is based on houses, and the housemaster a boy lands with at 13 will be with him for five years and inevitably have a huge impact on his life. Some can be understanding and inspirational, others less so, and most contemporaries agree that Piers was unlucky. He was allotted to Nigel Wykes, or 'NGW', a classics master who had a rather stern and straightforward approach.

"Wykes was a very unsuitable person to be Piers's housemaster," says Sheridan Thynne, who was two years ahead of Piers. "He was very mainstream, but very artistic – he embroidered some very sophisticated silk pictures. He only taught me for one half, and he was quite the wrong sort of person for me. Very old-fashioned, very harsh, and not a very inspiring person. Piers didn't come across many masters who were very good at getting things out of people who weren't very mainstream. There is a certain amount of luck in coming across the right teachers and the right people to get the best out of you. So he didn't value Eton as much as I did."

Nevertheless, like Piers's prep school headmaster Wykes soon got a firm idea of the Courage personality, as his first report made clear:

"He is an amusing companion, and despite his diminutive appearance he is well able to stand up for himself. He might easily become something of a character; at any rate he has the makings of a natural comedian. We all like him very much, though as yet we find it difficult to take him seriously!" Less pleasing for mum and dad was the notion that Piers was "...in many ways barely mature enough to deal with the problems of public school life." Not long after that report was written, much interest was aroused when a number of Courage beer barrels were delivered to NGW's house. The harmless explanation was that they had been donated for use as oversize flower pots...

Academically it was clear that Piers had a lot of catching up to do. Maths master Mr Lawrence, who'd known the Courages when they lived in Windsor, was clearly exasperated after the first term: "I have met few lower boys here with quite such a private school aptitude for covering self and neighbourhood with ink."

While his studies bumbled along, Piers soon made friends both within NGW's house and amongst the other boys he came across in lessons. He had a less active involvement in sport than at St Peter's, but he enjoyed swimming (especially after the Queen opened the impressive new outdoor baths), and mucking about in boats. He would eventually get elected to the Sailing Club.

One activity which wasn't on the official curriculum was skiffle. Thanks to Lonnie Donegan the home-made music craze swept the country during 1956, and Piers was one of hundreds of thousands of young men who got their hands on an acoustic guitar and Bert Weedon's 'teach yourself' book.

"I can remember him coming home and infuriating my father," remembers Charlie Courage. "He had just bought himself a Grundig radiogram, and this was to play Bach and Mozart. But Piers would attack it with Lonnie Donegan and goodness knows what else. My father didn't take too kindly to that..."

At 14, friends are an enormous influence on any young man. In July 1957 a Liverpudlian called Paul McCartney, just 21 days younger than Piers, ran into a fellow skiffle fan called John Lennon. Although Piers tried teaching one of his pals how to play guitar, he didn't find the same sort of musical soul mate at Eton. But his associates turned his life in another direction.

In 1970 he recalled when he first discovered motor racing. He said that after a particularly uninspiring Latin lesson one of his schoolmates loaned him a copy of a book called *The Vanishing Litres* by Rex Hays, a well known model car maker. Taking its title from the downsizing of engine capacities over the years, the book told the story of the first 50 years of Grand Prix racing, from 1906 through to the Fangio/Moss era. Piers said that he was instantly captivated, his life changed overnight.

However, he erroneously recalled reading about "Bentleys rushing round Le Mans," a marque and race which don't get a mention in the Hays book, so it may be that he confused it with another tome. Leading further credence to that argument is a letter he wrote home in March 1957, in which he thanked his parents for sending him a copy of the *Automobile Year* annual, adding that his mates were envious of it. *The Vanishing Litres* was certainly published during '57, but it seems unlikely that by March Piers would have been able to borrow the brand new book from a pal, become an instant convert to motor racing, and request the annual as a present.

Above *Happy days at a fancy dress party in Windsor. Piers is in the back row playing Johnnie Walker, while younger brother Charles wears the jockey's colours in the front. Somewhere in the picture are the children of Group Captain Peter Townsend.*

Right *The cheerful Courage personality was already very evident when he was just eight years old.*

TEL: SEAFORD 2664

ST. PETER'S SCHOOL.
SEAFORD.
SUSSEX.

13th October, 1950.

Dear Mrs Courage,

Now that Piers has completed his first three weeks here I expect you would like a report on his work and general behaviour. He has adapted himself to the ways of the School very well, considering his tender age, and I love his gay, cheerful attitude to things. He has been well taught, and I think he is probably quite intelligent, but he is not exactly a world's worker as yet. He exerts himself by fits and starts and he needs periodic prods and digs to keep him up to the mark. I think it is probably true to say that he has ability and is by nature lazy – a criticism which applies to many of my friends. In English his reading is fairly good and likewise his spelling, but he has careless lapses, and he can write quite neatly when he is not in a slap-dash frame of mind. He knows a little French already and is always bright and eager in form.

I like his general attitude to school life. He is a most friendly little person and always a cheery soul, entering into everything with much zest and popular with his fellow creatures. So far he has not proved himself a nuisance in any way, but I expect he is keeping something up his sleeve for us.

Don't take these observations of mine too much to heart because they are based on only a short acquaintance.

Yours sincerely,

P. Knox-Shaw.

P.S. Could you let me have your new telephone number and also Piers's National Health Medical Card if he has one.

Whatever the truth, it's certain that one of his school friends turned Piers onto racing at about that time, and the sport soon became the main subject of conversation amongst his pals. His initial interest may well have been sparked by long time class mate Mark Fielden, the son of Air Vice-Marshal Sir Edward Fielden, Captain of the Queen's Flight and one of the RAF's most respected pilots. In 1937 Fielden Snr had flown the Duke of Kent to see the Silver Arrows dominate the Donington Grand Prix, a job he almost certainly enjoyed more than most routine trips since he had raced motorbikes himself at Brooklands. Mark had inherited his dad's love of speed.

Through Fielden Jnr, Piers became friendly with a bunch of other Etonian petrolheads. Mark had been at prep school with David Wansbrough, whose father ran the Jowett car firm, and would later own the Gordon Keeble marque. Others in the group included Fielden's close neighbour from Goring, Peter Rose, and two cousins called Tim O'Rorke and Tom North. This little gang ate, slept and breathed racing cars.

"It was Mark who had the car bug first," recalls Wansbrough. "Initially I had the motorbike bug. He and I lived close together, and we used to build Ford specials and things like that. Mark's father was certainly very keen and encouraged his motoring activities. We were all nutty about cars, and used to read *Autosport* every week, and chat about it over a coffee.

"Piers was like he remained, a lively, smiling, cheerful, enthusiastic sort of guy. I don't think I ever heard him be nasty about anybody – he was just fun to have around."

The boys could hardly have grown up at a better time. Stirling Moss, Mike Hawthorn, Peter Collins and Tony Brooks waved the flag for Britain in Grand Prix racing. Vanwall was beginning to find real success, and Jaguar was winning Le Mans. Motor racing enjoyed the highest profile it had ever had in this country.

The Eton boys were luckier than most, since they were able to focus their attention on the school's extremely active Automobile Society. It held regular meetings, which were usually either racing film shows, or visits by famous names from the sport, who could hardly turn down such a prestigious invitation. There was a restriction on numbers, and boys usually couldn't be elected as full members until their final year, but the big meetings were generally open to anyone of whom the members approved. Piers and his chums soon became regular visitors, and thus would have come across the then secretary, Sheridan Thynne, who by co-incidence lived close to Rose and Fielden.

"Piers certainly knew who I was at school, and I just about knew who he was," says Thynne. "I was rather senior and authoritarian! I was chastised because I was unaware of the Automobile Society regulations which said that not more than half the activities in any term

could be associated with motor racing. I genuinely didn't know this, and I got called up before the headmaster. He said he understood the fixtures I'd arranged were a talk from Ron Flockhart, a talk from Duncan Hamilton, a motor racing film show and an opportunity to go to AC to see their Le Mans car being built. He asked which of those was a non motor racing activity?"

The passion for speed and racing took over Piers's life away from school as well. "I know my father always bitterly complained about the amount of money spent on *Autosport* and *Motor Sport*," says Charlie Courage. "There were racks of these things built over what seemed like a millennium, but in fact only a year or so. He kept every single volume. I can still remember there was one cupboard in his bedroom which was *Autosport* and *Motor Sport* and the occasional *Autocar*.

"When he was younger he was given an air pistol. He made a chequered flag out of his bedroom ceiling; the black squares were drawings or photographs of racing cars. He was terribly bored one day; he'd lie back on his bed with his .22 air pistol and shoot the people in the cars! Mother really took a terribly dim view of that..."

A year after he first caught the bug Piers finally got to see racing cars in the flesh. Getting to a race track during term time was impossible, but he took advantage of the holidays and on Easter Monday in 1958 the 15-year-old left Fitzwalters at the crack of dawn on an epic journey

St Peter's School
Seaford
Sussex

Dear Mum and Dad
    Thank you very much for the lovely letter you sent me it was very nice. Today we a having a service in our chaple and the Bishop of Lewis Iam shaw it is going to be very nice. On Wednesday we had a match against Pilgrims a school with only forty boys in it, but they won and we lost quite heavily. Our gardins are groing very well + the mustard and cress will soon be ready for piking, and the radishes we are getting on very well. On Saterday we had a match against kingsmead, again we lost very heavily one boy called Baxter scored 73 not out he hit two sixes! and lots of fours. Give my love to Charles + Andrew + William. I hope Charles soon gets over his chiken pox. With love from Piers

& 7/3/57

Dear Mummy and Daddy
Thank you so much for taking me out
on Saturday it was great fun and lovely
seeing you again with Stubbs.
Thank you so much for sending my
Guitar Tutors and the song books,they
will be very usefull because Ix am giving "Fifi" lessons this morning.
We had a very good days beagling on
Teusday and we chaased the same hare all
day and eventually killed it at the end
of a very exiting chase.
XXXXaa XXxxSchol Plaxxxxxx vas
The School Pláy was very good indeed
and it was so popular that it is having
another performance to-night,we clapped
for ten minutes atthe end because they
had a very clever way of showing all the
carachtures;they all went across the stage
with thee lighting so that they were sil-
oeted in charaaturistic postures,the result
was very efective.
I have received a latter from Gran telling
me that she is coming down on the16th,which
will be great fun.
The Automobile Year is a frightfully good
book and well xxix worth the money;everyone
ixxxx is very envious of me especially "Fifi"

With lots of love from

Piers.

OXFORD & CAMBRIDGE

SCHOOLS EXAMINATION BOARD

General Certificate Examination

THIS IS TO CERTIFY that   COURAGE, Piers R.

born   27 May 1942   attended   Eton College

and has satisfied the examiners in the following   single   subjects of the General Certificate
Examination of the Oxford and Cambridge Schools Examination Board in July 1960.

ADVANCED LEVEL: English

Signed on behalf of the Oxford and Cambridge Schools Examination Board

T.S.R. Boase

H. Butterfield

VICE-CHANCELLOR OF OXFORD   VICE-CHANCELLOR OF CAMBRIDGE

G.J.R.Potter.   A.E.McKenzie

SECRETARIES TO THE BOARD

THE MINISTRY OF EDUCATION accepts the Examination as reaching the approved
standard.
Signed on behalf of the Ministry of Education

T.R.Weaver

UNDER-SECRETARY

The young ones

Piers in his first road car, a Triumph Gloria that he bought for just £5. He customised it with a plastic Courage cockerel mascot, borrowed from a pub advertisement!

Free at last of the demands of Wykes, Piers lounged around Fitzwalters for most of the summer of 1960, preparing for the next step in his education. The previous year his father had been elected Chairman of what was by now known as Courage, Barclay and Simmonds Ltd. Through the fifties the company had expanded rapidly, mainly through acquisitions, and Richard naturally expected his oldest son to join him eventually. It was hoped that first Piers would complete his education, and he was steered towards a crammer course for the Cambridge entrance exams.

Work didn't start again until mid-September, and on 25 August Piers set off on a grand European tour, accompanied by a friend. No one can remember who went with him, but it could well have been Mark Fielden. Whoever it was, he was able to persuade his grandfather to lend a cherished MG Magnette to a couple of eager 18-year-olds who had little or no idea about the rigours of continental motoring.

The highlight of the trip was to be a visit to the Italian GP, and despite the poor roads of the time the pair duly made it all the way from Cherbourg to Monza. When they arrived they were disappointed to discover that the British teams had boycotted the race on safety grounds, because the organisers insisted on using the dangerous banked track. Still it was better than nothing, and they watched Phil Hill give Ferrari the last ever Grand Prix victory for a front-engined car.

Disaster struck on the way home when the MG's front bumper was lost in an encounter with a VW in the Alps, and the rest of the journey north was spent in silent contemplation of how they were going to break the news to the grandfather. But worse was to come. They reached Paris late at night, and unable to afford a hotel began looking for somewhere where they could park up and sleep in the car. Unfortunately Piers displayed the same lack of concentration which had frustrated so many school masters.

"I failed to notice a Renault Dauphine beside the road," he explained a decade later. "There was an appalling sound of rending metal and, feeling sick, I got out to assess the damage. Half the side was ripped off the MG and I had hit the Renault fair and square up the back. We spent two hideous days tramping round Paris trying to find the Dauphine's owner but, fortunately as I see it now, without success. Finally we gave all the particulars to the police and left it to them to sortit out with the insurance company while we scooped up the remains of the MG and returned it to the grandfather."

During that summer Piers took his first tentative steps in motor sport, although not in the sort of event of which the RAC would approve. Tracks like Silverstone, Goodwood and Snetterton had grown out of former airfields, and Piers found out about some highly unofficial racing going on at an ex-RAF base called Chalgrove. It wasn't quite abandoned, for it was the base of Martin Baker Ltd, the leading manufacturers of ejector seats, and their products were regularly test fired out of the cockpits of fighter jets. The company didn't operate at weekends, and there was little security, so enthusiasts would sneak in and blast round a makeshift course on the main runway and perimeter roads.

The handy hole in the Chalgrove hedge was originally discovered by local car enthusiast Martin Ryan: "If the security guards were out, you were in trouble, but otherwise you'd just drive in and help yourself, and spend the afternoon having some fake races. Anyone who fancied driving fast could go. There was only ever one plane, or sometimes two, but they were just being used by Martin Baker to test their seats. BMC had a big scrap heap where they dumped all kinds of prototype bits and pieces, and as I was in the motor trade, that's how I discovered it. As I had an Austin Healey I used to go over and nick things occasionally!"

Old Etonians Mark Fielden and Peter Rose lived just down the road from Chalgrove, and it's possible that one of them first told Piers of its delights, but it was Ryan who first actually brought him along.

"I met him in the pub that two or three of us used to meet at," says Ryan. "I think he wanted to go racing, and he'd heard from friends about people meeting up at this riverside pub, Ye Olde Leatherne Bottel, at Goring-on-Thames. And we just got chatting."

As word spread, so more and more eager young men would turn up on a Sunday morning. David Wansbrough was a regular, as was another former Eton Automobile Society secretary who lived locally, Fielden's pal

Piers was not always happy in his latter days at Eton. This is his 'leaver' – a specially posed picture that every boy gave his mates at the end of his final term.

Sheridan Thynne. Piers and Mark had been two years below Thynne at school, when age was all-important, but now all that mattered was their shared interest in cars.

"One tended to know half or two thirds of the people there," says Sheridan Thynne. "And the rest just appeared. It wasn't much monitored, and we just blasted round."

Most would-be racers on the Chalgrove 'grid' had perky little two-seaters, but there were also more mundane cars like Minis and VW Beetles. Piers caught the eye by turning up in the family's Morris Minor Traveller. It was hardly the ideal machine with which to kick-start a racing career, but he tried hard.

"Being a bit younger he was still in his parents' car," says Ryan. "But he obviously had a good touch, because he could make that thing go extremely well."

"Piers used to bring his mother's Morris along and perform wild things with that," recalls Wansbrough. "He was quite a press-on sort of driver. When we were all fooling around at Chalgrove Piers showed enormous enthusiasm, but I wouldn't say he showed any special talent. He'd go for it and try like hell, and my guess is that he later polished that into real racing talent."

In September 1960 Piers made a pilgrimage to the Italian GP, but was disappointed to find that the British teams had boycotted the race on the banked circuit. Less than four years later he was racing at Monza in his own right.

The only performance enhancement the humble Morris enjoyed was the application of chequered flag stripes, which had to be carefully peeled off when Piers went home to Fitzwalters. His parents had no idea what their son was getting up to on his weekend trips.

"I can remember him parking the car very carefully back in the garage," says Charlie Courage. "There wasn't much left of either reverse or perhaps first gear – I just know that whoever got into it the next morning knew that there was something seriously wrong!"

"He showed me these photographs of a Le Mans start," recalls Andrew Courage. "And the Morris was one of the cars. There was one of him coming round a corner with a tremendous amount of opposite lock. He said you must not show this to mother or father. My dad would have really hit the roof! It was all very hush-hush."

In September 1960 Piers began his Cambridge crammer course at a college in Notting Hill called Davis, Laing and Dick. He found a cosy London base at his grandmother's house at 29 Montpelier Place, and he would cycle to the college from Knightsbridge each day. The area around Notting Hill had yet to be fully redeveloped after the war, and many of the bombsites were occupied by car breakers. During his lunchbreaks Piers would poke around the old wrecks, and one day he found a machine he could hardly resist. It was a 1934 Triumph Gloria sports car, with the registration number RC1936.

"The only major blemish was a badly bent front axle which gave it a sad, knock-kneed look. Its cockeyed

headlights gazed appealingly at me, and I felt that the least I could do was save it from an ignominious end."

For the princely sum of £5, Piers became the proud owner of his first car, although he later had some regrets when he found out it would cost three times that to put the axle right. Still, he was finally a motorist in his own right, and a Courage Breweries cockerel proved to be the perfect radiator mascot.

"It was unbelievable," says Andrew Courage, just 11 when this new plaything arrived back at Fitzwalters. "My first memories of Piers and cars are digging around old wrecks looking for parts for the Triumph to try and keep it running. The back seat was so rotten that we put two armchairs in the car!"

Piers's fellow pupils on the Cambridge crammer course included Australian-born motor racing enthusiast John Hogan.

"You wouldn't believe it now, but in those days Notting Hill was a real dump," he recalls. "Every other person was a total car nut. We had Grands Prix around the square at lunchtime! The Austin-Healey Sprite was a favourite car, and there were Ford Anglias and Morris Minor convertibles. I didn't know Piers that well, but we were both part of the car gang. He was a very, very nice man, but I wasn't aware that he wanted to race at that time. I think his car had three different size wheels on it, because that's all he could afford!"

To no one's great surprise Piers failed the Cambridge exams that winter, and thus a rethink was required as to his future career path. But he still had plenty to occupy his time, and meetings with his motoring chums weren't confined to visits to Chalgrove. Mark Fielden and Sheridan Thynne were studying in London, at the Chelsea College of Aeronautical and Automobile Engineering in Flood Street, known to all and sundry as the 'College of Knowledge.' Through them Piers gradually got to know some of the other would-be engineers. Among them was a slightly built young man called Jonathan Williams, who was to become one of his closest friends.

Born in Cairo, Jonathan had grown up not far from the Courages in Colchester, where his parents ran a private school. He and Piers clicked instantly, and soon found that they had more in common than their Essex roots. Not only was Williams another racing fanatic, he'd already done a bit of real motor sport in a Mini.

"My father was a squadron leader, and after the war he came back and settled in Colchester and bought a school," says Williams. "He took me to Silverstone in 1951, and I saw Gonzalez, Fangio and Moss, who was my hero. It was great. My parents thought it was not a good idea for me to go to his school, so they sent me to one on the far side of the land – Cheltenham, an absolute bastard of a place!

"Then I went to the 'College of Knowledge'. It was the place where you sent boys who didn't know what they wanted to do, and were interested in cars. Years earlier

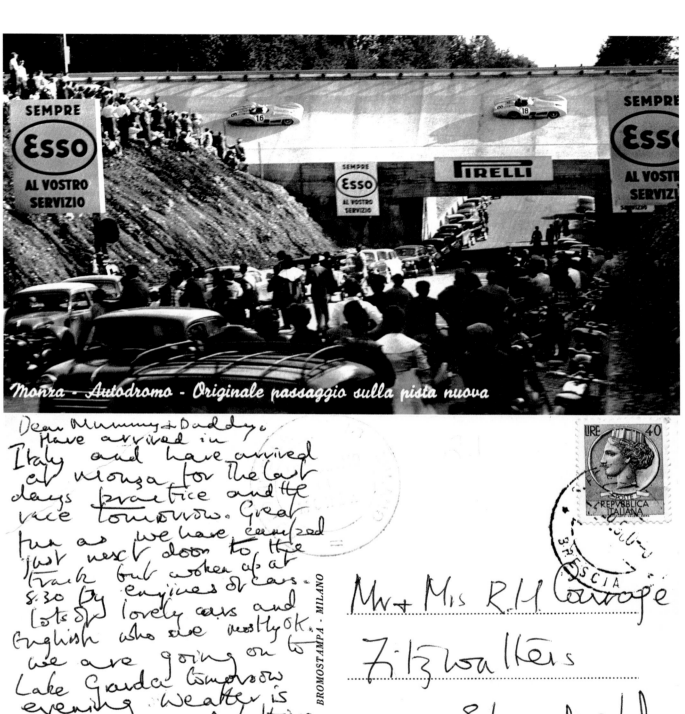

Monza · Autodromo · Originale passaggio sulla pista nuova

Dear Mummy & Daddy,
Have arrived in
Italy and have arrived
at Monza for the last
days practice and the
race tomorrow. Great
fun as we have camped
just next door to the
track but woken up at
8.30 by engines of cars.
Lots of lovely cars and
English who are mostly OK.
We are going on to
Lake Garda tomorrow
evening. Weather is
marvelous and bathing
good here as it is national
park. Car is going OK only
doing rather a lot of
juice. More late
Lots of Love Pieus.

BROMOSTAMPA · MILANO

Ed. ris. Cartiera S. Cesario (Vismara)
Via dei Mille, 2 - Monza

Mr & Mrs R.H Carrage

7.13 Walters

Shenfield

Essex

England.

Vera fotografia

Mike Hawthorn had been thrown out, and Moss went there for a bit. There were also a lot of people from the colonies who probably went back and became Minister of Transport or something! You learned everything – welding, pouring molten metal to make bearings, electrical stuff. I don't think anybody ever completed the course – we just fiddled with our cars in Sidney Street."

Jonathan soon got to know fellow student Mark Fielden, and through him was introduced to Piers and the rest of the gang.

"Mark realised that we were going in the same direction car-wise, and one day he said, 'You've got to come out this evening and meet some other friends.' He took me to a coffee bar in South Kensington, just behind the station, where every evening all these motoring mad people would turn up. And Piers was one of them. He had some ramshackle old banger, with its boot full of Castrol R and destroyed clothing. He wasn't a tidy young man at all.

"But everybody had cars like that. Peter Rose had an MG TC, and you could buy those for about £150. David Wansbrough had a dreadful thing he'd built, a Tornado with a plastic body on top of some junk. At one point I had a diabolical car – a Berkeley B105 made of plastic. Went like hell when it went. But I'd done some hill climbs and little sprints in one of the very first Mini 850s, so they all looked at me as if I was the guru! Follow him and everything will be alright.

"One of the places we used to go to was the Crown and Sceptre pub, just opposite Harrods. Piers lived near there in Montpelier Place with his grandmother, Lady Watson, who was a charming old lady. We used to come around and meet in the pub and have a couple of drinks."

Although the faithful Triumph Gloria was not as impressive as some of the other cars, Piers could at least hone his driving skills, as school friend Tim O'Rorke recalls: "I remember him showing me how he could slide it round Hyde Park Corner, quite effortlessly, and I was terribly impressed. He had terrific control."

Piers was still in an academic limbo, but Richard Courage didn't want to leave his son idle for too long, and it was decided that he should spend a few months in Paris perfecting the French he had grappled with since the St. Peters' days. To Piers this was "...quite the best idea for my education yet put forward."

Richard knew the Chairman of WHSmith, and arranged for Piers to get a job at the bookshop's Paris branch on Rue de Rivoli. On 4 April 1961 Piers headed by ferry to Calais, from where he caught a train to Paris. He was to stay with the wonderfully-named Mme Wolkonsky Mortimer Mannier, who rented out rooms at 25 Rue du Calvaire in St Cloud.

For someone who so clearly loved being away at boarding school, Piers initially found Paris an unhappy and lonely place. He may have been able to mix with the opposite sex, but he missed the College of Knowledge gang and the endless chats about cars, especially now that Jonathan had started to do some serious racing in a Mini. And he particularly missed the Triumph Gloria, which he'd left at Fitzwalters. A letter he wrote home soon after his arrival made his feelings pretty clear. A decade earlier he'd send regular urgent requests from St. Peters for sweets – this time, he needed money:

"I am now down to 10 francs and a week behind in rent. Smiths is pretty tedious. All I do is sit and stick labels into books or mend bookshelves from 9 till 6.30. I met one Etonian whom I knew vaguely. He was working in the knife and fork department of a store. Madame M.M. is still very pleasant despite the rent and we have 3 new arrivals, two English girls and one American, all pretty deadly. We went off to Chartres last Sunday, which I have already seen, then we missed the train and had to wait two hours which we whiled away in a shocking cinema. The train was so tight that there was hardly even standing room and no one would allow us to open the windows!

"I went down to the racetrack at Montlhéry on Saturday but discovered from a paper on the way down in the train that the race had been postponed until October, so I walked four kilometres to try and find the track, then gave up and came back by bus. Nothing ever seems to happen after dinner here (during which everyone sits and eats in silence or talks about what happened during the day which is usually nothing) and everyone tends to go to bed fairly swiftly. One consolation is that I can borrow books from Smiths for free and so I have read about 10 already as there is nothing else to do. I shall always regret not bringing my car over, as I would have had something to think about."

"Piers had an extremely woebegone face when things weren't going his way," says Sheridan Thynne. "I imagine during his time at WHSmith he must have looked a misery guts all the time!"

After a few weeks Piers graduated to dealing with customers, or specifically British and American tourists who were after the sort of books they could not readily (or legally) find at home. Nevertheless, Piers was still thoroughly bored after two months in Paris. On 2 June he had a chance to recharge his batteries when he went back to Fitzwalters for a lightning weekend visit, returning two days later, this time at the wheel of the Triumph.

After the disaster with the borrowed MG Magnette the previous August, Piers was hoping for better luck at the wheel of his own car, but the Triumph kept him busy. Vibrations from French cobblestones caused the windscreen to fall into his lap, the doors had to be held on with rope, and a corroded petrol pump required a hefty hit from a hammer every time the car stuttered to a halt.

Piers must have had a heart-to-heart with his folks on his brief trip back, for within days of returning to Paris

he handed in his notice at WHSmith. He seems to have enrolled at some sort of college instead, presumably to work on his French. He was much happier now that he had transport, and that access to a car soon won him a lot of friends amongst the student types he hung out with. The Triumph also enabled him to pay a visit to the Le Mans 24 Hours race for the first time, an event he described in another letter home:

"On Friday we set off for Le Mans with the two girls and John. We arrived there and drove round once or twice to the cheers of spectators at the corners and in the pits. We were just looking around when two chaps in a Mini asked us to their tent for a drink. We accepted and they were very helpful having been there for a week, and everything was just so, one of them having been in the army, and owning a marvellous blow-up tent. They lent us lots of blankets and extra clothes as we were very poorly prepared as the girls were only meant to stay for one night before going onto Tours and the Loire chateaux; however the atmosphere was so exciting that they decided to stay on. Race day was rather dim and wet, however still very exciting. The start was terrific with national anthems and flags then all the cars (60) coming past the pits on the first lap in a bunch at 150mph. Very exciting!"

His parents could hardly fail to notice the change in their son's mood. Piers suddenly had a busy social calendar. He'd taken nine people in the Triumph to the Auteil races, where he won money on horse number 13. He asked for his evening clothes to be sent over as he had been invited to a "smart dance," and was "...going out to a nightclub of sorts tonight in a large party, again in the car."

Chocks away at Chalgrove Airfield. Piers gets a good start at the wheel of his mum's Morris Minor, complete with temporary go-faster stripes.

On one occasion he even bumped into the original American in Paris, Gene Kelly, who was directing the movie *Gigot* in St Cloud. The Hollywood star apparently took a liking to the faithful Triumph Gloria, and asked if it was for sale. Piers had no intention of disposing of the car – not least because Kelly was only willing to offer an autograph by way of payment!

Le Mans took place on 10-11 June, and if a little piece of motor racing folklore is true, Piers must have returned to the UK towards the end of the same month, despite the fact that he was obviously having the time of his life. His old passport contains no exit stamp for that trip, and there's no sure way of knowing how long he and the Triumph stayed in France. However, on 1 July Jonathan raced his red Mini in a 'clubbie' at Mallory Park, and he recalls that Piers came along to watch, in which case he must have already returned to the UK by then. The significance of placing Piers at Mallory rather than in Paris on that day will soon become clear.

"We were great chums by then," Jonathan explains. "And Piers just tagged along to offer moral support. He

DRESSING ROOM

Above Piers in the paddock at Brands Hatch at the wheel of the Triumph.

Opposite The Chalgrove racers pose with their machines. Piers waves in the middle while also in the shot are Old Etonians Peter Rose (second from left) and David Wansbrough (far right), seen with his Tornado.

hadn't got anything to drive himself at that juncture. He was just trying to learn something, just be there. He helped unload the thing or load it up.

"I don't think it was pissing down for the race, but there were some damp patches. I just cocked it up at Gerard's, and then just sat on top of the bank watching the race. This lunatic was coming around in a grey Austin A35, using more and more opposite lock. I didn't know him, but I was certain that it wouldn't be long before we were talking! He was getting wilder and wilder, and then he rolled it completely. So there we sat on the bank on the outside of Gerards, with our mangled cars. We had a bond, having wrecked our cars in exactly the same place."

So it was that Jonathan Williams met namesake Frank Williams for the first time.

"He'd gone off on the first lap and was standing on the bank," Frank confirms. "Eventually I joined him, and he helped to pull me out of the back window. I didn't know anybody when I went racing. It was just about my very first race. But we just got chatting, and became friendly."

Jonathan is convinced that after the race he introduced Frank to Piers back in the paddock, but Frank himself is not so sure: "I thought that I met Piers in London, or at another race meeting."

Whatever the truth, Frank was soon accepted into the Eton/Chelsea College circle. Piers had found his John Lennon.

"We got on well straight away," says Frank. "Piers clearly came from a very different social background. He was a very bubbly and charming person, and made everybody around him laugh. He was very amusing. But he loved his motor racing, he lived for motor racing."

Born in South Shields, Frank was the son of a bomber pilot who had left when he was a baby. His mother had devoted her attentions to Frank's upbringing, and he was educated at a strict Catholic boarding school in Scotland, where he first developed his passion for cars and then racing. In his teens he'd hitchhiked to circuits from the special school his mother ran near Nottingham. On leaving school, with good qualifications, he had undertaken a series of jobs to raise cash for his racing activities with the A35. But he was always broke.

"At that level everybody was mates," says Jonathan, "We were all trying to do something and enjoy ourselves. Everybody was the same age, born in 1942. Frank was terrific – a really super guy. He probably had the least chance of making it, because the others could sometimes separate their parents from a few bob. But not in his case."

After the Mallory shunt Frank's Austin A35 was soon repaired, but having fitted a demon go-faster carburettor, he wrote the car off against a lamp post en route to his next race at Oulton Park! The engine was just about the only item Frank could salvage, so he set about building a replacement based on an A40 shell.

Meanwhile Piers finally had to pay serious attention to his future. A life in the family company beckoned, and to that end his father steered him towards accountancy. Bearing in mind the lack of interest in maths he'd displayed throughout his schooldays, this was probably not a very sound plan, but Piers was found a post with accountants Price Waterhouse.

Before life got really serious there was time for another continental road trip, a sort of final fling for the Eton Automobile Society gang. On 9 September Piers, David Wansbrough, Peter Rose, cousins Tim O'Rorke and Tom North plus a French friend called Dietlam, piled into three cars and set off in search of a little adventure. The Triumph wasn't deemed fit enough for the trip, so Piers planned to travel in Wansbrough's trusty Tornado, but it didn't get much further than the other side of the channel.

"The big end ran about two miles out of Dover," David recalls. "We had to get it across to France, and I spent a day trying to rebuild the engine in Boulogne. We couldn't get the bit we needed or something, and then we realised I'd taken out breakdown insurance. We went round to the local Renault place and hired a Dauphine, at the expense of the AA. Between us Piers and I spun it six times in a fortnight – once on the Monte Carlo Grand Prix circuit! We went down to St Tropez, all over the place, behaving like complete lunatics."

Piers and David eventually made it to Paris, where they met up with their colleagues in the Champs Élysées. O'Rorke's MG had broken its suspension just outside Boulogne, and he had already spent a couple of days searching for a garage that could help him out.

On Sunday Piers finally got to see Montlhéry, having failed to reach the banked track on foot five months earlier. O'Rorke wrote a letter home that tells the story of that day: "Sunday was scorching hot and there was not a cloud in the sky. Having met up with some girls Piers knew, we decided to motor out to Montlhéry and have a picnic, Tom managing to fit four people into or onto his car. Unfortunately we discovered on arriving that there were only motorbike races, which don't interest me as much as cars."

"It was fairly obscure, and we had a lot of trouble finding it," says Wansbrough. O'Rorke also remembers that day well: "My father was also interested in old cars, and he told me that there was a fabled collection of antique cars hidden away under the banking at

Montlhéry. We thought it would be great fun to go and have a look at it if we could. We were staying in Paris and we drove out to Montlhéry. We climbed over all sorts of barriers and barbed wire and eventually we found them. It was almost like a private museum – a huge collection of every sort of car you could imagine, Bugattis by the dozen. We took a photograph of Piers pretending to drive one of these cars."

After another night in Paris, they set off for the south.

"I drove down a lot of the way with Piers," recalls Tim O'Rorke. "I had an MG PB; it broke a front spring when we went to Paris, but apart from that it went fine. However, it had cable brakes, and they were very inefficient. The handbrake was a very tall lever that stood up on the passenger side, and worked on all four wheels. When Piers was driving round the mountain passes he would shout 'Brake!', and I would act as a sort of anchorman, and heave on this thing.

"We got down to St Tropez and we actually stayed in a hotel. My parents had been going there since before the war, and said we must go and stay in this little hotel. Having driven with the windscreen down we arrived looking absolutely shattered, and covered with road dust, as if we'd just finished the Mille Miglia! Of course I wasn't going to stay in the same hotel as my parents, as it would be too boring. So we went swanning round all the other hotels, but they took one look at this gang of vagabonds and it was clear there was no way they would let us stay with them!

Old Etonians go mad in France! Piers at the wheel of an old crock under the Montlhéry banking, accompanied by Peter Rose (standing) and Tom North. Tim O'Rorke took the picture.

"Eventually I capitulated and went to the hotel my parents stayed in. They looked a bit askance when we arrived, and I said in my best French, 'Je suis le fils de Monsieur O' Rorke,' and they were absolutely delighted to have us! They hadn't actually got space in the hotel, and they put us all up in the garage. It had bunk beds and a basin in the corner. It was absolutely perfect for us, because we could tip back any time day or night, without disturbing the other guests. It was quite fun."

In fact his 1962 letter reveals it cost 8NF per night, including breakfast!

"Accommodation was always a problem," says Wansbrough. "I do remember sleeping in a garage on some fairly basic Lilos!"

One member of the party had friends in Paris, and the boys stopped off there on the way back. The senior members of the family were away, and that nearly led to some rather serious trouble.

"I remember going back to the flat at night," says O'Rorke. "The daughters had all climbed into our beds, and there was giggling coming from underneath the sheets! We weren't quite sure what we were meant to do.

In that innocent age we hadn't got a clue, so we all scampered off…"

It was a great holiday, and over all too soon. But the guys were now all 19, and had to get on with life. Wansbrough had got into Cambridge, and would drift away from the rest of the gang, while for Piers the puzzling world of balance sheets beckoned.

"I think Piers just thought about having fun, like most of us did," says Wansbrough. "Some occasionally spent a few minutes thinking about what we might do as a career, but I don't know whether Piers did. But I don't think he thought in terms of a racing career at that time, any more than any of us did really. We weren't doing it that seriously. I know he didn't like work very much, and he hated Price Waterhouse when he went to do his accountancy."

Another era ended around that time when the Chalgrove authorities realised what had been going on, and put a stop to the unofficial weekend racing.

"It all came to an end because of our use of the runway," says Thynne. "One way or another we'd spread a bit of gravel onto it. The aeroplane they did the ejector seat testing with ingested some gravel, and the Martin Baker people had a long think about it. The guarding on the Sunday morning got a little bit more severe after that…"

Although his grandmother's house was a free and very comfortable London base, Piers decided instead to join some of his pals in a flat in Lower Sloane Street. Thynne, Mark Fielden and Jonathan Williams were there, as was Peter Rose for a while.

"I had shared the same flat with a couple of other people who were slightly more mature," recalls Thynne, "but I persuaded the landlord to let Piers and Jonathan and Mark arrive. I was constantly reminded how unsatisfactory we'd become as tenants. The guy had got some rather unpleasing pale teak furniture which we covered in coffee stains!" But it wasn't just the coffee which provided cause for complaint: "There were engines all over the corridors," says Jonathan.

Although he had to commute to Price Waterhouse, and conduct a correspondence course in accountancy, Piers could now really immerse himself in racing. Jonathan had upgraded to an Austin A40, Sheridan was campaigning a Mini, and Mark had an open Buckler. From time to time Frank Williams would stop by too.

"I hitchhiked down to London a couple of times to meet up with Jonathan, who was sharing the flat with Sheridan. And Piers was staying there, hiding from his father."

"Frank appeared like a genie from Nottingham periodically," Thynne confirms. "Usually on the Friday night before a Brands Hatch meeting or something, and spent the weekend with us. I can remember him several times eating with us on a Sunday night, and finishing about 11.30pm or something. He'd left the Austin somewhere near Brands and had come up with us. We were then quite keen to go to bed, and at that stage Frank used to set off from Sloane Square to hitchhike to Nottingham. We did think that was a bit strange..."

Frank had no money at all, but despite their more privileged backgrounds the others were hardly living the high life.

"I don't remember thinking we were lucky or different particularly," says Thynne. "We just had a great desire to get on with it and do some racing. In the Lower Sloane St flat we talked about very little else. Racing was very inexpensive in those days, but on the other hand we had no wherewithal.

"Our respective parents provided us with a certain amount of money while we were studying, so we could live in a way which they thought was appropriate. We probably spent only a third on food, and saving the rest meant that we were able to buy a set of tyres and go to a club meeting.

"We used to eat every single night in a place in Pimlico Road run by three very fat, elderly Turks. It was cheap even then. You got soup, and a main course with two veg, and a pudding – which was very frequently plum crumble, I remember – for five shillings. A coke

was sixpence, and two rounds of bread and margarine were sixpence. It was a lot cheaper than the sort of place our parents thought we were going to eat at, but it assisted us in making money available for more important things. None of us drank, because in those days it was a waste of money."

Piers longed to have a go at racing himself, but first he had to get himself a suitable car. The chance came when he somehow persuaded his father to fork out for what was ostensibly a 20th birthday present in the autumn of 1961, albeit some seven months ahead of schedule.

His choice was a Lotus Seven, then regularly advertised in *Autosport* at £399 in kit form. When the packages arrived Piers and his father laid all the pieces out in one of the sheds at Fitzwalters. Although the Triumph had required constant maintenance, Piers was by no means qualified to put the Lotus together, and his dad agreed to give up a few weekends to help him complete the jigsaw puzzle, which included a 1-litre BMC engine.

"The final insult for my father was that having bought it, he had to build it!", jokes Charlie Courage. "In fact it gave him the most enormous amount of pleasure. Father and myself were engineering orientated. He loved anything to do with mechanics. Piers wasn't as keen on that side of it, and just wanted to get in and drive the

thing! I think in those days purchase tax was not levied as long as there weren't any plans with it. But father built it himself, having sworn and cursed, burning his fingers on live wires that shouldn't have been live and short-circuited…"

"It really frustrated him," says Andrew Courage. "All of us were longing to finally start it up."

Jonathan Williams also came along to help, and says he ended up doing much of the work. When the project was finally complete, the Seven was successfully registered as OO 9149. The first thing Piers did was drive his pride and joy to the Lotus factory in Cheshunt for the recommended initial check-up. The inspector could hardly believe what he saw.

"You could take the car round to Lotus and they'd sign it off as being OK," says Jonathan. "I believe we had put something on upside down in the front suspension. It looked funny anyway!"

Aware that Piers was planning to go racing, the Lotus man also told Piers that on no account should he try to compete on standard road tyres. Since there was no budget for luxuries such as racing rubber, Piers could only shrug his shoulders. Keen to put some miles on the new toy, he and Jonathan motored to Nottingham to show the car to their pal Frank Williams.

"I remember once we'd finished the Lotus we drove up to see Frank," confirms Jonathan. "It was freezing – I don't think it had a roof. His mother wouldn't speak to us. She didn't like racing drivers and she didn't like Frank's friends."

"My mother ran a school for mentally retarded children, on a hill north of Nottingham," says Frank. "They rang up one evening and said we're on our way. I believe they were running-in the racing engine. My mother wasn't very happy but she found a spare bedroom or dormitory where they could kip. They came quite late, had a sandwich, and were gone very early in the morning, because they – or at least Piers – had to be back at work."

Piers could hardly wait for the new racing season to start, but in the interim he had plenty of opportunity to hone his driving on the public roads.

"I only once went in the Triumph," says Thynne. "I do remember Jonathan and I were both keen on Piers getting something with better brakes than the Triumph, little realising that with the Lotus he was going to go that much quicker, so we weren't going to be better off in terms of safety! I remember being driven from Shenfield to Brands Hatch. The passenger seat of that Lotus, when he just had it, was not a restful place to stay."

When the new season finally rolled around, Piers was at last able to use up some of his energy on the track, and on Sunday 8 April 1962 he made his official competition debut at Brands Hatch. It was not a race meeting as such, but a minor sprint organised by the joint efforts of the Allard Owners' Club and the North London Enthusiasts' Car Club.

Sheridan was also there with his Mini: "At the best organised sprints, the ones that made the best use of time, they had a grid of four cars half way down the bottom straight. You'd do half a lap of warm-up from the paddock, and then went off at 15 second intervals. You'd do one standing and one flying lap, timed again on the bottom straight."

Some 101 competitors turned up on a wet and blustery day, split by marque or engine capacity into 15 classes. Not all categories were fully subscribed, and indeed Classes 9 and 10 were cancelled due to lack of entries. Piers was out next in Class 11, along with a bunch of other Lotus Sevens. The man they all had to beat was one Clive Lacey.

"Clive Lacey had a very non-standard Lotus Seven," Thynne recalls. "It was built for Colin Chapman, and I think it had special suspension and all sorts of things."

Piers knew that his home-built machine was never going to keep up, not least because it was very much in standard road trim, but he threw everything into his brief run, as he explained in 1970:

"To tell you the truth, it didn't feel all that different from driving on the road except for two things. The first was that I experienced a sense of freedom that I had not known since the days on the airfield. The freedom was the freedom from fear of somebody coming the other way. I was able to go as fast as I liked without worrying about somebody coming equally fast in the opposite direction. The other thing that was different from driving on the road was that great lumps of rubber kept flying past my head. The Lotus man had been right to warn me against driving on road tyres – they simply disintegrated."

Lacey not only left the other home-built Sevens trailing, he also set the overall best time of the day. R.C. Neville and D.B. Porter tied for second place in Class 11, while despite his tyre troubles, Piers finished fourth. The organisers decided that as Lacey had won overall he shouldn't get the class prize as well, so the others all moved up one. Thus Piers recorded a top three placing on his maiden outing, and even a spelling mistake could not disguise his delight at earning a first mention in an *Autosport* report: "Pearce Courage, making his first appearance, drove very well to take third place."

There it was for all his friends to see – he was a racing driver at last.

This sporting life

Piers knew that proper racing would be rather more challenging than sprints, and to that end set about making the Seven into a more potent machine. His upgrading consisted of forking out for a set of second-hand Dunlop 'R5' racing tyres, which were already almost bald but nevertheless sturdy enough to last a season. He couldn't afford to keep the road tyres as well, so the R5s stayed on the car at all times. The other big tweak was painting the car so that it matched Jonathan's A40.

"Initially it was aluminium with a green nose cone and green mudguards on the front," says Jonathan. "But later he painted the plastic bits black. My A40 was black – it was the done thing to be a team."

While the Austin had been sprayed with meticulous care by Jonathan ("I spent nights and nights in a freezing garage, rubbing down filler!"), Piers did the job at Fitzwalters with a pot of paint and a brush, so the effect wasn't quite as pleasing on the eye as he'd planned. Nevertheless, in some ways Piers had already moved a step ahead of his chums.

"We were still doing touring cars," says Frank Williams, "and he was doing something a little more elitist, i.e. sports cars, the next level up. In those days kids like me thought my first season will be touring, then I'll go into sporty cars, and then I'll go bigger sports cars then eventually I'll go single-seaters.

"I remember once carrying the Seven's nose up Exhibition Road with great pride – I had to go up to what was then John Sprinzel's rally business, just the other side of the park. He used to do Sprites and bits of bodywork and whatever, and I had to take it there for repair or bring it back after being repaired. So there I was, assuming people were thinking 'He must be a racing driver.' I was very proud of it!"

Piers later recalled that he competed in 20 races in 1962, but tracking down the full details of his appearances in obscure 'clubbie' sports car events is a near impossible task, for only on rare occasions did he merit a mention in the weekly press.

However, a few races can be pinpointed. He was at Castle Combe on 9 June, then on 1 July he finished third in a Lotus Six and Seven event at Brands Hatch – Jonathan pipped Frank to the same position in the same day's saloon event. On Saturday 7 July he contested a 5-lap scratch event at a Goodwood Members' Meeting, and he would have finished eighth but for missing the chicane. The ensuing one minute penalty left him 13th – in a field of 15 finishers. He was only a couple of places behind the Austin-Healey of one Chris Irwin, who was to loom large in Piers's future.

The following day Piers was at Snetterton, and even got his picture in *Autosport* for the first time, although purely by chance as the Lotus swept past the photographer at the start of the Jack Fairman Trophy Libre event. On 22 July, the day after Jim Clark won the British GP at Aintree, he returned to Brands Hatch, and was delayed by a first lap skirmish with R. Payne. The mistakes were all part of the learning process.

"He was extremely carefree, with a huge bubbling enthusiasm, and massive energy," says Thynne. "We were all quite worried about him because he used to spin quite a lot on the road, as well as on the track. Road going journeys in the Lotus Seven were never relaxing."

The season ended on a low note when he and Jonathan made their long trip to Aintree in September; Piers in the Lotus running in convoy with his pal's Volkswagen pickup tow vehicle and trailer combination. They chose to make the journey by night to avoid hotel costs, and driving rain did not make Piers's progress any easier. Only afterwards did he realise that travelling at night was not ideal preparation for going motor racing…

Piers was distinctly unimpressed by Aintree's bland layout, and his negative opinion of the place was not helped by a disaster in the race, for the gearbox jammed and he careered into a sturdy Grand National fence. The battered car was undriveable, but Jonathan and Piers managed to load it onto the VW pickup. They duly headed South with the Austin on tow behind.

It was apparent to both men that it was time for Piers to trade up from the Lotus. Jonathan himself had ambitious plans; he had his heart set on Formula Junior. Indeed he had already ordered a Merlyn Mk5, as announced in *Autosport* on 14 September. The company was handily placed not far from his home town of Colchester, and he was confident of receiving good service.

"Father said we could have a go at Formula Junior," Jonathan recalls, "and I bought a Merlyn, because they made them up the road. Selwyn Hayward, who I'm still

A thoughtful-looking Piers with Roger May, sometime assistant to mechanic Roy Thomas.

friends with, was a very plausible salesman! They made them in a barn – it was a cold, horrible place, low tech to a high degree. They made about three Juniors in 1962, and I don't know how Selwyn survived.

"He laid on a test session for me at Snetterton in Andre Pilette's 1962 car. I immediately felt at ease in a single-seater, and was quick. It was logical to assume that the new car would be even better, but it was let down by the dampers used with the new inboard front suspension, which was the undoing of it all. I raced it at Boxing Day '62 at Brands, and it was so-so. Instead of saying sod it, put the springs on the outside, we carried on like that! If I had raced the old car, I think I would have had a good 1963 season."

With less experience than Jonathan, Piers wasn't yet ready for single-seaters. But Merlyn was also in the sports car business, and it was apparent that a proper racer would be a huge step up from the Lotus. Jonathan sang Merlyn's praises and introduced him to Hayward, and a deal was soon agreed. Next job was to find the money to pay for the new machine, and the two youngsters set about persuading Richard Courage to invest in his son's future.

"Piers said he wanted to go racing, and my father said, 'Don't be so bloody stupid,'" says Charlie Courage. "'You're training to be a chartered accountant, and I'm damned if I'm paying for you to do something I don't want you to do.' My mother then threw a wobbly. She said, 'Unless you buy him a car, I'm leaving.' When he said, 'No,' she left. She went and lived with my uncle and aunt for a week before father gave in!"

Jonathan Williams recalls: "His mother said she would leave unless he coughed up. She did leave, and he coughed…"

It was to be the last time for quite a while that Courage Snr was to offer his son any financial support.

"I remember Piers came along and he decided to buy the car," recalls Hayward. "He said to me one day, 'My daddy is coming down on Sunday to pay you.' I thought that's wonderful, that's exactly what we want! On the Sunday afternoon the father duly arrived, in a beaten up old Rover. He came into this little office that we had. He was a very important man, Mr Courage, and he had a beautiful suit, and a rose in his buttonhole.

"Tugging the forelock, I said, 'Mr Courage, I would have expected you to have come in a different car.' 'Well.' he said, 'I can have any car I want, even a Rolls-Royce. But what do I want an ostentatious thing like that for?' This was true; his attitude was obviously one of economy, because he kept poor old Piers on a shoestring as far as I could see. Piers was always in my office, borrowing a stapler either to do up the seams of his trousers or put a patch on. There were always holes in his shoes. I remember on one occasion repairing them as best we could…"

The Merlyn cost £950, and a second-hand 1,100cc Cosworth engine was found for £250. Having sold the Lotus Piers also need personal transport and a tow vehicle, and he acquired what he described a "real Rajah's car", an elderly Jaguar MkVII.

"I went with Piers to buy it," says Jonathan, "somewhere where the used car men lurked up near King's Cross Station. We contravened every law of buying cars, because it was night, and it was raining! But it ran, and it did sterling service."

The white beast came equipped with a trailer, and thus the racing outfit was complete. Jonathan and Piers hung around the Merlyn factory as their cars were being built, and both men accompanied Hayward to the Racing Car Show at Olympia at the end of January. Their new cars were the focus of the company's display.

"We had two black cars, and it was not the most spectacular sight!," says Hayward. "After putting the cars on the stand that night, we decided we were going to have a sandwich and a beer in the pub next door. We were scratching around, we were hungry and thirsty, and as there was a pub next door, we thought we'd go in there and have a sandwich and a beer. We didn't realise until we stepped inside that it was a Courage pub.

"This was when the pubs closed at 10pm. We just about made it, I think we had about five minutes to spare, and the guy exploded on us. He said, 'You come in here at five to 10 asking for food – you've got to come in at a proper time!' Piers looked at him, and said 'Sorry, sorry…' I thought, 'My God, your father owns this place!' But he just, 'OK, all right, sorry,' and we left. He could have said to the guy, 'Do you know who I am? My father will have you slung out,' but he said nothing. Then he turned to me as we walked out the door, and said to me in the most humble way, 'I shall tell my daddy about this.' He was a lovely, wonderful character."

Jonathan and Piers enjoyed buzzing around the show and meeting people.

"Everybody went to the show," says Hayward, "In case you met someone you should know, or who might give you something – even a can of oil! I remember Frank Williams would be hovering in the background, with no sign of financial support."

Among the people they encountered was Roy Pike, an aspiring driver from California who had been racing an Ausper Formula Junior. They soon established a rapport with the red-head, whose technical grasp of racing far exceeded their own. Pike was soon convinced he should become involved in the Merlyn operation, as Jonathan recalls: "I wanted to get him on board the Merlyn team because I thought I'd learn a lot."

While Piers's father had offered somewhat reluctant encouragement to his racing activities, Jonathan's parents were supportive not only of their own son, but all of his mates as well. Their house became a welcome haven.

"Piers and I spent a lot of time with Jonathan's parents in Colchester," says Sheridan Thynne. "They were second parents to both of us because they were great supporters of racing, and great supporters of helping the unwise young to get on with what they wanted to do."

"It was open house," says Jonathan. "People used to come and go. My father was mad on cars. He wanted to race when he was young but didn't have the money, and I was acting out his thing for him. And my mother just put up with it, poor thing. I think she worried a lot."

Piers didn't take delivery of his completed Mk4A until shortly before his first outing with it. He didn't get off to an auspicious start; some 200 yards down the road from the factory, the front bodywork was blown off the trailer.

"He reversed it onto the trailer," says Charlie Courage, "and as we got going all of a sudden there was a huge bang. He'd forgotten to tie the front down, and the wind got under it. It didn't do it any good at all as far as the bodywork was concerned..."

Luckily the damage was only cosmetic and Piers did his best to cover it up by applying stripes of white tape to the nose. He was entered for a race at Brands Hatch on 24 March – he planned to follow the fairly prestigious Guards Championship – but he was only a reserve, and probably didn't start. It's not known if he actually fitted in another proper outing, but he was

definitely in action at the Nottingham SCC meeting at Silverstone on Easter Monday, 15 April.

Piers ran the black Merlyn in a 12-lap combined Formula Junior and sports car race, and he battled for class honours with a well-known lady club racer who'd first competed as a sidecar passenger in 1923! *Motoring News* reported their tussle thus: "In the sports racing car class Bluebelle Gibbs driving a Lola and P. Courage (doing justice to his name) in a Merlyn fought for first place. The final stages saw Courage pulling away from Gibbs to win his class."

Autosport raved about him: "Piers Courage in his new Merlyn put up a grand show, finishing fifth in his second race this year." Closer inspection of the report revealed that the author of this glowing prose was none other than school pal Mark Fielden, who was hardly an impartial judge!

He got a less biased mention in a Snetterton report, when in an event on 28 April "...a gigantic spin at Coram by the Merlyn of P. R. Courage lost sixth place." A week later he was back in action at the Norfolk track, and this time he actually battled for the overall lead: "Robyn McArthur's private dice with Piers Courage (Merlyn) ended prematurely when the Lotus 23 coasted to a halt at the hairpin. The Merlyn was just in front of Ken Baker for the remaining laps until Courage did it all wrong at the Esses." Baker was not driving a proper

sports racer like the Merlyn, but a Jaguar E-Type. At least Piers had the consolation of setting fastest lap.

Although the Merlyn was a step up, Piers still wasn't taking racing too seriously, as Hayward recalls: "At one of the early Silverstone meetings I got there just about as practice was starting. Piers was standing looking very pale and very chubby in his overalls. I asked, 'What's the matter?,' and he muttered something about just coming from a party. He still had his dinner jacket on under his overalls."

Early in 1963 Jonathan and Piers realised that having moved up the ladder, they could no longer get away with DIY preparation, so professional assistance was sought. Through Roy Pike, Jonathan had heard about a skilful mechanic cum fabricator who was happy to tackle any job on a freelance basis. His name was Roy Thomas, although he was known to everyone as 'Tom the Weld.'

Thomas was based in a yard off the Goldhawk Road in Shepherd's Bush, behind a showroom owned by well-known sports car racer and car dealer Cliff Davis. A former German POW, Davis was one of the true characters of British motor sport and was a close friend of Graham Hill and, in earlier times, the likes of Mike Hawthorn and Ruth Ellis murder victim David Blakeley. Like a benevolent uncle, Davis rented out garages and offered moral support to racers or would be racers from every level of the sport, including the two-wheeled variety.

"Cliff enjoyed himself no end keeping an eye on them," recalls his wife Sylvia. "He was always very keen to help. It was really wonderful at that time."

Their son Chris, who was around 12 in 1963, loved the unique atmosphere: "It was a schoolboy's dream. It was a long yard, with lock-ups on each side, some of which had been knocked together. There were all sorts of cars being built there. There was a Formula Junior car called the Ausper, and basically the guy just did a runner. All these cars left behind were brand new at the time, but by the time my father could prove that rent hadn't been paid and he got a court order to claim possession of the goods, the cars were years old and out of date. It was like a tomb!

"Bonfire night used to be quite memorable. People used to get penny bangers, about a dozen at a time, and tie the fuses together. Then they'd lob them round the workshops and over each other's garage doors. When you think of the petrol and oxyacetylene and all that around, it was a bit daft…"

In one garage a mechanic called George was painstakingly rebuilding Dick Seaman's Delage on behalf of its patient owner, Rob Walker, the project having already dragged on for several years. Other tenants even included a pukka Grand Prix team in the shape of the underfunded Scirocco-Powell outfit.

Its small staff included the bespectacled Anthony Horsley, a frustrated racing driver who was hoping to get his career going despite the handicap of his Billy Bunter proportions. Later he would pick up the nickname Bubbles, after buying a car from Bluebelle Gibbs: "I was 'sales manager' at Scirocco in 1963, selling off the old Emeryson F1 cars. When they were all sold I didn't have a job, and then I got promoted to van driver!"

Another familiar character was Aussie Steve Ouvaroff, who worked with Davis: "We used to call it disaster alley. If it hadn't been for Tom the Weld, we would all have been on bicycles! It was great fun. Dreams were made and died there."

At the end of Cliff's yard stood the busy premises of Roy Thomas. He'd previously worked for Graham Warner's Chequered Flag team, running Graham Hill and Mike Parkes, and he had built the Gemini Formula Junior cars – including the one used by Jim Clark in his first ever single-seater drive. Tom started his own business in 1961, and although he was only in his late twenties, he was regarded by everyone as a guru who could perform miracles with metal. He never seemed to leave his workshop, a perception encouraged by the fact the he was never seen without his brown sweater.

Tom, who sadly died of cancer in November 2001, recalled the unique atmosphere of the place: "It was a meeting point for everyone involved in motor racing. They used to congregate in the yard and talk. Those who hadn't been around in the daytime would turn up at 7pm or 7.30pm. And we'd all go off for a meal somewhere, and talk about motor racing – what we were going to do and what we weren't going to do. That dinner party would usually be about a dozen people, and it was every single night."

Piers, Jonathan and Frank slipped easily into this informal circle, and Cliff's yard and the adjacent Seven Stars pub became a second home to them. They soon became friendly with Horsley, while at around this time Jonathan also introduced another racing pal to the yard, someone he'd met during a particular boring exercise at the 'College of Knowledge'.

"You had to cut a square hole in a block of metal, then you had to make a square so accurately that would go in the hole eight different ways and you couldn't see any chinks of light around it. It was just to teach you to file straight and fettle stuff, but it was a pretty exasperating job. I couldn't see that that would be useful in my future! Across from me was this other boy who turned up even later than I had. He was a bit chubby. He looked at me, and the first time he ever spoke he said, 'Let's go and have a drink.' Meet Charlie Lucas! So we legged it across the street to the pub..."

Lucas was an ambitious would-be racer who was due to come into a huge inheritance on turning 21 in 1964, his late grandfather having founded a successful concrete business. He was soon convinced to spend some of it in advance on the purchase of a Merlyn sports car –

Jonathan was a good salesman on behalf of his local manufacturer!

"In the country of the blind, the one-eyed man is king," says Jonathan. "I was the only guy they all knew who had done any racing, and they thought, 'He knows more than us.' Totally misplaced confidence, like me with my stockbroker..."

"He ordered the car, but it was very difficult to get money off him at that time," says Selwyn Hayward. "One day I said to him, 'I really have to have some money,' and he said, 'don't worry, when I'm 21 everything will be alright.'"

More significantly 'Charlie Luke', soon shortened to just 'Luke', was yet another Old Etonian, although he didn't actually know Piers until they met at the yard.

"I never met Piers at school," he recalls. "He was a year older than me, and at school that's a lot. He was also a lot brighter. I wasted most of my time at school doing very little, apart from being secretary of the Automobile Society and working in the engineering block. For some reason they let me keep my car there."

There was an instant rapport between Piers and Luke, and since they had identical Merlyns, they began travelling to races together. This was an ideal arrangement, as Jonathan's Formula Junior commitments meant that he was now usually at different meetings. On one occasion Luke asked Piers to try out his car on a practice day at Silverstone en route to Oulton Park. He duly crashed it at Woodcote, and so loaned Luke his own precious car for the next event, only for the engine to blow up! With a year's experience, albeit in a humble Lotus Seven, Piers was the senior half of the partnership.

Piers leads in his new Merlyn at Silverstone. Here the car is in its first incarnation, painted black and with white stripes on the sharply raked nose. Roger Boote and Robyn McArthur follow.

"He always believed in himself, he always believed he was a racer," says Luke. "Although we tried to tell him that he wasn't! He did have a lot of self-confidence. We just came in at the wrong time. We thought we were Hawthorn and Collins, when we started just after school, to the extent of even buying corduroy caps and folding them in the middle. It sounds so pathetic – walking around and calling each other 'Mon ami mate'! But that was the sort of approach...

"I briefly shared a flat with Jonathan just off the Fulham Road somewhere. It was pretty horrendous. My mother came down and saw a Hewland gearbox on the bed, and I knew there would be trouble. She said she wouldn't have worried had it been a woman or something, but a *gearbox*!"

At some point Piers changed from the original black Merlyn bodywork to a newer shape, which was painted red. Meanwhile Jonathan was coming to terms with the works-backed Merlyn Junior.

"Jonathan was the first person who drove for us who didn't have another job," says Hayward. "He was a trainee professional racing driver. I think Piers had something like £500 a year allowance, and he couldn't make ends meet, and there was never any money. His father never came to his aid and said you need a bit more money – he let him get on with it. The problem was they were all driving the van and working on the cars themselves, so they always arrived with nothing really finished, and hungry!

Jonathan's first overseas race was the prestigious Monaco GP support event on 25 May, and to make the trip cost effective he teamed up with fellow Merlyn racer Roy Pike. With no race of his own that weekend, Piers went along to help out.

Opposite top Piers's own scrapbook caption tells the story: 'Selwyn returning something to the stores after Lucas had been discovered pinching it.'

Opposite middle Overhead view of the Merlyn cockpit with its new red bodywork.

Opposite bottom Roy Thomas, known to everyone as Tom the Weld, was a master mechanic. He's pictured here in his workshop at Cliff Davis's yard, complete with trademark welding goggles.

"We all went down in a lorry," Roy recalls. "It was actually the ex-Rob Walker/Moss lorry that Alf Francis had used, which had been sold to Scirocco-Powell. Piers came along because he had nothing else to do. The exhaust pipe broke near Lyons, so the whole thing filled up with fumes."

"Piers came down in the lorry with us, with Pike driving like a maniac," says Jonathan. "Roy and I had bought it, half each. We had two cars one above the other. My father had the school carpenter make a set of bunks, and there was enough room to fit them between the cars and the rear doors! There was no question of hotels."

Hayward followed the trio down later, and met up with them in Monaco: "Piers taught me to drink Cognac with coffee at about seven in the morning! It was after the first practice. I thought that's a helluva time to start drinking."

There was much enthusiasm, but the weekend ended in disaster. First Roy had a suspension failure, and then Jonathan had a huge accident at Tabac Corner following a similar breakage.

"I woke up in Princess Grace hospital," says Jonathan, "in the middle of the operating theatre, so they weren't too good at calculating the dose! Grace Kelly came to see me, and I was the only customer. I had a tremendous bash on the head, and was scalded down one side because water came out of the pipes, and I think I had a broken leg and wrist."

"The car was not very badly damaged," says Hayward. "I was in the hospital minutes after he was there. I don't think he was very badly hurt, I think it was more shock than anything. He tells me now, 'Oh yes, it was a bad accident,' but it wasn't. It was a slow corner in those days. There was a kerb, and they jumped the kerb from the road to the pavement. It was the shock of jumping the kerb, which they all did, which led to it breaking."

"The car was totalled," Williams insists by way of denial. "There wasn't a single piece that you could use again. And I had a hole in my Les Leston helmet that you could stick your fingers through."

With Jonathan hospitalised, Roy and Piers made their own way back to England with the truck. Pike remembers the trip well: "Somewhere near Paris the doors came open, and the bunks Jonathan had made fell out. We had to go to the police station to find everything."

Pike says that there was a design flaw in the Merlyn suspension, but Hayward insists that a sub contractor had supplied below standard parts: "At that time we farmed out certain parts for manufacturing, and the company which made the lower wishbone did not adhere to a drawing. I said, 'I'm very sorry...' Jonathan had lost confidence, naturally, and I said, 'The best thing is if we just take it off you,' and gave him back his money."

Jonathan's injuries did not take long to heal, but without a car, he was back to square one. However, finding a replacement did not prove too difficult. Tom the Weld's expertise in fixing bent space frame tubes extended not only to building replacement chassis, but also complete 'replica' racing cars – for considerably less than an original would cost. So Jonathan found himself the owner of a brand new Lotus that did not exactly carry Colin Chapman's seal of approval.

"Tom built slightly forged Lotus 22s," says Lucas. "He just knocked the chassis up, and bits seemed to come out of Cheshunt at night over the fence. He built me a beautiful Lotus 23 sports car!"

"There was an Irishman who worked in the stores at Lotus," says Jonathan. "We'd say, 'Have you got anything for us?,' and he'd bring out a wishbone..."

"There was no security at Lotus at all," says Pike, who helped Tom with some of his projects. "There were even stories that people who worked up there would build a car, and gradually move it nearer the door. One day out the door it would go!"

Tom's other customers included a fresh-faced young American who occasionally hung around the yard, and who had aspirations to be an F1 driver.

"I also built a Lotus 23 for Peter Revson," he recalled. "Revson was a nice guy – I wasn't that keen on his brother Doug, who was a real American cowboy. But I got on very well with Pete. He went back to the States with this sports car, and did ever so well with it."

Jonathan's Monaco shunt had reminded the youngsters that motor racing was dangerous, but a much harder lesson was to come in a freak accident in practice at Silverstone on Friday 5 July. Mark Fielden was sitting in his car in the unprotected pitlane when the Hon. John Dawnay – the future Viscount Downe, and by tragic co-incidence yet another Old Etonian – lost control of his Aston Martin. The ex-works DBR1 spun into Fielden's Lotus, killing him instantly.

"It was the Aston Martin Owners Club, one step up from a clubbie, and thus quite a big meeting," says Thynne. "Mark was in a Lotus 17, which he acquired very cheaply, because it was a fairly bad racing car. He was parked in the pits minding his own business, and the Aston arrived from behind. I doubt whether he knew what happened. It was traumatic for me. My future wife was Mark's girlfriend, and arrived at Silverstone to discover that he'd died. It was heavy stuff, and a huge blow to us."

"It was his first time out in the Lotus," says Fielden's friend Martin Ryan. "The impact squashed it to about three foot long. I was amazed when his father told me to pick up the remains, put it on the trailer, and bring it back. Later he buried it."

Despite the tragedy, everyone carried on. Indeed, the very next day Piers shone in a support event for the prestigious Brands Hatch Six Hours saloon race, behind veterans like Keith Greene and Roy Pierpoint. It prompted an enthusiastic report by Mike Kettlewell in *Autosport*: "Piers Courage had climbed to seventh position in the Merlyn. Courage was living up to his name and was driving as fast as he could on the streaming wet track. By lap three he was sixth, to move up to fifth when Morley lost two places after going wide." Later it went wrong: "Courage explored the grass after Paddock on the eighth lap, revolving his way up Pilgrim's Rise. Piers restarted immediately, but only got as far as Bottom Bend, where the red Merlyn pirouetted thrice, blocking Geoff Oliver's DRW, and retired after a brave showing."

Although Piers was enjoying his sports car racing, he was soon missing two of his closest pals. Once he was fit enough, Jonathan chose to forsake the domestic scene to join a select band of gypsy racers on the Continent. It was the only way to make Formula Junior cost effective, as there was little cash to be earned from racing at home.

The more ambitious could travel around Europe, surviving on starting money and the occasional generous prize fund; Junior was usually either the main support event at a major meeting, or the headliner at smaller venues, and organisers wanted to provide the paying punters with good grids. So having sold the lorry that he'd taken to Monaco, Jonathan resurrected his VW pick-up, loaded his Lotus 22 onto the back, and set off in search of adventure. Having run out of funds for his saloon car exploits, Frank Williams agreed to go along for the ride.

"When Frank first turned up at Cliff Davis's yard," says Bubbles Horsley, "he was trying to get some money to go off with Jonathan. The only thing he had to sell was an overcoat – in June! I said, 'Do you know what month it is?' 'It's cheap,' he said..."

"I believe Frank was very keen to come because he had someone wanting to knee-cap him!" says Jonathan.

"In Monaco I got bashed on my head, and I couldn't remember which day it was. I was completely loopy, and Frank was my minder, mainly, although he likes to say that he was my mechanic! It was a great help, because by lunchtime I couldn't remember getting up in the morning. I suppose he was very patient, because I would ask him ten times a day, where are we racing this weekend Frank? We used to sleep in the back of my VW pickup on two Lilos between the wheels of the Lotus.

Below Piers presses on in the wet at Mallory Park.

Opposite Chasing Robin Benson's Elva in the Guards Trophy support event at the prestigious Brands Hatch Six Hours.

"He'd drive the Volkswagen a bit, polish the car and keep me company. We didn't go back to the UK until the end of the season. We had no base whatsoever – a self-contained unit. We had minimal expense. We had enough bits to rebuild the thing after a not-too-major crash. If you lived, you could rebuild it! And you could borrow bits like wishbones, and crow bar the chassis straight. One hundred pounds was about the average start money, and it went a long way. You'd scrounge loads of petrol at the end of the meeting, so you probably didn't have to buy fuel for your tow vehicle. You slept in the back of it, and ate a ham sandwich once a day, and thought you were having a great life. Which you were.

"But it could get tight. I went to Enna from a hillclimb in Trieste with Frank. We had 100,000 lire, but it was a long way. We had to save enough money to get across the ferry to Sicily. And we ended up sleeping on the beach under the VW for a week, and literally living on grapes we'd nicked in the dark from the local vineyard. To not have had the price of the ferry, we'd have failed. We'd not have got the next £100 which then kept us going to the next place."

"There was a lot to see," says Frank. "It was fun, always very enjoyable. It was a little bit of hand to mouth financially, and we really did sleep in between the wheelbase of the car, either side, in the VW pickup. It wasn't that comfortable, a little claustrophobic in there. The canvas cover, which was a good piece of kit, literally kept the weather out. But when you're young you don't really feel the cold! I can remember waking up in the Dolomites at seven in the morning in a lay-by, no traffic coming by, getting up and going to the nearest little place down the road and having a lovely hot roll and marmalade. It was great."

On their travels the pair got to know a bunch of aspiring young drivers, including a tall and slightly aloof Austrian to whom money did not appear to be a problem.

"I first met Jochen Rindt in '63 when he was driving a Formula Junior Cooper on an airfield track," says Frank. "I thought, 'Shit that bloke's quick.' It was a

long left hand corner, I was watching from the outside. I think I went and had a word with him, and I'd been a fan ever since."

Piers heard the tales of the continental adventures, and having got a taste of it in Monaco, longed to be able to join his friends. But he barely had enough money to compete in Britain with the Merlyn, and his tedious accountancy commitments didn't help.

"His father wanted him to be in the city, so I think he did a pretend job somewhere," said Roy Thomas. "He would turn up in a pin stripe suit, and we would tease him something awful! He had such a sense of humour, but if someone was going to get caught, it was Piers. We had fun with him, and he enjoyed the fun as much as anybody. I don't think anybody would have ever been cruel to him."

At some stage Piers had upgraded to a 1,500cc engine, and that just about exhausted his funds. All told he contested just 13 events in 1963, and a third place at a damp Oulton Park on 7 September was one of his few solid results.

"He was always very forceful and determined," recalls Merlyn boss Hayward. "I'm not too sure that he had the best equipment. Unfortunately the dampers didn't do what we were told they would do, so we had to bring them out again. I have no recollection of him ever crashing it – he would have spun it for sure, but I don't

remember it ever coming back or spare parts being sold for it."

What Selwyn probably didn't know was his customers were getting their spares made to order by Tom the Weld!

Sheridan Thynne suggests that Piers matured while driving the Merlyn: "I suppose he was pushing incredibly hard in those days. I think there was a sign of tremendous commitment and effort, and a desire to discover where the limit was. I don't think in the Lotus Seven days we quite realised that it was talent. When he got the Merlyn he got a lot neater and more cautious."

Thynne says at this stage there were no serious aspirations to make it to the top: "When you're club racing, you didn't decide at 16 that you wanted to be a Grand Prix driver and programme yourself to be so, you decided that you wanted to go racing. I don't think we talked about it much, but I suppose we knew that Piers and Jonathan were better than us. But it didn't hugely affect our enjoyment."

"He was certainly getting better," says Frank. "It was a quicker car, but I don't know how competitive. It was not acknowledged to be the best in its class; the Lola and the Lotus were."

Jonathan came to regret that he'd sent Piers down the Merlyn route, and says that he could have found something better for the 1963 season.

"The Merlyn was a mistake, but that was through everybody thinking I knew more than they did, because I'd started to do hillclimbs and sprints and five-lap races probably a year before they got going. So they thought I was the oracle! I had a Merlyn, so he had a Merlyn, and Charlie Lucas had a Merlyn."

By now it was clear to Piers that there would be no more subsidies from his father. In fact there was strong parental pressure in another direction – it was made clear that it was time that Piers concentrated on his accountancy, a part of his life that had been neglected, to say the least.

"Piers was expected to do something," says Charlie Courage. "Dad was a great stickler – if that is what he expected you to do, you had to do it."

Exams were coming, and in November he was dispatched to a crammer course at Car-Rhyn Hall near Conway in North Wales. It must have seemed like the end of the world at a time when so much seemed to be going on. Prime Minister Harold Macmillan resigned, JFK was assassinated, *That Was The Week That Was* ruled the TV roost, and *She Loves You* raced to the top of the charts as Beatlemania was getting into full swing.

Far away from London, the racing scene and his growing circle of pals, Piers could see little point in continuing with the course: "I began to assess my knowledge of accountancy and came to the conclusion that it was zero. My chances of passing the exams made a neat equation with it."

He felt his future lay in motor sport, and a phone call from Jonathan tipped the balance. Ever the persuasive salesman, Williams rang up and convinced Piers to abandon his studies and start planning for the 1964 season. Desperately worried about how his parents might react, Piers packed his bags, climbed aboard the Triumph TR3 he was using at the time, and headed back to London. There could be no turning back.

In his pocket he had the address of the house where Jonathan was now staying; Flat 6, 283 Pinner Road, Harrow. Piers knew that he'd find a friendly welcome, although he hadn't actually met the landlord until he knocked on the door. When Charlie Crichton-Stuart appeared Piers introduced himself, and announced that he'd come to stay.

Crichton-Stuart was a Formula Junior racer who Jonathan and Frank had met on their continental travels. He was three years older than the rest of the gang, and was also a genuine, blue-blooded aristocrat, as he was a grandson of the fifth Marquess of Bute, and nephew of the sixth. He had flown Provost and Vampire fighters in the RAF before taking up racing, and had even baled out. The Vampire didn't have an ejector seat, so if you were in trouble you had to tip it upside down and topple out! The discovery of high altitude deafness cost him his

frontline job, and unwilling to drop back to Transport Command, he left the RAF. He discovered motor racing by chance, and soon realised that it could in some way replace the buzz he'd got while flying.

Always on the look out for ways to finance his sport, he had acquired the flat in Harrow and then sublet beds – or in some cases sofas or floorspace – to his racing pals, or any friends of a friend who happened to be passing.

"Piers turned up one day at Charlie's place in Harrow, where we were all hanging out," Jonathan recalls. "He said he'd given accountancy up. He'd gone missing. His mother rang up and asked, had I seen him? He was standing about a foot away from me. 'No, not at all...' – it was only time I lied to her, dear lady. But I did ring my home and say, 'Courage has quit!' At that point there was nothing else to do but have a go at the racing..."

Piers was under considerable stress for the first few days at Pinner Road, and worried that he'd "...be cut off without a penny." He snuck home to Fitzwalters to pick up some clean clothes, and eventually wrote his parents a letter explaining the situation. He was as aware as anyone else in the family that six generations of Courages had run the business, and that by opting for something as apparently frivolous as motor racing he would appear to be letting the side down. But even Richard realised that times were changing. In the post war years the company had grown, largely through acquisitions, and the Courage family's shareholding and therefore direct influence had shrunk.

"Chairman is a very high position to attain in a big company," says Andrew Courage. "By 1960 there really wasn't so much room for the family any more. I can't imagine my father even entertaining thoughts that Piers could be a future chairman or even a director. All he thought was that he could be someone who could contribute something to the company. With Piers he suggested accountancy as a good base with which he could come in as a management trainee. Later he suggested a career in marketing for me, because my maths was worse than Piers's!"

A couple of weeks after receiving the crucial letter, Richard rang the Harrow flat, and naturally Piers expected the worst. He was more than relieved when his father said that he was free to abandon accountancy and pursue his motor racing dream. But from now on, Piers would have to pay for it himself.

"It was sad in a way because Piers had a wrong perception of his parents," says Thynne. "They were upset, but it was never conceivable that he would be cut off without any money at all. They were too fond of their children, so that just wasn't ever going to happen. I always thought it was a pity that he got confused about what was likely to be their reaction. Within a few months he and the family were perfectly amiable with each other."

Left *Fellow Old Etonian and Merlyn driver Charles Lucas soon became a close friend.*

Right *The unglamorous exterior of 283 Pinner Road, Harrow, where so much motor racing history would be made.*

A hard day's night

Piers would remain with his friends in Harrow through the winter of 1963–64, although there were occasional forays to his grandmother's place in Knightsbridge when he desired some home comforts. Thanks to the famous names that passed through it, Crichton-Stuart's flat was to forge a little place in motor racing history. For reasons no one can fully explain Innes Ireland was a regular visitor, despite being an established Grand Prix driver and a generation ahead of the rest of the inmates. Crichton-Stuart, who sadly died in July 2001, described how it all worked.

"It was a three-bedroom flat in a cheap area of Harrow. The phone number was Underhill 2080; I can still remember it! It was the ground floor flat on the left as you went in, and there were some garages at the rear backing onto a railway line, where a little tube train went past fairly regularly. There were eight lock-ups, and we kept our cars in there, preparing and cleaning them and polishing them.

"I had a room of my own, because it was my place.

People like Frank were lying on the floor or sleeping in a garage, while those who paid some rent like Charlie Lucas, who would pay for Piers and Jonathan when he was there, got the other rooms. People were always moving around doing different things. There was a bunk bed in one room – and different people every morning. It was fairly disgusting looking back on it. But we were all young, we were all healthy, we were all normal! There were always five people in the flat, and often ten, and we were doing something that I suppose people found unusual. There was the usual turnover of girls, and a certain amount of swapping...

"I think the neighbours were pretty tolerant, but there would be the odd row. The flat caught alight one night. We'd all been to the movies, came back and the bloody fire brigade was there. There was a hairdresser above us, and the first he knew was smoke coming through his parquet floor!

"I had a daily called Mrs Buckland. I didn't worry about anybody else, but she used to make my breakfast and generally looked after me. I think the others used to pester her. It was one of those things where sometimes somebody had some money and sometimes other people did, and it was share and share alike. Sometimes somebody went to the shops to get food for everybody, and other times you went out. There was a café in Rayners Lane where you could have a three-course lunch for five shillings. We weren't great drinkers, except Innes. The rest of us if we had two beers we were pissed, literally! I'd not been drinking because of flying, and they didn't drink because they were trying to be serious about their racing.

"Innes was a star, because he was the only big name we had. He turned up because one of us was going out with his girlfriend or he was going out with one of our girlfriends – I can't remember! As he'd driven a Grand Prix car he was a bit of a God. He stayed for a bit and then he stuffed some sports car in America and broke his leg quite badly. He was laid out permanently and couldn't move for three or four months. So we all got to know him then. He was a good sport, good fun, and he treated us like normal people."

Pinner Road was to leave a lasting impression on all who stayed there.

"It was a little block of six flats," says Bubbles Horsley, "with a big parking place at the front, and a yard at the back with lock-up garages, and if we weren't in the back of Cliff Davis's, we kept our cars there. There was quite a lot of partying, but at the same time from early April to October, it was literally a transit camp, because people would come and go, as we were away racing. Then in the winter Frank and I would be dealing away making the money to do the next season."

"Charlie was a very good landlord," says Jonathan. "People gave him five pounds a week, and came and went as they wished. That was a lot of fun. We had the odd party, nothing that would curl your hair! If you didn't have the money he didn't seem to make a song and dance about it. A very nice person, through and through. But Innes could be a grumpy sod, throwing his weight around. He didn't have any money, and that was the problem. He had an aeroplane, and that had gobbled up some. So he crashed there, took over the best bedroom, and didn't pay his rent. He was funny, but he had a temper."

"Innes was probably hiding from somebody else's angry husband!," says Frank. "There were a gang of us who shouldn't have been there. I don't think the

Tom the Weld and Roy Pike help out as the Lotus 31 is loaded onto the trailer at Shepherd's Bush, ready for another Continental trip. The tail of Piers's trusty Zodiac can just be seen.

neighbours were very happy! It was motor racing morning, noon and night. Nobody had any real money. Everyone was always worried about how to pay their bill or buy their lunch, or pay for a set of used racing tyres or so on. But it was fun. And Charlie was a great host in his own way, a very charming person."

With his accountancy career abandoned, Piers set about planning his future. The timing was right, because for 1964 the FIA was replacing Formula Junior with new 1.6-litre F2 and 1-litre F3 categories, and thus it was clearly a good time to get into the latter. With the benefit of his experience from the previous summer Jonathan convinced Piers that an F3 season in Europe could pay for itself. He sold his Lotus 22 to Kiwi Roly Levis, who took it to the Tasman series, while Piers managed to sell his now unwanted Merlyn for a respectable £1,000. That gave him a head start, but with no more subsidies from his father all he could rely on was £500 per annum from a trust fund that had come into operation when he turned 21 the previous year.

Jonathan and Piers thought about buying a pair of Coopers, but that proved to be out of their financial reach, so the obvious alternative was to go back to Lotus. Colin Chapman had launched his contender for the new F3 regulations at the Racing Car Show. It was based on the existing 22 Junior, but was known as a 31. It was cheap, but Jonathan and Piers still couldn't afford new examples. They turned instead to Tom the Weld, who set about creating a pair of replicas for them.

"We had Tom make us two Lotus 31s to order," says Jonathan. "They were a mixture of parts, some of which came illegally out of Lotus – things that would fit in a raincoat pocket. Tom would have made the wishbones, engines mounts, steering column, anything connected to the radiators. We had to buy the chassis, because they didn't fit in a raincoat. In fact our 31s were slightly better than the real ones because we put a few more frills on them."

Piers said later that he managed to get Tom to build his entire car for £75! Both men bought Holbay engines at £250 apiece, while Piers also found a spare for £100. Having sold his old Jaguar MkVII tow-car for £70 he invested £360 in a Ford Zodiac, bought on HP, and another £30 on a trailer. Throw in a spare set of tyres, and he was ready to go. From the start the plan was to concentrate on mainland Europe, and there were solid financial reasons for so doing.

"You got £10 a start in England," said Crichton-Stuart, "but on the continent you'd get £150, or if you went somewhere like Enna you got £300. Don't forget a new engine in those days cost £250. You didn't make money, but you didn't lose money either, as long as you finished in the top 10 and got some start money."

The canny Jonathan had correctly surmised that they had a better chance of getting race entries and starting money if they gave themselves a flashy team name rather than run as humble owner-drivers. Inspired by Crichton-Stuart, who ran as Anglo-Scottish Racing, they came up with the rather grand moniker Anglo-Swiss Racing. It was chosen because they intended to have a summer base at a Lausanne garage owned by Charles 'Chuck' Graemiger, a former pupil at the College of Knowledge.

"Charlie Graemiger had a Lotus Elite, which he worked on and fettled but it never went more than a hundred miles," says Jonathan. "His father was an ambassador for Switzerland in the Philippines. Charlie was always complaining because his father had a Ferrari but he drove it so slowly that it was never on more than about five cylinders! He had a place in Lausanne, which geographically seemed very good to us, because we wouldn't have to come back to England to mend something. So we called ourselves Anglo-Swiss Racing, which was rather pretentious..."

Some pals would later suggest Anglo-Swerve as more appropriate title! The pair decided to keep their financial arrangements entirely separate, but they certainly looked like a team, as Jonathan recalls: "The cars were black; mine had red wheels and a red thing on the nose, and Piers had blue wheels and a blue thing on the nose. Otherwise they were identical."

Their plans were revealed in a brief announcement in *Autosport* on 7 February 1964: "Jonathan Williams and Piers Courage have teamed up to run a pair of Lotus-Fords this year, while Frank Williams, well known for his driving of a hot Austin A40, will handle a 1961-type BMC Cooper." Showing that the magazine had a curious concept of what constituted hard news, the item appeared *above* the following one-line story: "The F1 Constructors Association has been formed, founder members being Brabham, BRM, Cooper and Lotus"...

Piers and Jonathan weren't the only ones making grand plans. In January Frank's new friend Jochen Rindt turned up and stayed at the Harrow flat for a while, and during this visit he went to the Racing Car Show, where he handed Jack Brabham £4,000 cash in payment for a brand new F2 car. The brash Austrian looked a bit flash in his camelhair coat and pink shirt, and the penny counting Brits had good reason to be a little envious of his apparent financial security.

It was in early 1964 that Crichton-Stuart surprised everyone by acquiring a steady girlfriend. The others were mightily impressed. Not only was she a beautiful blonde who was just getting into modelling with Mary Quant, she came from a titled family and was the daughter of one of England's best known pre-war racing drivers. She was Lady Sarah Curzon, known to everybody as Sally.

Although her father was Earl Howe, winner of the 1931 Le Mans 24 Hours and latterly chairman of the

BRDC and the RAC's competitions committee, Charlie Stu had not met her through motor racing.

"I met Sally through my sister," he recalled. "She was the most beautiful girl I'd ever met, came from a good family, and was altogether really lovely. And she obviously had a racing connection, because of her dad. I used to go down to their house at Penn, but he'd had a stroke and he couldn't talk. He was an extraordinary man, and still ruled that house with a rod of iron. He had a silver whistle, which he blew when he wanted something. He couldn't talk, but he could understand. His wife Sybil, who was a very strong character in her own right, used to jump when she heard the whistle!

"The Howe family were descended from Admiral Howe, and the Curzons were Viceroys of India. I know nothing about art, but in their dining room they had these fantastic marine paintings, which were all ships, done by somebody called Montague Dawson. They're now worth 150 grand each. All his cars were painted in the same colours, blue and silver, and there were two at the house in Curzon Street, an Aston Martin DB2 and a Mercedes 300SL."

Sally confirms how they met: "Through his sister, Angie. I met her and then Charlie came round and he was frightfully dashing and wonderful, and amusing. I was very young and my eyes were sort of like stars. It was a very strict upbringing in those days. One didn't go out too often, and certainly had to be home at 12. He was a very strict father!"

It was with some trepidation that Charlie introduced her to his racing pals. There were two concerns in his mind – firstly she might not be too impressed by the conditions in which they all lived, and secondly, one of the gang might try and nick her. But he couldn't hide her forever, and when they rolled up one day in her new Alfa Romeo, everyone took notice.

"I came down to this incredible flat in Harrow where they were all camping, Bubbles, Luke, Charlie, Jonathan, some other bods were all in this flat, all skint, all trying to race, all having their cars stuck together with glue."

They were all struck by Sally, none more so than Piers, who had seen Earl Howe on his visit to the Eton Automobile Society four years earlier. She recalls that Piers didn't make any secret of his interest: "Apparently Piers turned round and said to one of them that's the girl I'm going to marry. Very romantic!"

Crichton-Stuart confirmed the story: "I took Sally up the flat to meet everybody. Piers was trying to change some gear ratios, and said to Luke, 'I'm going to marry that girl.' Luke said, 'Don't be so fucking stupid. Just look at yourself; oil from head to foot.'"

Luke: "Sally was this dinky, Twiggy-like model, who looked as if she'd come from another planet. Piers was smitten…"

Bubbles: "I do remember the occasion. We were all down at the lock-ups at the bottom of the garden. She was a pretty girl, and we were scurfers, we were all oily rags. Here was a bit of quality!"

Jonathan: "Our jaws dropped in unison. Nobody had seen anything like that. We didn't buy fashion magazines, so we couldn't understand this at all. She was delightful."

In fact Piers had already met Sally when he was still a teenager at Eton, and they both attended a party at Frinton in Essex. However, Sally admits she had no recollection of an event that had clearly registered with him: "It must have been one of those parties when you're young and you're introduced to boys – in those days it was very conventionally done. I don't remember the dance, but he remembered the dress I wore – he told me when we got together."

Crichton-Stuart was soon engaged to Sally, but he had nothing to worry about, as Piers was far too gentlemanly to attempt to steal a mate's girlfriend. He would just have to bide his time.

"I'd never have said he was a great ladies man, as were some," says Horsley. "He was much more into the cars, and getting it organised."

"He wasn't interested, frankly," agrees Lucas. "He wasn't as predatory as some of his mates were. It sounds corny, but he was too nice a guy."

Top *Piers splashes round the soaking Vienna airfield. He finished sixth in the poorly* *supported event. It was the second 1,000cc F3 race ever held, and the first on the Continent.* **Bottom** *Although they kept their finances separate, Piers and Jonathan really looked like a* *team in Anglo-Swiss livery. Here Jonathan works in a sunny Monza paddock.* **Opposite** *Piers took this snap of a smiling Jonathan.*

Crichton-Stuart confirmed that Piers could still be a little naïve around women: "He was very wild, very charming, always had a smile on his face, hugely talented, but clumsy in everything he did. We sat in a bar in France once, and there was a barmaid who looked like Brigitte Bardot and had the lowest cut dress we'd ever seen. We were staring down the front of her dress for about ten seconds while she got some ice for us and Piers knocked this bloody coke over, straight down the front of her. That summed him up…"

However, Piers may have been something of a dark horse, deliberately keeping any female companions away from his pals. In late 1965 he made an interesting revelation to Anthony Marsh in an interview for *Sportscar* magazine: "I never bring girl friends anywhere near motor racing. I've seen so many friends bring fabulous girls to a racing weekend and have them set upon by a pack of wolves and lose them! Racing suffers from too many men chasing too few girls, most of whom have done the rounds before with other racing drivers! If you really care for a girl, don't mix her up with motor racing."

Later Piers would always insist that Anglo-Swiss Racing made its debut at the Nürburgring, but in fact his own personal scrapbook reveals that his first single seater race took place a little earlier, at the Aspern airfield track near Vienna on 12 April. For reasons he's now unable to recall, Jonathan could not make the trip, so Piers made the brave decision to tackle ASR's first meeting without him.

It was quite a trek down to Austria for the Zodiac, and Piers was possibly persuaded to go by Frank, who had his own reasons to make the trip – Aspern was to be Rindt's F2 debut, and he'd offered to help out. In fact he'd agreed to ferry Jochen's brand new Brabham to Vienna. Frank remembers the journey well:

"Instead of being grateful to me for getting the car from the Brabham factory in time for its first race, I got a bollocking from Jochen for damaging two tyres on the van. It was a 24-hour drive non-stop from the Brabham factory, starting at 8pm, to the middle of Vienna, and the autobahns then were quite brief, I can assure you, large parts were missing, especially in Austria. And that's all he said. 'You've cost me two fucking tyres!'"

The venue itself was hardly worth the long journey, as F2 contender Richard Attwood recalls: "Aspern was a really bad circuit, an airfield, in very bad repair. It was a real boneshaker. It had a tight hairpin and some faster bits, but it was a makeshift circuit, and the surface was the worst element of it."

The main event was the second race held to the new F2 rules. A small 15-car field included Jack Brabham and Denny Hulme, while bizarre legal reasons saw World Champion Jim Clark stuck as a frustrated spectator. Rindt had problems and didn't record a proper practice time, and nor did he figure in the race.

From an entry of 21 just nine cars turned out for the F3 support, and Piers was the only Briton on a grid that included a couple of Frenchmen and three East Germans in Melkus-Wartburgs. The organisers loaned him a local mechanic called Rudi, but even with outside help Piers was in at the deep end on his first F3 outing, almost literally after a downpour made the bumpy runways even more difficult come the race. He qualified sixth, and finished in the same position, three laps down on winner Guglielmo Bellasi.

Still, it was a start, and being on the same bill as Brabham and Hulme was a huge step up from club racing. He and Frank then headed north for the altogether more prestigious event on Nürburgring's 4.8-mile South Circuit a fortnight later, supporting the Eifelrennen F2 race. This time there was a much more representative F3 entry, including Jonathan, who had travelled over from England. It was here that Piers first encountered many of the European racers who would be his regular rivals over the next couple of years. He also met Nina Lincoln, Rindt's Finnish girlfriend.

"I was living at Belgium at that time, and I drove there to meet Jochen," she recalls. "I met Piers too. He was living in the back of a truck or something – the first impression was, 'Gosh, he's dirty!' He was very, very funny, a funny jolly guy, always jumping around and making jokes. He was lovely."

Above left *Roy Pike, Jonathan and Piers waiting for the race at Rheims on 5 July. The car is John Ampt's Alexis.*

Top right *Piers performs high tech preparation in the Rheims paddock as Aussie John Ampt offers advice.*

Bottom right *Piers made his first F3 appearance in England at Brands Hatch on 3 August. His race ended in* disappointment *when the throttle stuck and he collided with Roger Mac at Paddock Bend.*

Overleaf *Two fascinating pages from Piers's own scrapbook, including shots of the inside of 283 Pinner Road and* the lock-ups behind it, plus views of Piers's first trip to Monaco in 1964. It was the only race his parents attended.

The 25-lap race distance was more than the Lotus's fuel tank could manage, so Piers rigged up an auxiliary tank that sat above his knees. Belgian Jean-Claude Franck took pole and led away, while Piers surprised even himself by getting up to second. He was demoted a spot by Australian John Ampt, and although some reports said he spun off, Piers later wrote that he'd come to a halt after he tried to switch to his extra tank and his amateur plumbing let him down. Jonathan provided some cheer for the fledgling ASR outfit by taking third place.

That night they became involved in celebrations in the bar of the circuit's Sport Hotel with some of the star names from the F2 event, in which their pal Rindt had finished third. During the evening's festivities a policeman's moped found its way into the building.

"It was so cold that we decided not to sleep in the car, and so we found a guest house," says Jonathan. "Piers overdid it on the booze, not being used to it. We had a lovely time, because we were sitting next to Jim Clark, and that all went to our heads rather. Piers was a bit unwell in the night. He said we can't tell them... so we shoved some cash on the table, opened this window, and descended into the garden and legged it."

Next stop was Monza, and the trip gave them a first chance to drop into Chuck Graemiger's place in Lausanne.

"Every time we passed we'd pitch up there," says Jonathan. "We were always going to Italy or up from Italy; geographically it was an excellent place. He was a pretty good helper as well, but we were just using his place."

The first visit to Monza proved uneventful, although Jonathan did at least pick up third in a heat for the Coupe de Milan. From there they drove across to Monaco, for the prestigious Grand Prix support event. This was by far the biggest and most competitive F3 field yet gathered, and for the first time the humble ASR outfit came across the highly professional Tyrrell Racing Organisation and its ambitious lead driver, Jackie Stewart. With his works BMC support Ken Tyrrell was seen by some to be contravening the spirit of F3, which many regarded as a preserve of privateers.

"We were a total shambles," says Jonathan. "Tyrrell knew about motor racing. We didn't know anything. His cars were perfect and well prepared. But Ken was nice, and he could talk the hind legs off a donkey. He'd always spare some time to chat to you."

Monaco was a big weekend for Piers, for his parents were holidaying in France and agreed to come along to watch – possibly the only time in his entire career that they did so, certainly at an overseas event. Piers was determined to show them that he could make a go at motor racing. Unfortunately the meeting got off to a bad start when a lapse of concentration saw him stick the Lotus in the barrier at Mirabeau early in practice. The incident caused some amusement, as Frank

Williams recalls: "We heard later on that Piers had got out, scratched his head, picked up all the bits, and looked forlorn. It was such an act there was a titter from the crowd..."

Fortunately damage was cosmetic. There were two 16-lap heats, from which the top 11 finishers in each would qualify for the big final on Saturday afternoon. Jonathan finished sixth in the first, while Piers got involved in a fraught battle for second with John Ampt, Philippe Vidal, Bruno Deserti and Jean-Pierre Jaussaud. Eventually his exhaust worked loose. He finished 12th, and thus failed to make the final, which was dominated by Stewart. Still, there were clear signs that he could mix it with the quick guys.

Next came one of the biggest challenges faced by the travelling circus – the trip to East Germany for a pair of back-to-back races. The Cold War was at its height and the British drivers felt like 007s or Harry Palmers as they edged their way across the border into a world that was totally alien.

Charlie Lucas went along for the ride: "We got to that corner of Austria but we couldn't find the border. It was getting dark, and there were no lights anywhere, so we pulled into this field and went to sleep in the Zodiac. In the morning I got out and went to have a slash. There was a post behind me and I walked out by the road, and it said 'Achtung Mienen' on it. We had actually parked in a minefield!

"I was trying to figure out whether I should ask Piers to back it out gently or whatever, the idiot got out and started looning around. It scared the shit out of me! I still have this mental picture of this lunatic running across this field – not carefully trying to follow the car tracks or whatever – just bolting like hell across this field. It could have been the end of a beautiful relationship..."

Once you made it across the border, things ran surprisingly smoothly.

"You only got in if they invited you, but once you were in you were well treated," Charlie Crichton-Stuart explained. "It was full of goon towers, barbed wire, and people who'd just changed their uniform from a Nazi one to a communist one. We were all given a helper. Mine was a guy called Max, and he couldn't speak a word of English! But then he got pissed at the prize giving and his English was better than mine, so they were obviously put there to hear anything we said..."

"You were put up by the state," says Bubbles Horsley, who went there the following year. "We were paid huge sums of money, but in East German marks, which we then had to use to buy cameras, lenses and china. We'd smuggle them back into West Germany and sell them for useful money."

There were two venues on the East German trip. Bernauer-Schleife resembled Berlin's legendary Avus, in that it was essentially two sides of a dual carriageway.

Williams . Charly . Luke . Frank . Self .
Brands driving Luke's Mark VIII

Len + Charly.

Bub   Frank.

Frank driving the Zodiac back home Vienna.

Rear view of an Autobahn.

Mum. Jonathan. Me. John P.

Me   Mum

↑   ↗
MONACO.
↓   ↘

John P. Williams, Me

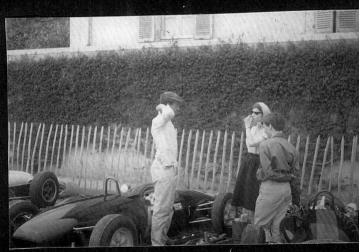

Me   Mum J.J.W.

"You just went down one side, and there were bales, and you buggered off in the other direction," says Jonathan. "It was a very grim place, no fun whatsoever. The local cars went like hell in a straight line, but they were in trouble because they had no proper tyres, and they didn't have disc brakes. But show them a long enough straight, and they went well! We went because it was a race and we got some money, and it kept us going. There was very little you could do after you'd bought an imitation Black and Decker drill and a load of petrol."

Despite encountering mechanical gremlins Jonathan finished third, but the race was won by John Peterson, a colourful American who was known to everyone as John P.

"I think he had faulty judgement," recalls Jonathan, "because he came over and got a Cooper and instead of putting a Ford in it he put a DKW motor. He had a DKW station wagon to tow it with, and the back was full of broken DKW engines covered in oil and filth and mess. As so was he – he wasn't a tidy chap! But he liked Germany, and based himself there."

Meanwhile on the same weekend Jochen Rindt was using Pinner Road as a base during his visits to the Mallory Park and Crystal Palace F2 races. With Frank giving him pit signals, Rindt won the latter event, and set himself on the route to stardom.

The second stop on the East German trip was very different, for Schleize was a dramatic road course that really tested the nerves. Piers described it to Barrie Gill in 1968: "It was a fantastic circuit, about five miles long, like a sort of Spa over cart tracks with open sweeping bends and one hairpin. At one point the road went through a farmyard between two large walls. There were chickens penned off on one side, and straw scattered all over the place. I came hurtling through there, hit the straw, went up the wall, shot out of the farmyard and disappeared into a ditch!"

This time the locals dominated, and most of the Brits were out of luck. Then before leaving it was a question of spending the local currency on things like fuel: "It was terribly expensive – about eight bob a gallon – but I used to carry about 60 gallons in cans strapped all over the Zodiac. They all leaked, and that petrol smelled like dead fish. It really was the most foul stuff. Even Jonathan's Volkswagen pinked on it!"

While Piers and Jonathan ended their trip to East Germany without major mishap, that very weekend tragedy struck one of their friends back in England. Old Etonian Peter Rose, who had shared Piers's early adventures at Chalgrove Airfield, had not pursued motor sport with the same fervour as his former school mate. But like Sheridan Thynne, he'd dabbled in club racing, and had acquired an Austin-Healey from his friend and

Chalgrove ringleader Martin Ryan. On 14 June Rose was practising for a minor event at Silverstone when brake failure pitched him into the sleepers, and he was killed instantly. Coming almost a year after his close neighbour's Mark Fielden's death – at the same circuit – it was a major shock.

"We were more affected by Peter Rose's accident," says Thynne," not because we liked him better or knew him better, but because Mark's accident was clearly not a motor racing accident in the conventional sense. We were more affected by somebody who was racing and had an accident than what was clearly a freak. It was very traumatic, but the fact is that when you're 21 and 22 you are not as long term affected by those things as when you're older."

"Peter Rose was a good driver and very enthusiastic," recalls school friend David Wansbrough. "He'd done very little racing so it was too early to tell what his potential was. But he was a great, great character, and a lovely man. I think his interest was more in the cars and the mechanics and the engineering than in the pure racing."

"It was very sad," says Jonathan. "He never intended to be a professional driver, but he was such a very nice person."

It's not known when news of his accident reached the F3 boys, as they would have been on the road from Germany to southern Italy and unlikely to be in close contact with the UK. But the next venue on their schedule, Caserta, was almost as scary as the one they'd just left, and not the ideal venue for anyone mourning the loss of a friend. The exceedingly dangerous road course would claim several young stars during the sixties, although there were compensations.

"That was a popular race because we got very good starting money for going down there, and everybody liked going to Amalfi and Positano," said Crichton-Stuart.

"It wasn't a fun place at all," says Jonathan. "It was about 30kms north of Naples; one of the little kingdoms before the unification of Italy. There was a huge palace. It was very hot, especially for us in those days, because we were not used to it. It was on public roads, with a sharp right hand corner. The coming back bit was bad because in the middle of that you went through a farmyard with a brick wall on both sides…"

"Caserta was not a place to go off," Bubbles Horsley confirms. "It was a sort of triangle. You went down a long straight, there was quite a tight corner, then another long straight with a couple of bends through an orchard, where later I had an accident with a guy in a black Lola, who unfortunately was killed. Then you went under a railway bridge; turned right again and went through the village, where 'Geki' had a fatal accident in 1967. There were kerbs to hit, which would launch you."

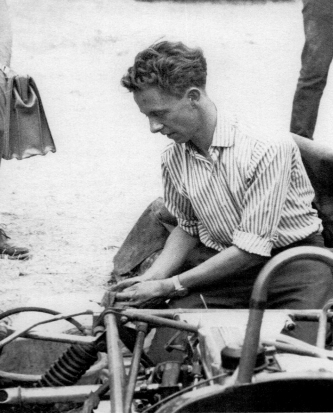

Piers had begun to demonstrate that he was at home on such a track, and his fifth place – and best Brit – was further proof of that. He was one of several drivers who ended up in jail on Sunday night. High jinks in the town square got out of hand when members of the group attempted to sabotage a police vehicle.

"We took the wheel nuts off a police van," says Bubbles Horsley, "and then got arrested. It turned over with us all in it."

"We got jailed for mucking around in the town before the race," Crichton-Stuart recalled. "They told us they were going to interview everybody, write down a few details, and then you can bugger off. Everyone was bored because it was 2am by this time. The first guy they called out was David Prophet. They said what's your name, he said, 'Prophet, David,' where were you born, 'Hong Kong'. Which was all true. But they threw us all back in jail because they thought the guy was taking the piss! They kicked us out at 6am…"

The trip back north nearly ended in disaster for Piers, as Charlie explained: "I followed him up from Caserta. He was in front of me in his Zodiac, and I could see his head dipping as he started to fall asleep in the midday sun. I thought this is going to be funny, so I dropped back 20 or 30 yards and I watched him fall asleep at the wheel, then hit the armco on the outside, which woke

him up. He got such a fright that he nearly jumped through the roof…"

Next stop was a return trip to Monza for the famous Lotteria event, where a fatal accident to local Norberto Bagnalista was another reminder of the risks involved. Piers finished fourth in his heat, and fifth in the final. On paper that appeared to be his most consistent outing to date, but *Autosport* reported it thus: "Courage went up a bank and into the woods at 100mph on the first lap – emerging with a grin!"

At Monza Piers indulged in a spot of DIY car maintenance, as Jonathan recalls: "The chassis was bent like a banana, so he reversed the Zodiac into it. It was actually quite an intelligent thing to do! He was quite handy. They were simple things to run in the end, and if there was an engine problem then we'd all chip in and sort things out. Money was tight, but possible. Expenses were low, except for things you broke, and petrol to get to the next race. A set of tyres would go for a year."

Piers described the way of life thus: "We had very little idea of how to set the cars up and the technique was to go as fast as you could for as long as the car held together. We were our own mechanics and we always arrived on the grid worn out and filthy. Every now and then it became necessary to repair to Lausanne to have the effects of some catastrophe rectified, and it was lovely to have a meal of cold milk and corn flakes and the supreme luxury of a bath."

Switzerland was a handy pit stop on the drive from Monza to Rheims for the support event for the 12 Hours and the F2 race. This was perhaps the biggest race after Monaco, and Jackie Stewart led an unusually dull race from start to finish. However, third place for Piers was further proof that he was getting better. There was a summer break in the continental calendar, so Piers and Jonathan headed back to the UK to catch their breath and allow Tom the Weld to work his magic on their battered machines.

"I'd arrive on a Monday or Tuesday morning to find three or four cars lined up outside the garage, with wheels cocked in the air and broken bodywork," Tom recalled. "We were continually straightening Piers' car. He used to go on these continental flings, and he was forever having accidents. He would come back with a very bent motor car and very limited funds to put it right, so we had to do the best we could. A lot of the time it was, 'I can't pay any more than this – it doesn't matter what it costs, that's all I've got.' We used to work round it."

Tom wasn't unduly worried about Piers's chassis-straightening efforts at Monza: "I think he learned that trick from me! We used to do appalling things. Health and Safety would go absolutely ape if they knew what we were up to in those days. I had a huge iron frame just outside the garage which I used to hang the chassis on. I'd put a pivot bar under the back, put weights on, heat the tubes, and pull it all back square. It was the only way to get them out racing again!

"Sometimes they were so twisted that we had to drive road cars up a ramp to put some extra weight on to bend them back again. But they always survived, although sometimes they used to have funny locking brakes between lefthanders and righthanders. But lots of the cars when they came out from the manufacturers weren't much better…"

Once back in London, Piers didn't sit still for long. None of his friends can remember how or why, but he linked up with David Prophet for a trip to Ireland, where he campaigned an unfamiliar white Lotus 32 at Dunboyne and Phoenix Park. The dramatic first venue was the home of the prestigious Leinster Trophy, and Piers must have found the damp, tree-lined village streets as testing as any continental street circuit.

An 18-year-old Ulsterman called John Watson drove an Austin-Healey Sprite in that meeting: "It was a triangular circuit, on little more than B-roads. When I first went to

watch as a child, it was just breathtaking to see these cars on a proper road circuit, and you could tell who was a good driver. Piers turned up and seemed to wander round as if he was rather lost in this strange place – he looked uncomfortable in the car, I have to say."

Exactly how Piers fared at Dunboyne is not recorded, but in the Hawthorn Trophy race at Dublin's Phoenix Park a week later he finished seventh overall, and second in the 1,100cc class. It was all good experience.

During the summer pit stop Piers also got swept up in the usual partying at 283 Pinner Road. On one occasion Frank Williams showed the rest of the gang the assets that would get him to the top – by which I mean his fierce determination and will to make a buck. The exact date is not known and a few details are sketchy, but the legendary Williams streak definitely happened, as various expert witnesses testify.

Bubbles Horsley: "He was paid 10 bob to run round the garden naked. Opposite in Pinner Road there was a church, and the whole thing was timed for when the congregation emerged from matins on Sunday morning. He got his 10 bob, set off naked, then the church emptied, and we wouldn't let him back in. The trouble was he couldn't hide at the back because every time a train went by there was this crouching figure."

Crichton-Stuart: "That was my bet. It was quite simple. I bet him 10 shillings that he wouldn't go out there with nothing on. He rushed out and I locked him out. He called my bluff because he went back down the road and I opened the door and said, 'For Christ sake, get back in here!,' because there were people going to church on the other side of the road."

Jonathan Williams: "The true story, because I was there, is that he accepted an offer of cash to go out with no clothes on when the commuter train from Pinner or I don't know where came past, and to jump up and down. I'm sure they all enjoyed it greatly. Then we locked him out. He was very cross about that."

"There was no big deal to it," says Frank himself. "Bubbles or Charlie bet me that I wouldn't do it, so I did it. Then they locked me out, which was very unfair, because it wasn't part of the deal. The train didn't stop. But it did go by quite slowly. I think it was for £5, which is a lot of money if you haven't got any…"

Frank was usually up to something in his quest for funds, as Crichton-Stuart recalled: "He was always on the main chance, trying to do deals and hanging around wherever there was any opportunity. But he was hard working, with a huge amount of energy, and was pretty amusing in his own right. We found him humorous in the nicest possible way. There was always some adventure that he was up to, and he was always hustling away."

Sally Curzon had quickly become part of the Harrow circle, occasionally attending races with Crichton-Stuart, but despite his long illness, Earl Howe's death in late July – at the grand age of 80 – came as a shock.

Another frequent visitor to Pinner Road was Charlie Lucas's sister, christened Charlotte but known to everyone as Loti. "Piers was relatively clean and sanitary looking compared with the lot who lived in the flat," she recalls. "It really was a rat hole. Frank was very quiet, he would follow along behind. He wasn't one of the instigators, one felt. He came to stay with us for Christmas one year. I can't remember him actually saying anything, and he was just sort of there. But he borrowed 2/6d off my mother to buy me a present – and she's never had it back! Frank was living so close to the edge."

Anglo-Swiss Racing made its British debut at Brands Hatch on 3 August, in a support event to the Guards Trophy sports car race. It was a not a great day for Piers, as a stuck throttle saw him slam into Roger Mac at Paddock Bend. That sort of incident somehow vindicated the decision to complete his racing education overseas, away from serious media attention.

In the middle of August Piers and Jonathan set off for the continent again. First stop was Nogaro, where Piers disgraced himself by crunching his car into a wooden fence in practice. He was able to borrow a Ford France-owned Lotus 27 for the race.

With his own car damaged Piers had the good fortune to find another ride, and at Zolder he turned up in a brand new Brabham entered under the name of Radio Caroline, the pirate station that had begun broadcasting in the spring. The deal was put together by colourful Irishman Derek Kavenagh, who was a regular at Cliff Davis's yard, and it involved Piers supplying his own engine. However Zolder was another disappointing outing, a driveshaft breaking on the line.

Below *Piers working on the Radio Caroline Brabham in the Zolder paddock on 23 August. His Zodiac can be seen in the background.*

Opposite *Piers sitting in Bubbles Horsley's F3 Ausper in the garages at the Nürburgring. The wide cockpit would allow two 'normal' people to sit side-by-side, much to Horsley's embarrassment...*

His luck was to change the following weekend on his first visit to Zandvoort, where he had another outing in the Radio Caroline car. After one minute's silence for Dutch hero Count Carel Godin de Beaufort, killed a month earlier in practice for the German GP, Piers burst through to take the lead from pole man Jackie Stewart. The Scot had been two seconds clear of the field in practice, and soon demoted Piers to second. But despite intense pressure from behind, Piers grimly held on, as *Autosport* reported: "Courage was in dreadful trouble with a locking brake on the nearside front wheel, and it says a lot for his skill and determination that he maintained his second position for two-thirds of the race."

He was eventually demoted by John Rhodes and talented Zandvoort specialist Rob Slotemaker, but fought back to reclaim runner-up spot: "Courage pulled out all the stops and rocketed past to take the chequered flag and set the seal on a fine drive in the face of adversity."

Zandvoort was truly a turning point in his career, and colleagues who hadn't taken him too seriously had to admit that he'd made great progress. "That was the best race of his life so far by a long chalk," says Jonathan.

Piers had a third outing in the Radio Caroline car at Crystal Palace, before returning to his faithful Lotus for the final continental fling of the season. First stop was the bleak Wunstorf airfield in Germany. By now Frank and Bubbles were on the road as a team, towing a pair of cars on a double deck trailer behind an elderly Morris van. Bubbles had acquired his bright green Ausper from Steve Ouvaroff mainly because it had a cockpit large enough to accommodate his bulky frame.

The huge driver's seat gave the others some cause for amusement, as Jonathan recalls: "At Wunstorf he'd gone off for a hot dog and a coffee, and when he came back Charlie Stu and Frank were sitting in his car side-by-side! Bubbles was extremely aggrieved, but it was the only sort of car that he could get in to..."

It wasn't the only laugh at Horsley's expense that weekend: "We camped on some waste ground near the track, and Bubbles slunk off into the darkness to have a crap in a cabbage field. We had lined up our vehicles and everyone put on their headlights, which resulted in a repetitive cry from the field of, 'You shits!'"

Crichton-Stuart recalled that meeting: "Frank used to rent out the back of the van for us to sleep in at night, so you didn't have to sleep in your car with the feet sticking out. At Wunstorf we all paid out 10 bob and went in there, Piers, Bubbles, Frank and myself. And the blankets were so bloody polluted with whatever Frank had had in there before!"

A visit to Vallelunga near Rome and then a return trip to the Nürburgring's South circuit on 27 September were next on the agenda. The latter event was something of a works outing for the Pinner Road brigade, with Piers, Jonathan, Charlie Stu, Frank and Bubbles joined by Charlie Lucas, who turned up to have his first crack at F3 in a Lotus 22 that he'd acquired from Roy Pike.

At the Nürburgring Luke had a close-up view of Piers the mechanic at work: "Tom had pop-riveted some aluminium sheet inside the cockpit area of the 31s to stiffen up the chassis. Piers thought it would be a bit of a tweak to save weight by taking this out, without realising of course that it was the water pipe that it was riveted to. So when he filled it back up with water again it just pissed out. He actually started the race with matches stuck in all the rivet holes to stop the water coming out!"

Eddie Fletcher, another member of the gang, blew his engine in practice. However, in order to earn his starting money he went onto the grid and, having got moving via the starter motor, coasted down to the first corner. When he got there he alighted from the car, took out the sandwiches, drinks and cigarettes he'd stashed in the cockpit, and proceeded to watch the race in style. When Piers's match sticks failed to stem the flow he pulled alongside Fletcher and, borrowing some handy tape and bits of tyre, attempted to plug the holes again! Jonathan eventually finished fourth, but the rest of the Brits were out of luck.

"Frank was driving a Brabham I owned," says Horsley. "I was driving round in my Ausper and I saw this familiar green bodywork all over the place, and then on the next lap there was Frank grinning at me out of a tree. I thought, 'You bastard, you've written my car off!' It upset me so much I went off shortly afterwards. I was chucked out of the old Ausper, and I winded myself landing, and I hurt my leg. I obviously didn't look too good, so they shoved me in the back of the ambulance, and set off for the hospital.

"They had to stop to open the gate, by which time I'd got my breath back and was *compos mentis* again. So I got up, got out, shut the door, and went back to the paddock. They took off at high speed and when they got there, there was nobody in the back. Actually, they were furious. They came and found me and I got the most terrible bollocking. They insisted on driving me to the hospital for a check-up..."

However, it wasn't always funny, as Crichton-Stuart recalled: "There were great moments of amusement, and great moments of tragedy. I remember a race at the Nürburgring when we had to go to the prize giving to get the start money. Somebody said something in German, so we all stood up. Piers suddenly realised it was one minute's silence for somebody. Then the guy got up again – it happened four times. Four people had been killed – one in the cars and three on motorbikes."

Lucas now had a taste for F3, and the following weekend he borrowed Piers's car for the end-of-season Farningham Trophy event at Brands Hatch. It was his first appearance at the Kent circuit, but Piers and Jonathan were on hand to offer advice and act as pit crew.

"Nobody told me Clearways was a righthander and not a lefthander," he smiles. "I drilled it straight into the bank on the first lap of qualifying. Next minute I was sitting in hospital, and I'd broken my left leg and left shoulder."

Aware that Piers was now stuck, Luke agreed that the decent thing would be to buy the remains of the crunched Lotus for a generous fee of £1,000. His stay in hospital was to prove expensive, as he was a sitting target for anyone with something to sell.

"The only person who comes to see me is Bubbles, who tells me, 'What you really need is an automatic American car, so you can sit on the other side with your leg up.' So he sold me a Ford Edsel. What a shyster!"

Sheridan Thynne paints an interesting picture of Piers at around this time: "I remember the first time Piers came and had dinner with us after we got married. He was about the second or third person to use our dining room. We had a sort of wine red carpet, and when we went in the next day to tidy up we found Piers had been scrabbling with his feet, presumably with nerves, throughout dinner. It looked like a minefield! Despite being 22 and by then in his first year in F3, successful, and well-adjusted, he was sufficiently nervous to scrabble up the carpet. This is no sense a critisicm, but he could be a very unrelaxed person."

With his own Lotus out of commission Piers was forced to contest the last two continental F3 events of the season at Innsbruck and Monza in a borrowed Alexis. On his return to London he went to see the still incapacitated Lucas, and the seeds of a grand plan were sown. "I was left some money by my grandfather," says Luke, "and it rather went to my head, I'm afraid."

Forget Anglo-Swiss Racing; from now on it would be Charles Lucas Engineering Ltd.

Those
magnificent
men in their flying machines

Piers dives down the inside of Trevor Blokdyk at Zandvoort on 29 August. The pair banged wheels, and Piers later retired after a tangle with a backmarker while leading. The Chequered Flag cars of Chris Irwin and Roy Pike follow here.

With a little prompting from Piers and Jonathan, Luke decided to invest some of his recently acquired wealth in his own F3 team. All three of them would drive, and the general idea was that together, they would have as much fun as possible.

"It was Piers who talked him into having this team," says Jonathan. "Luke admired Piers. He came into a lump of money, proper money, and that's when we took off."

"It seemed like they were having such fun going around to all these races, so I thought it would be fun to do it properly," Lucas admits. "It was because Piers was a mate of mine, not because he was an ace driver. And Jonathan rather the same, although he was considered the star, because he'd been racing in Europe longer than we had. Piers was the dearest friend I ever had, and you just wanted to have him around if possible, because he was always a laugh."

When Piers later finalised his 1964 accounts for the British taxman, he estimated his income from racing at

£1,000, and his running expenses at £1,040, including a hefty £340 for 12 cross channel trips. But no longer would he and Jonathan have to watch the pennies or sleep in road cars as they struggled from race to race. Now though they were effectively professional drivers, taking 40% of the start and prize money, with the rest going to Lucas. However, there was also a modest flat fee, as Jonathan recalls: "I remember Piers talked him into giving us a salary of something like £5 a week, so we would get our stamp and be in the system so we would actually get a pension one day!"

Piers no longer needed a heavy duty tow car, so in November 1964 he sold the trusty Ford Zodiac to Frank. He replaced it with a red MGB, bought from Cliff Davis on a three-year HP agreement. It would serve as suitably flashy transport to the races for himself and Jonathan. Meanwhile rather than commission more ersatz Lotuses from Tom the Weld, Lucas decided to buy a pair of second-hand Brabhams.

"They were actually F2 cars," says Jonathan, "which were just as good as the new F3s. I had Alan Rees's, and Piers had Denny Hulme's. And we got new Cosworth engines, two each. So we were really opulent."

Luke insists that the decision to go for older F2 chassis was a wise one: "It was rational, because it was a slightly stiffer chassis, with better front uprights. They were slightly better cars and they worked all right. Tom put the F3 engines in them, and off we went."

As his ambitious plans gathered momentum, Luke made matters even more complicated by adding a fourth driver, racing trainer's son Peter Gethin.

"I'd been driving the Lotus 23 sports car and Gethin was the king, he was the man," says Luke. "He won a thing called the Guards Championship. He was a nice

guy and you wanted him around. He had to drive the wretched old 22."

"I met Charlie when I was driving a Lotus 23, and so was he," Gethin recalls. "He had the latest big wheels and all sorts of special tweaks, and I had a standard car, and I still beat him most of the time!"

Gethin was obviously quick, but there was a more unusual motive behind his recruitment, as Jonathan suggests: "The only reason was that Charlie Luke fancied Gethin's girlfriend. He thought it would be easier to steal her away by having Gethin under his wing. And he did! I don't think Peter was too pleased at the time."

Even Gethin admits that he wasn't hired on talent alone: "They were all his mates, and I think Charlie invited me to drive because I'd beaten him quite a few times, and he liked me. And he fancied my girlfriend. I can't think of a better reason to employ someone, really!" As things turned out, the plan eventually backfired on Lucas, as Peter recalls: "She left me for Charlie, left Charlie for Piers, and left him for a postman…"

The Lucas team made its debut at the Boxing Day meeting at Brands Hatch, postponed to 31 January by the freezing conditions on the original date. For some reason only Jonathan was entered in one of the newly acquired Brabhams, while Gethin had Luke's old Lotus 22 for his first single-seater drive. He stripped first gear at the start and made a poor getaway, but Williams led from the off and became involved in a fraught battle with Roger Mac. After they tangled Jonathan spun and had to settle for second, while Gethin salvaged fifth.

It was not a bad start, and Luke now had nearly two

Piers poses for the camera of leading photographer and friend Patrick Lichfield. The stripy overalls caused much amusement in the F3 paddock.

months to get properly prepared for the season. He made sure that the team was as well presented as the cars: "Everything was red, white and blue. And we had groovy dark blue overalls with stripes down the sleeves. Everybody thought we must have been a bunch of pooftas! It was slightly over the top. Even our sweaters were red, white and blue. We also bought these stupid little scooters, Honda monkey bikes, for the convenience of the team. And we moved from Cliff Davis's yard to a railway arch a bit further down the road in Shepherd's Bush."

No one had seen anything quite like it before. Ken Tyrrell had pioneered professional preparation at F3 level, but there was nothing flashy about his operation. The Lucas *équipe* made its next appearance not at a glamorous continental venue, but at Yorkshire's windswept Croft Autodrome on 27 March. Gethin won in the old Lotus 22, while Luke's Brabham ran with the leaders, until a spin.

At this stage the team had more drivers than cars, so at the first major meeting at Oulton Park on 3 April Jonathan was absent while Luke and Piers had a go. It was at Oulton that Lucas first established a rivalry with Graham Warner's well-known Chequered Flag team.

There were several links between the two organisations; the Chiswick-based Flag was also from

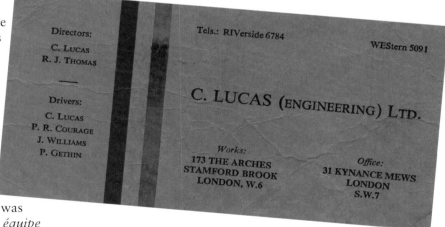

Top *Luke's camera catches Piers aboard an Alfa Romeo with team supporter Carol Crook, daughter of racer and Bristol Cars owner Tony.*

Above *The Lucas team had four drivers, but there were rarely enough cars to go round.*

Opposite *First time out in Luke's Brabham on Good Friday, and Piers leads John Cardwell down the hill at Oulton Park. He eventually finished fourth.*

West London, and Tom the Weld had once worked there, building Gemini Formula Juniors. And the number one driver was a Cliff Davis regular, Roy Pike, who knew Jonathan and Piers well.

Pike recalls that the colourful Lucas team's arrival on the scene caused some amusement: "He bought race suits, he bought booties for the drivers, he bought this, he bought that. He must have spent an awful lot of money. He never actually thought about making money out of it."

"We had a beautiful lorry he'd bought from Ian Walker, all these fancy overalls, the monkey bikes," says Jonathan. "One of the magazines said, 'The Charles Lucas team and the drivers with their gaudy overalls.' The world wasn't ready for this yet…"

Charlie Crichton-Stuart put his new Brabham on pole at Oulton, but the Lucas boys filled the next three places, with Gethin ahead of Piers and the team boss. However, come the race Pike charged through to win for the Chequered Flag. But with Gethin and Lucas both hitting problems, Piers upheld the team's honour in fourth, having briefly held the lead at the start.

Ever keen on the continent, Jonathan headed down to Italy for solo appearances at Monza and Imola, but the next outing for Piers was at Goodwood on Easter Monday, on the weekend that mods and rockers fought on the beach front at Brighton.

Hail, sleet and snow rather spoiled race day for the 50,000 strong crowd, but when the F3 event got underway it was Chequered Flag against Lucas. "We were the two teams with money to spend," says Jonathan. Pike and Piers battled fiercely at the front, as *Autosport* reported: "It was Pike versus Courage with a vengeance, and on several occasions the latter came within an ace of overtaking the American." Piers finished just 0.6sec behind, with Jonathan third.

At around this time the Lucas *équipe* scored one over its main rival when the team was invited to help with the filming of Roger Moore's *The Saint* TV series. Piers and Luke indulged a little stunt driving with the Brabhams, and had a great deal of fun doing it, as the latter recalls: "They wanted interlocking wheels, banging against the side of the cockpit, that sort of thing. It scared the shit out of us. Piers said, 'You go behind – if you hit my rear wheels you're the one that goes up in the air.' Thank you very much!" Ironically the episode was entitled *The Chequered Flag*…

Next on the agenda was a trip down to Pau, allowing Luke to stretch the legs of his latest acquisition, a gold Ford Thunderbird. He was fascinated by flashy road cars, and sometimes couldn't help himself, as Merlyn boss Selwyn Hayward recalls: "There used to be a lovely expression in London among the car dealers – clap hands, here comes Charlie! Every time we saw him he either had a Ferrari or a Porsche…"

Jochen Rindt and his F2 team-mate Alan Rees came along for the ride to Pau, but it was to prove a disappointing weekend, as the fortunes of Team Lucas hit rock bottom. Piers crashed in the wet, while the team boss retired after "about 12 spins," having qualified a respectable fifth. Later it was discovered that it wasn't entirely his fault, and that the car had some suspension quirks: "It was something to do with the way Graham Hill had set it up…"

Nevertheless his confidence had taken a battering, and he didn't race again that year: "Charlie could be very good one day, and forget it the next," says Gethin. "He was a young man who had a lot of money, a very nice, charming man. He enjoyed it, but it wasn't something he wanted to be a World Champion at."

Thus far the fledgling team had not set the world alight, but there was a change for the better a fortnight later at Zolder – and strong Belgian ale played a part.

"We used to stay at this grotty hotel," says Luke. "I seem to remember somebody throwing up in the corridor.

Piers leads the pack in the International Trophy support event on 15 May. He went on to score his first outright F3 win, although he nearly crashed as he set off on his victory lap…

But it couldn't smell any worse than it did already! On Saturday night Jonathan had been playing snooker and he got so pissed he fell asleep on the billiard table. We thought, 'Well, he's not going to be much use tomorrow.' He got up in the morning and he didn't say a thing from breakfast to lunchtime. Then the race came and he flew. He was fantastic…"

Jonathan led Pike home to give Lucas its first victory, while Piers set fastest lap before missing a gear shift and blowing his engine.

"That was where it all changed," says Williams, who paints a slightly different but equally colourful picture. "What happened was that I went out after practice with Picko Troberg and a friend of his, and we did a sort of pub crawl over the whole of that area. Eventually I got back in. I was sharing a room with Peter Gethin, and according to him I was making a lot of noise and fell unconscious on the floor, between the two beds, where I slept happily until 9am. Then I felt absolutely rotten until I got in the car. And I never drove better!"

The Lucas team returned to England in triumphant mood, and the celebrations continued at Silverstone at the International Trophy meeting on 15 May, the day that Jackie Stewart scored his first F1 victory for BRM. Piers and Jonathan were both in contention in the F3 event, as reported in *Autosport*: "Courage, Pike and Williams had a tooth and nail battle for supremacy and were never more than a few feet apart, the trio often being practically neck and neck, fighting for each corner."

Jonathan retired with a fuel pump failure leaving Piers to head Pike across the line. He remembers that race well: "We passed Pike going into Woodcote, both of us, one on each side, and that just wrecked him." Roy has

Top left *Luke always had a soft spot for flashy road cars. The gold Ford Thunderbird was one of his more memorable machines, and made regular trips to the Continent.*
Top right *Sporting his smart new jumper, Piers relaxes with Charlie Crichton-Stuart. Some people thought the colourful Team Lucas outfits were a little over the top...*
Bottom left *Piers compares notes with Chris Irwin, possibly on the subject of hats. The pair were to be regular on-track rivals over the next couple of years.*
Bottom right *Piers and Jonathan pose with the red MGB that carried them around Europe in 1965. It was a step up from the days of sleeping in grubby tow vehicles, and matched his trousers so nicely.*

his own version: "Jonathan got in the way, broke the tow and I just dwindled away."

It was Piers's biggest win to date, although he spoiled things a little by losing control and spearing onto the grass as he set off on his victory lap, distracted perhaps by the huge garland strung around his neck! In later years he would frequently have a laugh at his own expense while retelling the story.

Any trip back to Britain would invariably involve a stay in Harrow, which continued to be the focal point of action of all kinds. Frank Williams had found novel ways of raising funds, as F3 racer John Cardwell recalls: "One night Charlie Stu and I had been out for a meal, and we came back at about 10pm. There was a guy on the door of the flat saying, 'A pound a head please.' I said 'Charlie, what's going on?' He said, 'I don't know.' I said to the guy, 'This is Mr Crichton-Stuart, it's his flat.' He said, 'Hang on, I'll get Mr Williams.' Frank had blue movies running and was taking money off passers-by..."

"They were of a very, very poor standard," recalls Jonathan. "Old scratchy black and white things where the frames jumped! It hadn't become an art form yet."

"They used to come into the country in frozen chicken lorries," says Bubbles Horsley. "Obviously some dodgy F3 driver was in that business! The best customers were the Harrow police. We used to do their Christmas movie show, so they turned a blind eye to us..."

With their shares of the Lucas prize money stacking up nicely, and Luke paying expenses, Piers and Jonathan could now afford to travel around in relative comfort.

"It was brilliant," says Jonathan. "You could drive your own car to the race, and check into a little hotel. It didn't become more serious, in the sense that we still had our sense of humour, we just had better equipment, and it was rather nice. And once we'd won a couple of races, it became easy."

Next step was Montlhéry, the partially-banked track that Piers had last visited as a teenage tourist. He retired after clipping the chicane straw bales, while Jonathan had to make do with third: "Charlie Crichton-Stuart won it, and we didn't do particularly well. It was a jump on the brakes type track, no skill required."

After the race the boys headed into Paris to sample the colourful nightlife.

"It was all Luke's fault," says Jonathan. "He said he'd show us the sights of Paris, and dragged us off there. We went out in his gold Ford Thunderbird. We stopped outside somewhere, and the doorman turned up and called him 'Sir Charles.' So he was not unknown in the area!"

The evening proved to be a handy way for Jonathan to get rid of some unwanted East Germany currency he'd held on to since the previous year: "This particular girl was extremely nice, and I thought she deserved a present. You wouldn't have known – it said

'Deutschmarks' all over them – a bit unkind, but there you are!"

From Paris the group headed down to Monza for a double header – two lucrative races within a week that made it financially worthwhile to miss the clashing but more prestigious Monaco event.

Held on 27 May, Piers's 23rd birthday, the Vigorelli Trophy was promoted as the richest F3 race yet, with £1,400 available to the winner. Jonathan and Piers each won their heats, and after leader Andrea de Adamich spun off in the soaking wet final, Jonathan came home ahead of Kurt Ahrens and Piers.

"I won that race because of Frank," says Jonathan. "You couldn't see in the rain, it was awful. I had one of these clip-on bowl type things on front of my helmet, from which the water got blown away at speed, but I left it in the paddock. Frank went to get it. When the one-minute board was out he came across like a rugby player, dodging every official. He managed to slip it onto my hat before they dragged him away!"

The Lucas team was far better prepared than most of the local opposition: "The British were much more advanced than the Italian guys," says de Adamich, "because of the tyres, engines and so on."

Three days later, with some of their rivals having trekked off to Monte Carlo, Piers and Jonathan again won their respective heats of the Coppa Autodromo. Jonathan's victory in the final led to a brief if uncharacteristic dispute with Piers.

"We had a verbal agreement, and I broke it! We were great mates, and whenever he was quicker he was quicker, when I was quicker, I was quicker. There was one occasion at Monza where we were so much faster than everybody else I actually said to him that you can have this one. We were a bit cocky in those days! We were just driving round in the rain, and I don't know what came over me in the end – maybe I thought he was going too slowly – but I whizzed past him and disappeared into the distance. Piers was a bit peeved after that – he said, 'You told me it was my race.' I said, 'I meant it to the fingertips, but I couldn't sit watching your gearbox going that slowly round Monza.' But that was the only time – otherwise it was a straight fight. He didn't feel angry for long..."

One of the twin Monza victories actually earned Jonathan a car, although that wasn't as grand as it sounded: "A load of junk it was too. Innocenti built BMC cars under licence, and this was the one they couldn't sell. It was a sort of Morris Oxford type thing. They had a field full of them they couldn't get rid of! I couldn't put it on Italian number plates, as that was bureaucratically impossible. A friend of mine had had a tax free car in France with red number plates. He didn't need them any more so I put those on the car and used it when I was in Italy. Eventually somebody bought it for about 2/6d!"

Having lost out at Monza, Piers bounced back in style the following week. He won at Brands Hatch on the Sunday and Goodwood on Whit Monday – setting new lap records at both venues. At the Kent track £500 was up for grabs for a new record, and *Autosport* rather ungenerously noted that: "Courage's time of 53.6sec is an indication of how fast money can make a man go."

Jonathan had preferred to travel to the daunting Chimay road course in Belgium that weekend, ironically the sort of high-speed track that Piers would have loved. But a couple of weeks later the pair reunited at Caserta, for the grandly named Coppa d'Oro Pasquale Amato.

"I remember Jonathan and Piers arriving at Caserta, and they'd come down in Piers's MGB," recalls rival John Cardwell. "They were absolutely burned brown, as they'd driven right from the UK with the roof down!"

Making a rare appearance on this trip was Frank Williams, in what was described in *Autosport* as an "unstable looking Cooper" that he'd bought from veteran entrant John Coombs. Frank had gone to Coombs with a bag of money, but had been completely unable to find out the asking price for the car. However, the canny team owner wined and dined him and found out how much was in the bag. Frank left with a Cooper and £20 to his name. It was all part of the learning experience…

Once again Piers showed that he was a man to beat on fast circuits where bravery counted for much, leading home Cardwell by 19 seconds. Frank brought up the rear, and when he lapped him Piers entertained his friend by weaving from one side of the track to the other, like a jubilant Spitfire pilot making a victory roll.

"I remember seeing him at Caserta," says Frank. "He passed me on the slowing down lap. It was a very bumpy road there, and he was just showing off his car control. I was very impressed!"

After the race Piers was delighted to meet Juan Manuel Fangio, who had loaned his name to an Italian F3 team and was now actively seeking entrants for a series he was organising in Argentina for the following winter. Jonathan recalls a test day at Silverstone earlier in the season: "When we first had our Brabhams, at the very beginning we took them up to Silverstone for a practice day. It was wet, and when it dried out we started to drive round. Fangio had orchestrated a team for young Argentinian drivers, paid for by the YPF petrol people, and they were there too. I believe we got down to about 1min 40sec, and none of the Argentinians could get under 1min 44sec. They were saying, 'The English have sold us duff

engines!,' or something. Fangio got in one of these things, with no goggles, no crash hat, and he nipped out before they could stop him. He did a warm-up lap and his first flyer was 1min 39sec something. So that old man could drive…"

After Caserta Piers, Jonathan and John Cardwell headed to the nearby resort of Positano for a brief holiday. Piers had a go at water skiing for the first time, and there was even a sightseeing trip to Pompeii, which no doubt revived happy memories of Latin prep at Eton. Then the gang headed back to Monza for the Lotteria GP, and the third race there in a month.

Roy Pike recalls how Frank raised some extra cash in Italy: "He'd go down to the town and buy a crate of Cokes and come back to the pits and sell them individually. Fantastic! You can't believe that someone with so little, except great determination, could create so much. He was extremely talented, he worked very hard."

Once again Piers won his heat, although come the final he was handicapped by a broken steering wheel. The Lucas lads lost out in a slipstreaming dash to the line, Picko Troberg heading home Cardwell, Piers and Jonathan.

Wherever possible, the visitors tried to help each other on and off the track: "We were all very wary of the local heroes," says John Cardwell, "because they could be bloody dangerous. We used to try to protect each other. If these guys started getting in the middle of us we'd get them out of the way if we could! With 15 or 20 cars running wheel to wheel, you had to trust each other. And we had the best cars and the best engines. If somebody was stuck for a part, it was 'I've got one, here you are.' We used to drive like hell against each other, but we were good mates."

Bubbles Horsley recalls one of the more interesting drawbacks of racing at Monza: "A group of us would have to agree not to finish, and retire with about two laps to go. The idea was to lay siege to the guy who organised it – to stop him doing a runner with the gate receipts! For that, you received a percentage of everybody else's prize money. I think I was one of the volunteers…"

In June the Lucas team moved to new premises at Duke's Head Yard, just off Highgate High Street, which had previously been the home to the British Racing Partnership F1 team. It was another clear sign that the patron wanted to have a professional outfit.

"It was the smartest place I'd ever seen," Luke recalls. "We were moving upmarket a little bit, and we were doing quite a bit of work now as Tom had started to build our engines. Eventually we installed our own dyno. The trouble was that when you started the engines up at 11pm the whole of that valley where Alexandra Palace is acted like an echo chamber. People were going around wondering where the whine was coming from…"

happy to share a grid with the big names, and run in front of a 70,000 strong crowd. Piers was the fastest F3 qualifier and led the class from the off, but a loose electrical lead caused to him to retire on the second lap, leaving Pike to win from Gethin.

The final continental fling of 1965 was at Monza, supporting the Italian GP. Lucas had entered a third car for Cacho Fangio, and much excitement resulted when it caught fire in the paddock garage, as mechanic John Pettit recalls: "My concern was that all the guys' personal belongings were inside the garage, so I rushed in to get Piers's bag. That's when the fuel tank blew up, and blew me out of the door. We were right next door to Honda. Denny Hulme said, 'You should have seen the Japanese – they left everything and ran for miles!' I lost my sight for a few hours, and ended up in some sort of nunnery round the corner…"

Jonathan was now fit enough to make a proper comeback, and he won the first heat, held in the rain, but had a flat battery in the second, which handed victory to American Bob Bondurant. Piers was out of luck, and retired. In the afternoon the disappointed Lucas boys watched their old F3 rival Jackie Stewart score his first Grand Prix victory. Williams recalls that both he and Piers had a promising chat with Tim Parnell, who ran a semi-works BRM, about possible future F1 opportunities. They were now within reach of the big time.

The last few outings back on home ground brought a win for Piers in a clubbie at Silverstone, a retirement in the Oulton Park Gold Cup support event and another with gearbox problems while leading at Brands on 3 October.

Several members of the Pinner Road gang got a pleasant surprise with their corn flakes on 24 October when *The Sunday Times* devoted a page of its trend-setting colour supplement to 'The new men,' profiling ten of the most promising young racing drivers of the time. Piers, Jonathan, Charlie Stu, Roy Pike, Chris Irwin, Peter Gethin and John Cardwell each got a mention and a moody portrait. All good publicity, and something with which to impress friends and family.

With his regular Brabham now put up for sale Piers stepped into a Lotus 35, a recent acquisition by the Lucas stable, for a Brands clubbie at the end of October. In the Formule Libre race he was contesting second place with Alan Rollinson's F2 car when he went off, the ensuing damage also forcing him to non-start the F3 event, for which he had earned pole. It was a rather low-key end to the season.

One of those autumnal Brands Hatch meetings was to have rather more lasting significance. Piers was still determined to fulfil the promise he'd made when Sally Curzon had made her first visit to the Harrow flat. Piers would never have made a pitch when she was with

Charlie Crichton-Stuart, but one presumes he now felt that all bets were off. There was one small problem, however, for in the interim she had met someone in New York.

"There was a very nice American who I was going out with, and he came over to see me. Piers said, 'Come to Brands Hatch.' So I dragged this man down to Brands Hatch, and Piers decided to drive us back, or rather insisted on driving us back, in the most terrifying fashion. The whole thing was so embarrassing. The poor man was so traumatised by the drive that he asked to get out. He said, 'I'll give you a call.' When he'd gone I said, 'Piers, you can be absolutely shocking!'

"He did it on purpose, too. He was as pleased as punch. All he did was grin the whole way back, and then he said, 'I'll pick you up for dinner.' And that was it, that was the start. Piers had obviously decided to work out a plan to get rid of him...

Before long they were officially an item, and engagement soon followed: "Wasn't I lucky? I was swept up by this dashing young man who looked absolutely stunning and decided to take over, and that was it. The poor darling, he didn't have a bean. He was living with his grandmother. I was taken round there for tea, and then he crashed his car. He wasn't looking where he was going, and we were laughing so much he drove into a skip!"

Luke and the other F3 lads were mightily impressed: "They were a wonderful couple – what more could you ask for? You could look at Sally, and Piers made you laugh!"

Linking up with Sally was the icing on the cake during what had been an outstanding year for Piers. His achievements on the track were neatly summed-up when Luke advertised the Brabham for £1,900 in *Autosport*, noting that Piers had amassed 12 wins and five lap records with it. He was now regarded as a serious prospect by those who knew him.

"I figured in 1965 that Piers would eventually do good things," says Jonathan. "He had the speed, and he could stay on the road as well for prolonged periods. I think it took him until '65 to mature to that stage. At that time I thought that in Grand Prix terms he'd be sort of a Denny Hulme; very good, not a Jim Clark, but certainly win a few races if he kept at it. He had the enthusiasm from day one, he got the speed, and finally he got the dependability. I think he was at a high level."

Peter Gethin faded from the picture at Lucas as the season went on, but he too held Piers in high regard: "It was a fun year, driving with some nice guys. Piers was always going to be a top driver; he and Chris Irwin were the two who I thought would make it. Piers was just a natural driver, like a polished Rindt. He was very smooth and had good control on fast circuits, and he was fairly brave, but then you had to be in those days."

Meanwhile plans for 1966 were already well advanced, and the Lotus name figured prominently. Luke rightly felt that his organisation had achieved a degree of respectability, and wanted to step up a gear by gaining works status. There was no chance with Brabham, and instead he had his eye on Lotus, who hitherto had no official representation at F3 level. After initial contact at the Motor Show, a deal was set in motion by Geoff Murdoch, competitions boss of Esso and an influential supporter of Piers even in the Anglo-Swiss days.

During early discussions a new name cropped up as Piers's prospective team-mate – that of Roy Pike, who chose to leave The Chequered Flag. Both Jonathan and Gethin dropped out of the frame.

"Charlie was offered the Lotus works deal," says Jonathan. "A poisoned chalice if ever there was one! Part of the money was coming from Esso, and that was Geoff Murdoch. For some reason he didn't take much of a shine to me. Instead he greatly favoured Roy Pike, and he was over the moon about Piers's prospects. He told Luke, 'You have your driver, and I'll have my driver.' So I was more or less shouldered out. Everyone was saying 'Pike is the new Jim Clark.'"

It was also agreed that the team would spend more time in the UK and miss some of the less significant overseas races.

"The trouble was Jonathan only really wanted to race in Europe," says Lucas. "So it wasn't a great team effort. He couldn't wait to get back in the sunshine."

Jonathan did indeed have an independent streak, and had always preferred the gypsy lifestyle and the sun on his back. He had a good name in Italy after winning so often at Monza, and soon managed to land a works drive that would allow him to spend the full season on the continent.

"I managed to ask a chap I knew to tell de Sanctis that he could bribe me to leave Charlie Lucas! And that all worked very well. I went down to them and said force me to leave, make me an offer I can't refuse. And they did."

For Lotus, the attractions of the arrangement with Lucas were clear. A new F3 car, the 41, was on the way, and good results for a works-backed team would generate customer sales. Negotiations were conducted by team manager Andrew Ferguson, and a deal was agreed on 10 December.

"We were asked to the Lotus factory, so myself, Roy Pike and Piers went to see Ferguson and Chapman," says Lucas. "I wish I had a tape of it! They talked to Piers and Roy and said, 'Of course we want you to test the F1 car, race Lotus Cortinas, and we're not quite sure about

running you at Indy this year, but…' It went on and on and on. Piers's eyes were standing out on stalks. He couldn't believe it!"

So Charles Lucas Team Lotus was born, although as Luke remembers, it was a complicated arrangement: "We all signed contracts with Firestone, we didn't sign with Lotus."

Lotus also took options on the services of both Piers and Roy for 1967 and '68, and thus they would be available for promotion if they turned out to be good enough. Barely four years had passed since Piers had brought his homebuilt Lotus Seven in for its fateful first check-up, so the prospect of driving alongside Jim Clark must have seemed like a dream. In fact everything came together so quickly that it was decided that the new alliance should make its debut before the end of the year, in the Lombank Trophy at the Boxing Day meeting at Brands. The first Lotus 41 was hurriedly completed, and given a shakedown by Piers. He wasn't very happy with it.

"It was a really crappy car," says Luke. "We had to do an awful lot of work to get it to work before the first big race, which was Boxing Day Brands. The first time Piers drove it there was no way it would work. We had great trouble with the front suspension, because it was a very flexy old chassis."

The Brands event was made even more interesting by the appearance of Brabham's new 1966 model, in the hands of Irwin. It was in effect a showdown between the two manufacturers, and a good result would guarantee lucrative winter sales.

The 41 looked great in its green and yellow works livery, just like a mini version of Clark's title-winning Grand Prix car. In front of a large holiday crowd, and under unusually bright skies, Piers did the job for Colin Chapman, and overcame the car's faults. Helped by good tyres, he led home Irwin's new Brabham by 7.6 seconds, putting the Lotus firmly on top of the F3 shopping lists. For Piers, it was the perfect way to end a season that had really put him on the map.

In a winter edition of *Sportscar* magazine, Grand Prix commentator Anthony Marsh revealed how highly Piers was now regarded: "Courage talks quickly, eagerly, but he says he has not yet learnt to 'hard-sell' himself, as a professional driver needs to these days. However, his racing record this year and his classic, polished driving style must have made their mark internationally, without any self-advertising from him. This slight, cheerful young man is perhaps one of the few amongst today's up-and-coming who can safely be picked out as a top-line racing driver of the future."

Left Piers fools around on one of the Honda 'monkey bikes' that the Lucas team acquired in 1965.

Right Jonathan Williams was to be Piers's F3 team-mate for two happy seasons.

Un homme et une femme

A smiling Piers at the wheel of the Lotus 41, his helmet now carrying the Eton colours that were to become so famous. This first example was painted by Australian mechanic John Pettit, who was actually a qualified structural engineer having fun in Europe before settling down.

For Piers everything looked rosy at the start of 1966. As before he was to be paid 40% of any prize, starting and bonus money by Charles Lucas, while Esso's Geoff Murdoch provided a welcome retainer of £500. He also had a rather significant date looming on the horizon – marriage to Sally, although even she can't recall exactly when the subject first came up.

A March date was carefully chosen to precede the European racing season, but they would have limited time to enjoy each other's company in the build-up to the ceremony. Luke had accepted Juan Manuel Fangio's invitation to contest the Temporada, a new four-race F3 series to be held at various venues in Argentina, starting in Buenos Aires on 23 January.

"I'd met this dodgy old guy called Vannini," he recalls. "He used to be Fangio's manager, and was involved in putting the whole Temporada thing together. He asked me if he could rent a car for this guy Cacho Fangio to drive. He really was a son... You only had to look at him. He had those eyes."

A selection of South American drivers were found berths alongside the European visitors, who included Piers, Irwin, Crichton-Stuart, John Cardwell, Clay Regazzoni and, in his final fling with the Lucas team, Jonathan Williams.

"It was fantastic, because they had no other international racing in Argentina then," said Crichton-Stuart. "And apart from the Tasman series there was no other racing going on, so it got terrific publicity. The girls were pretty, the weather was great, so it was jolly nice."

Alas the expedition got off to a disastrous start for Piers, who was to drive the team's older monocoque Lotus 35. In practice for the opening event in Buenos Aires he first had a minor off, and then shortly afterwards had another more comprehensive accident, spearing off the track at the high-speed first corner. Two wheels were torn off and the chassis was badly crumpled, and while Piers wasn't hurt in the initial impact, a burst radiator dumped boiling water over his legs.

"He was obviously one of the favourites," says Lucas, "but he stuffed his car."

"It was a big sweeper with concrete on the outside," says Jonathan. "It was a really quick corner."

Piers maintained that the throttle had stuck open, a theory supported by mechanic John Pettit: "I'm sure the throttle stuck, and there were various theories as to why. It was a lovely car, and if he hadn't crashed it I think he would have been the one to beat in that series. He was running extremely fast at the time."

The boiling water left Piers with a badly scalded left foot, and he was in some discomfort as he hobbled round the paddock on a crutch. The race was won by the Chequered Flag car of Chris Irwin, with Crichton-Stuart second and Jonathan upholding Lucas honour in fourth.

The circus then packed up and headed for Rosario, leaving one member stranded in a Buenos Aires hospital on his own. Daily attention to the burned skin was not much fun, as Piers told Barrie Gill two years later: "It really was excruciatingly painful. They used to give me a bit of wood to chew on – no anaesthetics or anything!"

While the others went on tour, Piers had plenty of time to contemplate what Colin Chapman might now be thinking about his new signing. A couple of days after the race Sally turned 21 back in London, and with their wedding only two months away, he missed her. Things got even worse when he contracted jaundice. He wasn't in a position to fly home, so a sympathetic Lucas invited Sally out to join him. She didn't have much time to pack.

"Luke rang and said, 'You must come over,'" she recalls. "So I got a ticket and went. It was very expensive, and the journey seemed to take forever. I'd never been to such a grotty place in my life. Poor Piers was in a hospital, and couldn't fly home until he was better. He was in terrible pain, and terribly unhappy about not racing."

Piers admitted as much in 1970: "I quarrelled with her most of the time. I did not improve matters by drinking far too much of an Argentinian whisky called Old Smugglers, which I mixed with Coke."

As it turned out Piers was fortunate to miss the race at Rosario, a bumpy street circuit where any accident had a good chance of involving spectators, as Jochen Neerpasch found out when his brakes failed. "The bravest would just sit on the kerbs, exposing their toes to the running cars," *Autosport* reported.

After destroying his F3 car a mud-spattered Piers had to be content with riding around in primitive karts. There was no shortage of things to do in Argentina.

With his foot slowly improving, Piers began to cheer up. He and Sally were able to join the rest of the group, and once they got away from Buenos Aires, spare time was spent in relaxed circumstances. In fact it proved to be a very memorable holiday, with shooting, swimming, horse riding and lots of wining and dining.

"He had a wonderful time," Luke insists. "Sally flew out to look after him, and we stayed on various estancias, which were run by English people. I've got a picture of him sitting by the swimming pool with a sock on – he doesn't look very ill! He was running around in a go-kart. He wasn't in too bad shape, but he hadn't got a car to drive, that was the problem. It was a very pleasant way to spend a winter, although our ace Cacho Fangio wrote a car off somewhere."

Luke, Piers and the others spent time not only with Fangio Snr, but two of Argentina's other Grand Prix heroes of the fifties: "We had dinner with Fangio and José Froilan Gonzalez. He took us round his museum and showed us the first car he'd raced. There was also a guy called Carlos Menditeguy. He was the most charismatic man I ever met. He was fantastic; he was still an ace polo player and tennis player – the last of those classic South American sports playboys, who actually looked the part."

The third round at Mendoza saw Crichton-Stuart score a thrilling victory over Irwin, although once again spectators were involved in two separate accidents during the weekend but without serious consequences. An exciting final race at Mar del Plata on 13 February went to Frenchman Eric Offenstadt, while second place for Charlie was enough to win him the Temporada title. Jonathan was plagued by unreliability, ending a pretty miserable series for the Lucas outfit. For the third race running, spectators were hit by a spinning car after Frenchman Henri Grandsire spun off, and sadly this time there was a fatality.

That very week *Autosport* carried a profile of 'Charlie Stu', who noted that the F3 driver he rated highest was Piers. Inevitably the story also referred to Pinner Road, in surprisingly colourful terms: "The goings-on there can hardly be related here, but rumour has it that over 300 of the fairer sex have passed through the door and out again in the past few years!"

When Piers and Sally returned from Argentina there was the small matter of finding time for the wedding before the season got underway with the first big meeting at Oulton Park on 2 April.

"We came back and I didn't know if we were going to get married or not," she says. "There was so much

confusion. We had to fit it in between coming back from the Temporada, getting well, and starting at Oulton Park."

Just prior to the wedding Piers had another important date. On 15 March he and Sally went to London's Grosvenor House Hotel for the prestigious Grovewood Awards. First held in 1963, these were given to the three most promising young British racing drivers, as chosen by a panel of judges comprised of leading motor sports writers, namely Gregor Grant of *Autosport*, Philip Turner of *The Motor*, and Peter Garnier of *The Autocar*. Having finished third the previous year, Chris Irwin was no longer eligible, so Piers edged out Tony Dean and John Miles to take the £500 main prize for 1965. He received the cheque from Jim Clark.

The fact that he had caught the eye of such a distinguished committee was a clear sign that Piers was now held in high regard. Grant pointed out in *Autosport* that "...not only is the driver's performance taken into account, but also the facilities that are open to him and his driving ability in relation to his car."

However, the judges' decision sparked controversy. Some suggested that it was wrong that an apparently 'rich kid' like Piers should benefit from a financial prize, and it was obvious that many people still thought that every time they bought a pint of Courage Best, they were underwriting his racing. Not everybody appreciated the Lucas team's flashy approach.

"It was monstrous, that," Sally recalls. "That man had achieved absolutely everything with no backing from his father. He was so broke he used to sleep in his tow car. He earned money wherever he could. That's how determined he was."

"Everybody thought that he never had to struggle and the money was there," says Bubbles Horsley. "The popular press was a bit like that – 'brewery heir' and all that sort of thing. Although he had some help, it was very limited. He did resent that and found it quite difficult. You just had to swallow hard and put up with it."

"He was the son of a wealthy brewer and people thought our approach wasn't very professional," says Luke. "But he was beginning to think by this time that it wasn't just a game, and he really could do it."

"He deserved it," said Crichton-Stuart. "But I think having a silver spoon in your mouth was a disadvantage, even then."

Piers didn't worry unduly about the fuss, for he was deeply involved in preparations for his forthcoming marriage. Indeed, he drew up the seating arrangements for the reception on the back of his copy of the Grovewood Awards press release!

Piers had one other interesting appointment before the wedding, and on 17 March he found himself back at Eton – standing in front of the Automobile Society that

Top left Luke relays the bad news to Piers's anxious parents.

Top right Piers examines the Lucas Lotus 35 after crashing in Buenos Aires. Later that same day he completely destroyed the car in a second incident.

Bottom left Nursing his injured foot, Piers poses for Picko Troberg's camera in Buenos Aires. The Swede was a friend and rival of the Brits in the F3 days.

Bottom right Luke captures Piers posing by the pool in Argentina, his injured foot protected from the sun by a sock...

POST OFFICE

No.
OFFICE STAMP
BRENTWOOD
24 JAN.66

84/688 HA44 BAIRES 36 24 1228 Words.

MR R COURAGE FITZWALTERS SHENFIELD
BRENTWOODESSEX

PIERS HIT WALL IN LOTUS NO INJURY EXCEPT
SLIGHT BURN ON FOOT HAVE PUT HIM INTO BRITISH
HOSPITAL FOR OBSERVATION TO BE SURE WILL WRITE
TO GIVE ALL DETAILS CHARLES

TS 15/102 LN*

he had belonged to just six years earlier. The appreciative audience included younger brother Andrew, who was 17 at the time.

The visit was recorded in the club's minutes by then secretary Stuart Rolt: "Piers Courage and fiancée Sally (William Hickey) Curzon arrived with Charles Lucas in the latter's brand new ('I bought it this morning – couldn't resist it') Chevrolet Corvette Stingray. The President kindly gave them coffee before the meeting."

Lucas recalls the day: "I remember going down with Piers and Sal mainly because we were asked why the H16 BRM wouldn't work, and we hadn't a clue – any more than BRM! Piers put it down to vibration harmonics, which kept them quiet, and was probably right."

Piers and Charles must have put on a good show, talking about their careers up to date and the recent trip to Argentina. However, one suspects that most club members paid more attention to the third member of the party, as coming face to face with a Mary Quant model was a rare treat for the average schoolboy. Meanwhile the wedding was now just a fortnight away.

"Piers was a great romantic," says Sally. "I'll never forget when we were about to get married, I was late for work. I was racing along and I tripped on the pavement. Fell flat on my face, all my bags going everywhere. I knocked out my front tooth. I remember howling and

crying and saying he'll never marry me, he won't want to see me. I was in the hairdressers' boo-hooing, and suddenly this wonderful package arrived. Obviously somebody had told him you'll never speak to her again, and he went off to a jewellery shop in Sloane Street. I think I've kept the card somewhere – it said, 'I'll always love you, with or without your teeth.' So romantic!"

The wedding took place on Tuesday 29 March at Holy Trinity Church, Brompton. Luke acted as Best Man, and he and Piers arrived in the former's new Stingray, while Sally was given away by her brother-in-law, Derek Whiting. Official photographs were taken by none other than Patrick Lichfield.

As Sally was a model and the beautiful daughter of the late Earl Howe, and Piers was a member of a family whose name appeared on licensed premises in every high street, some attention from the society columnists was inevitable. But it was a quiet news day – the story of Pickles the dog finding the missing World Cup had just about run its course – and thus the wedding garnered extraordinary coverage in the national papers.

There were several reasons. Firstly the lack of suitable girls in their respective families meant that there were no bridesmaids, and instead the couple were accompanied by five very photogenic page boys in green velvet outfits – Little Lord Fauntleroys, as one paper dubbed them. Secondly, it was a windy day, and outside the church the press cameras captured Sally's spectacular veil as it flew many feet into the air. It looked a little like Cyd Charisse's fantasy dance with Gene Kelly in *Singin' in the Rain*, and the diamond tiara only just kept the veil on her head. Finally, there was the matter of the other man. Although he didn't attend the ceremony itself, due he said to a clashing lunch date with Stirling Moss, Sally's ex-fiancé Charlie Crichton-Stuart appeared in civvies at the reception. Everyone had remained friends, but inevitably his arrival caught the imagination of the media, and he received almost as much coverage as the couple themselves.

The *Daily Sketch* went to town, a full centre-spread combining the page boys, the flying veil and the Crichton-Stuart angle, although in common with some other papers it erroneously called him 'Chris' rather than Charles.

The Sun boldly stated: "The bride invites an old flame." The *Daily Express* named Sally "the season's E-Type bride", referring to the flashy sports cars jostling for parking space outside the church, and showed Crichton-Stuart giving her a good luck kiss. Even the *Daily Mirror* gave much of its second page to the flying veil shot of a "breezy bride in a breezy whirl." Page

Opposite Piers's status as a bright young talent was confirmed when he picked up the Grovewood Award from Jim Clark in London on 15 March. Some thought he didn't deserve to win.

Left Piers and Sally captured at the Grovewood Awards, just a fortnight before their wedding.

three opposite was devoted to the paper's mandate for a Harold Wilson Labour government – a General Election was due the following day!

Crichton-Stuart gave the Courages his blessing, however awkward the arrangement might appear to be.

"Piers was very straight and very honourable," he told me in 1999. "They were ideally suited, with the same background. I thought Porridge was jolly lucky to marry her – and she him, too. I know everybody was after her. She was very pretty and a jolly good catch."

Due to lack of spare funds and the upcoming date at Oulton Park, the honeymoon consisted of a single night at Claridges.

"The wedding was wonderful, hilarious," says Sally.

"It was great fun, and then Luke gave a wonderful party in the evening, a very amusing dinner, with all our friends, at *L'Ecu de France*. It was let's keep partying, let's enjoy ourselves. We had that night, the next morning, we had lunch, and then we had to leave, because we couldn't afford it any more! It was great fun though, a great cross-section of friends, all his friends who became stars."

Sally enjoyed a great relationship with Piers's parents: "Jean was the most wonderful mother-in-law you could possibly have. She was fun and she was sparky, she was young-at-heart, and she was enthusiastic about things that we did. Richard was much more staid, and couldn't quite understand his eldest son, but appreciated him tremendously. In fact he often used Piers as a sounding board when there was a bit of strife between the two of them, because Piers could understand his mother, and he could also understand his father. He was very good at soothing things, and he adored them."

Just three days after the ceremony Piers turned out at Oulton for the first F3 event of the year. He qualified second in the damp conditions, just ahead of new team-mate Pike, but then the weather turned really bad and the meeting was abandoned. Esso paid a £5 bonus by way of compensation.

"It was appalling," says Sally, with some justification. "It turned out to be a real damp snow squib!"

Thus the season got underway properly at Snetterton on Good Friday. Pike gave Lucas its first victory of the year, while Piers dropped out with overheating problems, after starting at the back of the grid. He was again out of luck in the Chichester Cup at Goodwood on Easter Monday, where Irwin won for the Chequered Flag. It was soon apparent that the new Lotus still had faults, as Pike recalls: "The 41 was a very difficult car to drive, and it was very unstable under braking."

Because they now represented Lotus and Brabham the rivalry between the Lucas and Chequered Flag camps continued to build, and there was a special edge to the competition between Piers and Irwin. Matters were complicated by the fact that Luke's sister Loti had become Irwin's girlfriend.

"They all hunted in a pack," she says. "I started going out with Chris, who was of course the opposition, driving for Chequered Flag Brabham. Then no one would talk to me. The Brabham people thought I was a spy, sent to find out what their gear ratios were, and the Lotus lot thought I'd changed sides!

"Sally and I were called upon to do the catering. There was one particular race at Goodwood, and Sally said let's have a proper Sunday lunch, which was a silly thing to do, as none of them wanted to eat, and we took a proper table and tablecloth, silver, china, glass, roast chicken, all the trimmings...which was great fun."

Sally's involvement also extended to timekeeping: "Nobody took a blind bit of notice," she says. "I was doing it and I thought I was being a frightfully good help. 'Yes Sal, thanks very much.' But nobody relied on my time keeping at all. They all used to think it was a huge joke, but it used to keep me quiet. My maths is so hopeless..."

After a frustrating start to the year Piers finally notched up his first win of 1966 on the streets of Pau, although it came in bizarre circumstances, after he'd had a spin of his own.

"Piers should never have won that race," says Pike. "Gethin went off, the yellow flags were a bit late, and I clipped Gethin. Then John Cardwell, who was a little bit behind, hit me. And Piers, who was fourth, won it!"

A wet race at Barcelona proved disappointing when Piers got caught on the wrong tyres, and there was more frustration in the Vigorelli Trophy at Monza, where he was slowed by a misfire caused by fuel vaporisation. He did at least catch up with de Sanctis recruit Jonathan in Italy. Later the boys would learn that on the same weekend Jacques Bernusset, a continental F3 regular, had been killed at Magny-Cours.

Piers was back on song at Brands Hatch, beating Gethin and Pike to take the Les Leston Trophy. However, a week later a broken oil pipe caused him to drop out of the lead of the Radio London Trophy at Silverstone, leaving Pike to win. By now the team had a new recruit, at least on paper, as Luke recalls: "Half way through the year Andrew Ferguson rang up and said, 'Look, we're running a development car for Jackie Oliver, do you mind if we run it under your name?' And I thought, why not?"

However, despite the show of unity there was to be a little tension between the camps, as Oliver recalls: "The drivers were not happy if I was quicker, and I wasn't Charles's driver, so it was a bit of a nose-putting-out

Sybil, Countess of Howe
requests the pleasure of
your company at the marriage
of her daughter
Sarah Marguerite
to
Mr Piers Courage
at Holy Trinity, Brompton
on Tuesday, 29th March, 1966
at 4 o'clock
and afterwards at
30 Pavilion Road, S.W.1

Stumpwell Cottage
Penn
Bucks.   *R.S.V.P.*

session. But it just went over the top of my head. And Piers never used to say anything about it."

Next stop was Monaco, where the presence of John Frankenheimer's Hollywood film crew and the cast of *Grand Prix* added a touch of glamour to proceedings. Charlie Crichton-Stuart brought a little to the F3 paddock as well by showing up with his new girlfriend – British film star Shirley Ann Field, who was about to make *Alfie* with Michael Caine. Bearing in mind their collective love of cheap nights out at the cinema, the Pinner Road gang was mightily impressed by her arrival on the scene.

"That was jolly impressive, absolutely," says Bubbles Horsley. "A proper film star! We were all on our best behaviour."

"She was very glamorous, a big star," says Sally. "Everybody was going 'Coo-err...!'"

"That was a goody!," said Charlie. "It was probably subconscious, but it was a sort of competitive thing. She'd made *Saturday Night and Sunday Morning* with Albert Finney, *The War Lover* with Steve McQueen, and *Kings of the Sun* with Yul Brynner. She'd done bloody well because she'd come out of an orphanage, and it was a big achievement to get there."

Piers in the Lotus 41 on the streets of Pau on 17 April. He scored a lucky victory after the three cars ahead tangled.

Two years earlier Monaco had been only Piers's fourth-ever outing in a single-seater, and he'd been a little out of his depth. After missing the 1965 event due to a clash with Monza, he was now back as one of the favourites, with a serious chance to impress Colin Chapman and the rest of the F1 team bosses. This was the most prestigious race of the year, and with only nominal starting money available, prestige was the only reason to turn up. There were 60 entries, with the fastest 40 from practice split into two heats, and the top 11 finishers from each making it to the final.

The Brits dominated practice, with ex-Lucas man Peter Gethin setting a slightly suspect fastest time in a private Brabham, ahead of Pike, Irwin, John Cardwell and Piers. Jean-Pierre Beltoise won the first heat for Matra, while Piers followed Irwin home in the second. That earned him third on the grid for Saturday afternoon's final, and a serious shot at victory with the entire Grand Prix circus looking on.

Piers made a great start, and shot into the lead ahead of Irwin and Beltoise. However, it soon went wrong, as Nick Brittan reported in *Autosport*: "Piers Courage had the honour of leading the first two laps of the final until he brushed the wall at Tabac and lost his front suspension. Irwin stood on all the pedals at once in order to miss him, and while he was doing so the wily Frenchman nipped through."

Beltoise went on to score Matra's most important win to date, while second place did Irwin's flourishing

reputation no harm. Piers knew he had let the side down, but Luke was never too upset by such incidents.

"I don't think it made any difference," says Pike. "I think it was the idea of leading more than anything. Luke never really got upset. He wasn't really a team manager – it just sort of happened around him. We didn't have pep talks or strategy meetings."

After Monaco Piers didn't have much time to feel sorry for himself, for he had to hurry back to England for a busy holiday weekend. He turned 24 on the Friday, and celebrated in style at Brands Hatch on Whit Sunday, where he picked up £500 after heading home Irwin, Pike and Oliver in the Les Leston Trophy. He also set a new lap record for the long circuit, and won praise from *Autosport*'s Richard Feast, who noted: "At the beginning of the year it was being said that the Grovewood Award winner was a little out of touch. It looks like Courage has had the last word on that."

The following day most of the contenders were in London for the big Crystal Palace meeting, and a milestone in Piers's career. For the first time there was a sign that the Lotus contract might lead somewhere when he was invited to make his F2 debut for the works team, run by Ron Harris. Jim Clark was busy at Indianapolis, so in effect Piers was stepping into the World Champion's shoes, and it was quite an honour.

Piers qualified an encouraging ninth, setting the same time as experienced team-mate Peter Arundell. However, it all went wrong at the start of the first heat when he was hit from behind by Richard Attwood, and slammed hard into the sleepers. Coming so soon after Monaco, the last thing he needed was another high profile incident. Second place to Irwin in the supporting F3 race was small consolation, although he did a good job to fight his way through the leading pack.

Mechanic John Fowler joined the Lucas team that week, to look after Piers's car. He confirms that the Lotus was far outclassed by that year's Brabham: "I suppose the 41 was the prettiest car of the year, but we used to say it was designed by a blacksmith! The front end would flex, and the suspension geometry was wrong. Roy Thomas should take the credit for sorting that out, to the degree that we did get it sorted. Colin Chapman just basically ignored us. But Piers could drive anything."

"I don't think we did much to it after beefing up the front end," says Luke. "It wasn't as easy to drive as the Brabham. It didn't slide around as easily, which made it quick in faster corners, which actually suited Piers."

Although Piers was still enjoying himself, a Grand Prix chance was now just a step away, and thus racing was starting to get more serious. Jonathan was no longer travelling with him, and while Piers got on well with Pike, there was also a healthy rivalry, and the

RON
HARRIS
TEAM LOTUS

Correspondence to Ron Harris Racing Division
Glenbuck Studios, Surbiton, Surrey, England
Telephone: Elmbridge 0022

RH/JC   24th June, 1966

P. R. Courage, Esq.,
25 Roland Gardens,
London, S.W.7.

Dear Piers,

    Please find enclosed accounting statement together with cheque
value £75. 0. 0d covering the Crystal Palace meeting. It is our
normal procedure to pay all the money over to the driver who, in turn
pays a small percentage to the mechanics. Would you be good enough
to send a cheque for the amount shown to John Hogan, Esq., C/O Ron Harris,
63-65 King Street, Maidenhead, Berkshire.

                    Thanks,

                    Cheers,

                    Judy

                    Judy Coombs.

RON
HARRIS
TEAM LOTUS

Correspondence to Ron Harris Racing Division
Glenbuck Studios, Surbiton, Surrey, England
Telephone: Elmbridge 0022

JC/R.A.11.   2nd June, 1966

ACCOUNTING STATEMENT

To: P. R. Courage, Esq.,   Month of: MAY, 1966

        May 30th   CRYSTAL PALACE

                        Starting Money   £75. 0. 0.

AMOUNT DUE TO DRIVER   £75. 0. 0d

AMOUNT DUE TO MECHANICS £3. 15. 0d

Left *A fine shot by Nick Loudon of Piers on his F2 debut at Crystal Palace with Ron* *Harris's Lotus. This must be practice, for he retired at the start.* **Above** *Piers earned £75 at Crystal Palace, and even had to give up some of that!*

Luke recalls: "I'm afraid we slightly took the piss out of them. We couldn't believe the way Ronnie Hoare ran it like a military operation, with briefs and debriefs and all that."

Just five years earlier Piers had been happy to be at Le Mans as a spectator, and here he was not just competing, but doing so in a Ferrari. His schoolboy dreams had come true.

"It was lovely," says Pike. "Ferrari delivered the car on a transporter, and Piers and I were standing there. There were three of them on it … and one of them was ours!"

However, once he got on the track, Piers was underwhelmed. He had never driven a closed racing car before, and he found the GT machine slow, especially when the pacesetters came swooping past on the straight: "The whole thing was so far from the man-battling-with-machine scene that from time to time I had to lower the window and let the fresh air in to stop me going to sleep."

Hoare asked Piers to start the race, and unable to see the man with the flag, he sprinted across the road when the others began to move. Unfortunately the next-but-one car did a half spin as its driver tried to get away, and the 275GTB had to wait until nearly everyone else had gone. When he finally set off, he was in for a shock. On the first lap he saw the sister car of Hobbs chugging along in a cloud of steam, and on the second he passed Piper in the team's 365P2, going just as slowly. Both would soon become official retirements.

There was more drama back in the pits, as Luke recalls: "I remember at the start Sally sitting in the pits, absolutely looking the part as only she could, with stop watches, clipboards and so on. Then floods of tears 20 minutes later when she'd lost track of Piers… She was setting her stall out to do 24 hours of lap timing, and to have lost it in the first 20 minutes was a bit tricky!"

There was more bad news to come for the team. When the quicker Fords lapped him, Piers was surprised to see that Rindt was still in touch with the leading GT40s. Surprised because the private car had only a 4.7-litre engine, when the works machines had 7.0-litre units! The Austrian's aggressive approach had worked the previous year for Ferrari, but this time it didn't, and before long the GT40 was parked at the road side. Ireland didn't even get a chance to drive. A team that had come equipped to service four cars now just had one to focus on, and there was a surplus of staff. "They all broke down and everyone transferred their affections to our GTB," Roy remembers.

"The trouble was that as soon as their cars were out, they came and leant on us all the time," says Luke. "So it wasn't a very happy experience. All I can remember about the race are arguments and fighting – are you running it or are we running it? That was the idea; we

supplied the mechanics and Tom and the drivers. It was a very miserable weekend. The other guys didn't have anything to do so they told us how to do it."

The Maranello cars weren't the only Ferraris in trouble. As the race went on the main works and NART (North American Racing Team) entries all fell by the wayside, leaving Ford unchallenged in front. As the final hours of the race approached, just two of the 14 Ferraris that started were still running – and one of them was the Courage/Pike machine.

"I really enjoyed it," says Pike. "But I never slept the whole time – I'm quite a nervous individual."

While the marque's chance of outright victory had long since gone, Piers and Roy could still at least salvage a GT class win, so all eyes were on them in the closing stages. It was common practice at Le Mans that whoever started the car allowed his team mate the privilege of taking the chequered flag, but the team boss tried to dispense with that tradition.

"Ronnie Hoare decided that Piers would finish the race," says Pike. "Sally told him, 'If you do that, Roy will park the car out on the circuit and leave it there.' Which was about the truth of the matter!"

Hoare followed that advice, and with rain now falling, Pike got in the 275GTB at the last pit stop. However, at the end of his first lap he was overdue. He eventually coasted in with no brakes, having had a huge fright out on the track: "I left the pits and got down to the Esses and there wasn't enough brake on the right rear wheel, because the brake pipe had been ground through."

Autosport's Gregor Grant described what had happened: "Apparently the pit had run out of suitable wheels, and mistakenly substituted one of LM type. This caused fouling of the brake disc, with subsequent failure of the calliper. A pipe line was hammered flat, thus the machine only had effective anchors on three wheels – not very amusing during the very wet closing stages."

Pike resumed and struggled on to the finish, although he had another scare on his last lap when a huge puddle drowned the electrics and left the car on six cylinders. But he made it across the line in eighth overall and as GT class winner, two spots ahead of the similar yellow car of Ecurie Francorchamps.

Piers and Roy were back in France a fortnight later for the Grand Prix support race at Rheims. Jim Clark was struck in the face by a bird during practice for the main event, and was out of action for the weekend. There was some suggestion that Piers might step in, but his lack of experience counted against him, so Pedro Rodriguez got the job.

Top *At Le Mans Piers and Roy Pike took Ronnie Hoare's new Ferrari 275GTB to eighth overall and first in the GT class. It was the first of four appearances he made in the 24 Hours.*

Bottom *Nina Rindt and Sally pictured at Le Mans, where Piers and Jochen were both driving for Maranello Concessionaires. It was the only time that they were team-mates, although they drove different cars.*

Piers qualified second for the F3 event, and come the race was in the middle of a thrilling battle that flummoxed Gregor Grant: "Words can barely describe the fantastic Coupe de Vitesse race for F3 cars, and anyone who could keep an accurate lap chart must be a genius, when more than a dozen cars kept chopping and changing every lap." Piers lost out in the final dash to the line, and had to settle for third.

However, a week later at Rouen he struck back, helped by getting away from the pack on the very first lap. Pike recalls what happened: "I convinced John Cardwell just before the final that Piers was so quick down the hill that if he wasn't second, right behind Piers, the race was lost. I told Piers what might happen and at the end of the back straight John went straight into the hay bales, scattering straw and the field, leaving Piers clear. I did feel a bit guilty!"

Piers duly scored a crushing victory, and set a new lap record. Once again he showed his mastery of daunting high-speed road circuits. There was a run of three free weekends during July, and while Piers was able to catch his breath, Chris Irwin landed a third Brabham seat alongside team boss Jack and Denny Hulme for the British GP. It was a priceless opportunity, albeit with an older, outdated car, and Piers must have wondered when his Lotus connections were going to generate a similar chance. Irwin duly qualified 12th and finished a very

respectable seventh. It was apparent that he had edged ahead of Piers and established himself as Britain's hottest prospect.

Although not a great football fan, Piers had time to follow England's progress through to the World Cup Final against West Germany on 30 July. He and Sally even went along to see the victory celebrations outside the nearby Kensington Royal Garden hotel, where Bobby Moore and the victorious team appeared on the balcony.

"It was just a wonderful thing that England had won the World Cup," says Sally. "The whole of London was full of joy, and we thought we'd just wander down and have a look. He loved the thought that England had done so well."

For a while it seemed that Swinging London was the centre of the universe, and Piers and Sally lived right at the heart of it. Piers had always had his own views on fashion, and he enjoyed the burgeoning Carnaby Street scene, although his indulgence in it usually extended only to colourful wide ties and slightly suspect suits.

The July break allowed Piers and Sally to move from their temporary home in her flat at 25 Roland Gardens to a new base at 15 Sutherland Street in Pimlico, not far from Victoria Station. The imposing house was a little further away from the King's Road and the heart of the London action, and was near to some rather basic post-

war council flats, but it was handily placed opposite a pub – although not of the Courage variety. There was a good reason to move, for they had received the welcome news that Sally was expecting their first child in the New Year, and a bigger property was now essential.

The narrow four-storey house was a huge improvement, and Piers established his office in the basement, which had its own access from the street. He decorated it not with pictures of himself but with sepia-toned shots of his father-in-law Earl Howe, and the Silver Arrows in action at Donington in 1937. There were also prints of historic naval battles and a London Omnibus. In the coming years visiting journalists would invariably remark on the lack of self-aggrandisement this décor reflected.

While he might have been a little envious of Irwin, Piers did not have to wait long for his own first Grand Prix opportunity to come along, although it wasn't a fully-fledged F1 chance. Despite the earlier Crystal Palace debacle Ron Harris invited him back to run a Lotus 44 in the F2 class at the German GP, alongside Pedro Rodriguez and Gerhard Mitter.

The F2 cars ran concurrently with the Grand Prix machines, so this was Piers's first chance to impress the big names since his abortive effort at Enna 51 weeks previously. There was nothing to stop a quick youngster from embarrassing lesser talents with more powerful

machinery, and that's exactly what Jacky Ickx did with his Matra. The young Belgian left the rest of the class contenders behind, qualifying at the tail end of the F1 pack. Piers was seventh, a respectable three seconds off experienced team-mate Rodriguez – not bad over a nine minute lap.

The race started in the wet, and on the first lap Ickx tangled with British F1 privateer John Taylor. The latter crashed heavily, and Piers had to dodge past the scene a few seconds later. Perhaps he was distracted by seeing the accident, but anyway, Piers slid off the road near the Flugplatz – without serious consequences – on the fourth lap. Taylor was badly burned in the earlier crash, and succumbed to his injuries in a Koblenz hospital a month later. He had raced against Jonathan in Formula Junior, and like Piers had driven Bob Gerard's F1 Coopers.

Putting the 'Ring disappointment behind him, Piers headed for the F3 double header in Denmark and Sweden in company with Roy Pike. The first race at Roskilde saw another win for Irwin, while Piers had a fraught time, as *Autosport*'s Paddy McNally noted: "Piers Courage was trying like mad to keep up with a car which was obviously far from suited to the circuit. Two laps later Courage overdid it at the hairpin and lost his chance."

Mechanic John Fowler recalls a disappointing weekend: "It was like a go-kart track in a quarry. Piers reckoned he could have driven his Lotus Elan and done better in that than in his 41. We enjoyed Denmark, we just hated that place!"

Piers made his Grand Prix debut at the Nürburgring on 7 August, although only in an F2 Lotus run by Ron Harris. His day ended with an accident.

Piers trailed home eighth, but the following weekend's Kanonloppet at Karlskoga was a little more successful, with Piers and Roy joining winner Irwin on the podium, having held off the attentions of local hero Freddy Kottulinsky. However, on the slowing down lap the two Lucas boys managed to collide.

"I don't know which way round it was, but they ran over one another," recalls Pike's Kiwi mechanic Roger Hill. "I couldn't believe it. They came round and one car was dragging along the ground…"

"One car climbed over the back of the other," says Fowler. "Kottulinsky said they drove for about 50 yards down the road like they were mating. We were dumbfounded. We asked them what happened, and didn't receive a proper answer. To this day I've no idea whose fault it was!"

"It was all my fault," says Pike. "I moved across in front of him. It had nothing to do with Piers – he was just going along, minding his own business. It was a bit of a mess."

The trip home brought further unexpected excitement, as Pike recalls: "Piers and I got arrested for bank robbery! We were whizzing through Sweden in the Lotus Elan at 100mph or so, and we went flashing through this

village and there was a police car. Suddenly there was a helicopter in the air. We came to a road block and the helicopter landed, and a lot of police ran towards us with guns. We didn't know what was happening – everyone was speaking Swedish. They threw me in the back of the police car, and Piers had to drive the Lotus. They took us to a station somewhere.

Above Piers and Chris Irwin were rivals throughout 1966, but were both part of the British team in the European F3 Challenge at Brands Hatch on 2 October. Here they celebrate overall victory.

Opposite Piers and Sally caught earlier in the year in Argentina.

"We thought we were being done for speeding, but we were charged with bank robbery, and they showed us lots of mugshots of criminals. It turned out they had escaped in a blue car! Eventually by ringing the circuit they ascertained we were racing drivers. We drove furiously back to Amsterdam and loaded the car onto the plane to Southend…"

"It was suggested that we had tipped off the cops to get even for the bumper cars!" says Fowler. "I do remember that we were pretty pissed off that we now had all this work to do. Doing it in the race is one thing, but on the slowing down lap wasn't too clever."

The two mechanics had to get the Lucas truck back to England as soon as possible, so that they could repair the damaged cars.

"We had a very important race at Brands Hatch coming up, and now we had to do two complete

rebuilds. We got back to Highgate and we stripped the cars out before we even went back to our digs, I remember that. Piers's chassis was quite badly twisted, and they both had to be re-jigged, so none of us got much sleep that week."

Irwin's double success in Scandinavia was another significant boost to his reputation. His girlfriend Loti Lucas was watching developments: "That was the most bizarre year, because Piers won one race, Chris won the next. I think they still hold the record for the number of lead changes in a lap at Silverstone – about four or five times in one lap!"

Although he spent time with the Pinner Road crowd, notably Frank, in some ways Irwin never really fitted in with them. He had a ruthless, determined streak that clashed a little with the more relaxed approach of the others.

"Chris was quite friendly with lots of people," says Loti, "But not close friends. He was very much more concentrated on what he was doing than a lot of them. He used to go to the gym in the days when nobody thought of it. He was the first F3 driver to have Nomex overalls, and everyone said, 'For heaven's sake, what are you wasting your money on those for?'"

"He was good, there's no question about it," says Jonathan Williams. "Potentially he was a World

Champion or serious points scorer in F1. He had a lot of natural ability combined with a steely determination that I think outstripped the rest of us. He really wanted it. But he wasn't necessarily the man top of your list to go out to dinner with."

The Lucas team struck back at Brands Hatch on August Bank Holiday Monday, where the mechanics' hard work since Sweden paid off. Pole man Pike dropped out, but Piers made a wise tyre choice for the wet event and disappeared into the distance, leaving Irwin behind. What made it even more impressive was the fact that with repairs to his own car not yet finished, Piers had actually qualified in a different chassis.

"We didn't test his own car before the race," says Fowler, "and it had not turned a wheel until he got in it on the warm-up lap. There's no way the car could be absolutely spot-on, and that speaks volumes for Piers's skill. We decided to go with wets, and everything clicked. The flag dropped, and he just disappeared into the distance. He was very good in the wet, especially if he had the right tyres. Colin Chapman came up and congratulated both of us afterwards. He called it a 'masterpiece performance.' It was just wonderful to win, but I was absolutely knackered."

Meanwhile that weekend there was good news from Sweden – Frank had stayed on for a less important F3

race at Knutsdorp, and had actually won. It was a success all his pals could all enjoy.

Zandvoort the following week proved to be the opposite story to Brands, Irwin winning as Piers dropped back when caught on dry tyres in the rain. He still managed to finish a remarkable sixth. Then it was a long trek south to Enna for a welcome reunion with Jonathan, who was doing great things with de Sanctis in Italy. He would win again in Sicily, with Piers in fourth, but the wild slip streamer had a dramatic conclusion.

"There was an Icelandic driver called Sverrir Thorodsson," says Fowler. "No one knew quite why he was so quick at Enna, and there were noises being made that he might have a big engine. Coming round the very last corner he was sort of in the lead. Jonathan was alongside this guy, who clouted the Armco barrier at the end of the pits, right where Sally and I were standing.

"It sounded like a bomb going off, and Sally screamed and leapt into my arms. Thorodsson then spun diagonally across the field, but still ended up second! The other cars were going all over the place trying to avoid him, and there was smoke everywhere. Sally wouldn't let go until Piers came round at the end of the cooling down lap and we knew he was OK. She was shaking like a leaf. Then Ernesto Brambilla attacked Jonathan as he was getting out of the car! It was like a movie."

Jonathan has his own viewpoint: "I got squeezed and went towards the pit wall, and saw everybody in the pits diving out of sight. I thought they were overreacting a bit! There was another guy inside me, which I didn't know, so they had good cause to disappear behind the barrier..."

Flamboyant Frenchman Johnny Servoz-Gavin won the next event on the new Bugatti circuit at Le Mans, after Piers stopped with a broken throttle cable on the first lap.

"I suspected at the time that it was sabotage," Fowler suggests. "We'd never had anything like that happen before, although I don't know when it could have been done. I'd never seen Piers so angry before, but he was visibly upset. He came back, and I remember we went and sat in the stands with Jimmy Clark. Piers was down in the dumps, and Jimmy put him right by saying, 'This sort of thing has happened to me when the World Championship's been on the line.' Shit happens, in other words!"

After Le Mans it was on to the last big continental event of 1966 at Albi, where Piers dominated both heats to score a fine aggregate victory. Having earlier won at Pau and Rouen, he collected the French Craven A F3 title.

At the same meeting Irwin's reputation was boosted further by a strong performance for Brabham in the F2 race, in which he qualified and finished third. Once again, he had made people take note. However, Piers had not been forgotten, and *Autosport*'s gossip pages suggested that he would become Jim Clark's F2 team-mate at Lotus in '67. The *Daily Mail* gave the story even bigger mileage, suggesting under the headline 'New boy Piers may race with Clark' that they would actually team up in Grand Prix racing.

The season ended with a major new event at Brands Hatch on 2 October. Dubbed the European F3 Challenge, this was to be an interesting contest with eight countries each represented by three nominated drivers. Two heats and a final would determine which team came out on top. For once Piers and Chris found themselves batting for the same side, for along with Peter Gethin, they formed the home team. A few superfluous Brits ran as independents, and they included Jonathan, making a rare return to the UK. Just to complicate matters he joined the rival Chequered Flag line-up to drive a Brabham equipped with DAF's unsuccessful 'variomatic' transmission.

Come the final France's Jean-Pierre Beltoise set the pace, but Irwin worked his way into the lead. Piers was determined to get on terms with him, but got caught behind the Matra for most of the race, as recorded in *Autosport*: "Ten laps to go and Courage decided it was time to go motor racing. For lap after lap the Matra and

the Lotus flew round, Courage searching everywhere for gaps, but there weren't any. Finally on lap 31, with four to go, Courage got by."

By then Irwin was a long way up the road, and while Piers was happy to be part of the winning British team, he would have preferred to be the man on top. A couple of days later Irwin married Luke's sister Loti at the very church where Piers and Sally had tied the knot seven months earlier, cementing the ties between the rival Lucas and Chequered Flag camps.

It was time to take stock and prepare for the new season. By now Luke's relationship with Lotus had floundered, for having earlier agreed to allow Jackie Oliver to run a works development car under his name, he discovered an unexpected drawback to the arrangement: "The advantage of the Lotus deal was that if we won a lot of races there was a terrific Firestone bonus. We got totally tucked up. At the end of the season they took half the Firestone bonus money, because they said Oliver's was the other car! We lost a lot of money over that. It was the end of a beautiful friendship..."

"That left a nasty taste in everyone's mouth," says Fowler. "It affected me and Roger as well, when it was time to pay us our share of the bonus money. I think it was Mr Chapman's plan all along to go after that money. The Firestone bonus was pretty good, and we produced for them, while F1 and F2 were a dead loss for Lotus. Luke was just a perfect gent and was treated pretty badly over the entire affair. He spent a considerable amount of money fostering these guys, and he was no mean driver himself."

Luke and Tom the Weld now harboured ambitions to build their own car, and over the coming months they would set the Titan project in motion. Meanwhile Piers knew it was time for him to move up from F3, and he waited to see what Lotus had to say about his own future. Despite the earlier rumours linking him with an F1 seat, Colin Chapman could not offer anything concrete. Contrary to his usual policy, he decided to hire a big name to partner Clark, in the form of Graham Hill. They would constitute a formidable line-up for both F2 and Grand Prix racing.

At some point that autumn Piers must have realised that it would be better to be free of the Lotus option for 1967–68. On 4 November his solicitor Malcolm Scott wrote offering advice on his contractual position. Scott said it would be difficult to show that Lotus had not used its "best endeavours" to find him a seat, and suggested that Piers should "...argue with Mr Chapman that you have no heart in continuing to race for Team Lotus at this stage and to simply ask him to release you at the end of the year." He added that it would be a good idea to have another deal, on the point of signing, before tackling the Lotus boss.

"He was testing it at Snetterton when he hit the bank and it caught fire," says Luke. "It was too good to be true. There was a problem with the oil pick-up on the engine, and old Ted Martin wouldn't let us modify it. I think there was a bit of a fall out between Tom and Ted, which is why we never rebuilt it after it went up in flames. It was a great pity, as it was an excellent little motor."

Snetterton was also the venue of the start of the F2 season with the Good Friday meeting on 24 March. Aware that his outings with BRM would be few and far between, Piers had found himself a drive with veteran Guildford-based entrant John Coombs, who had long been associated with Graham Hill. Coombs had acquired a brand new McLaren M4A for the programme, equipped with a Cosworth FVA engine.

The year would see the introduction of a European F2 Championship for the first time. It comprised ten events, and only non-graded drivers – essentially those who had not previously scored World Championship points – were eligible to score. Thus you could finish seventh, behind a dozen established Grand Prix drivers, and still pick up a maximum nine points. Now F2 had a lot more to offer a 'comingman' like Piers, although some major events still stood alone outside the championship.

Piers in John Coombs's new McLaren M4A at Silverstone on 27 March. He finished seventh in the first heat, but a tangle with Denny Hulme showed how hard he was trying.

"To be absolutely frank I can't remember how we got together to run a car," says Coombs, "But it might have been through Bruce McLaren. I've got a feeling that he had something to do with the introduction of Piers, and I think I got a very favourable deal on buying a car from Bruce. Also Frank Williams used to come down to Guildford. He was buying any of the bits and pieces we didn't want, and was selling them. I'd even sold him an old F2 Cooper at one stage. I think it was 50/50 on prize money with Piers, and I probably gave him about 30% of the start money. Lugging a car all over Europe was quite expensive."

The bright red M4A was prepared by Coombs mechanic Roland Law: "It was the first time Bruce had made a monocoque," says Law. "It was quite a nice little car, although it was hard to get the fuel tanks in and out, because it was very, very narrow. I was putting them in one day and I had to call across to someone to lift the monocoque up so I could get my arm out! It was quite nicely built, quite a sturdy little car."

Coombs liked Piers from the off: "I just remember this incredible scratching of his head – he was always scratching the top of his head. He was very upright, a very nervous person. He was fairly light on his feet, always tripping around, lots of hand movement. The scratching of his head became a joke with everybody! But a very easy chap to get on with, and a nice guy. So I've got very good memories of Piers and Sally. But it was the most terrifying year I've ever spent in racing, because I always thought he

was going to hurt himself. Eventually I suggested to Sally that the best thing for him to do was go back and work in his father's business in the brewery…"

It was indeed to be a year of heartache for all concerned, but there was little sign of that when the season got underway in Norfolk. An interesting comparison would be provided by the presence of Bruce McLaren in his own works car, but significantly the Kiwi used Goodyears – on which the M4A had been developed – while Courage and Coombs were contracted to Dunlop. That would prove to be a handicap for much of the season as Piers struggled to get the car to work on the tyres.

As usual established names like Clark, Hill and Stewart would tackle a full F2 season, while among those joining Piers in the title chase were Jacky Ickx, Jean-Pierre Beltoise, Frank Gardner, Alan Rees and the inevitable Chris Irwin, the latter having landed a works Lola-BMW ride.

In the first heat at Snetterton Piers came home seventh of 14 finishers, beating Irwin, while in the second event he dropped out with a misfire on the last lap. In the 40-lap final he finished in what *Autosport's* Simon Taylor called "an excellent seventh" behind Rindt, Hill, Rees, Hulme, McLaren and Brabham, and thus second in the non-graded classification behind Rees. While seventh also turned out to be last place, all those behind him had retired, and even Piers was lucky to make it after his engine had lost most of its water. Irwin rolled out of the race on the first lap – the balance seemed to be tipping back in Piers's favour.

Three days later the field was back in action in the BARC 200 at Silverstone on Easter Monday. This time it was two heats with an aggregate result rather than a final. In the first Piers finished a useful seventh of 17 runners, and once again he was second non-graded driver behind Rees, but in the second event he retired early on with fuel injection problems.

The first race had not been without drama, as Taylor noted: "Courage was not hanging about in the Coombs McLaren, and on lap 4 he nosed ahead of Hulme's car. The two cars touched and Hulme spun, dropping to the tail of the field, while Courage lost two or three places." Whoever's fault the bump might have been, it was another sign that Piers was running on the very limit in his efforts to impress.

"I went to the outside of the car and noticed that the rim had gone apart in about three places," says Coombs. "I said, 'Piers, you hit something.' He said, 'No. no, no.' Then Hulme came up and said, 'He hit me, why did he hit me?' He was unaware of it. Didn't know what happened."

More was to come a week later at Pau, where Piers had done so well in his F3 days. On Friday he struggled with fuel injection problems, the wrong gear ratios and excessive understeer, leaving him with much ground to gain in final qualifying on Saturday. Unfortunately he crashed

heavily at the entry to the long right-hander at Virage du Parc Beaumont, ironically on his lap back to the pits.

Piers painted a colourful picture when recounting the incident in 1970: "I went straight through some straw bales and found myself careering across the lawn of a public garden. It was an attractive garden and the beautifully mown lawn swept down to an ornamental lake. An ideal place for an evening stroll but not really designed to have racing cars hurtling across it. My intrusion came as a great shock to the ducks swimming peacefully on the lake. As I tore across the grass I had an impression of a cloud of squawking ducks rising with a flurry of wings and also of policemen fleeing in every direction. I came to rest with the car's nose jutting out over the edge of the lake."

Roland Law had to load up the wreckage: "He went amongst the trees and took two or three wheels off. When I arrived up there some bloody kids were jumping up and down on it. I couldn't believe it…"

The car could not be readied for the race, as *Autosport* reported: "Courage admitted the error, but error or not the poor McLaren was sorely bent, with two of its wheels torn off, a shattered driveshaft, and the suspension lugs bent enough to suspect chassis damage. At first it was thought that the car might be repaired in time, but later John Coombs withdrew the car."

Piers was in distinguished company – Stewart and Ickx both crashed that day – but that was of little comfort, and the team returned home and thus also missed the following weekend's race at Barcelona's Montjuich Park.

Coombs now harboured genuine fears that Piers might hurt himself, and thereafter set about persuading him to adopt a more careful approach or even give it up altogether. He meant well, but it was not the sort of message calculated to boost a young driver's morale.

"John doesn't like anybody to get hurt," says Law. "Most of that was held in private, but I knew it was going on. Tell that bloody idiot – he's going to kill himself."

"The confidence wasn't there," says Coombs. "I was very nervous about him, I hated the thought of hurting somebody. I had a heart to heart with Piers, and I said to Sally, 'For God's sake, get him to go back to the brewery, or get a job somewhere.' When you see somebody having so many accidents there's going to come a time when there's going to be a big one."

A few days after Pau Bruce McLaren gave Piers a priceless boost in his regular *Autosport* column: "Wally Willmott is managing our Formula Two activities and he is certainly impressed with Piers. He is one of those rare racing drivers who says 'Thank you very much' at the end of a test or race, and goes fast too."

By now Bruce and Piers had become firm friends.

"Bruce was always supportive of people," Pat McLaren recalls, "and particularly of Piers, because we had become close friends. I thought he was just a super,

super person. He was such a delightful young man, and had such great talent."

The following week Piers had his fourth outing for BRM in the Spring Cup at Oulton Park, an event that drew a meagre field of just ten F1 and F2 cars, albeit with top quality drivers. Still stuck with the old Lotus, Piers qualified last and finished seventh and last in the first heat, before retiring with a water leak in the second. In the final his engine blew up, and to make matters worse his dropped oil probably caused team-mate Stewart to crash. Even when Piers himself kept out of trouble, the machinery would let him down.

He could at least commiserate by telephone with Jonathan, who was having an equally miserable time at Ferrari. The Dino F2 programme was running late, and on his sports car debut at Sebring his car had lasted only five laps. Jonathan had also failed in his attempt to land Piers a works seat for the Monza 1000kms.

He expressed his disappointment in a letter from Modena: "I feel we would have doddled along pretty well. Also the drive for Monza is a seriously prepared one – not like the Sebring effort. This sort of thing is I'm afraid only too typical of Ferrari policy – tell nobody anything until the last moment and then if possible still change the plan. In your case the trouble was our new Director Sportivo, [Franco] Lini, who started to play talent spotter on his own account and procured somebody called [Günther] Klass."

Three years earlier the impoverished Anglo-Swiss team mates could only dream about works drives with Ferrari and BRM, but it wasn't turning out how they had expected it to be. Perhaps by way of making up for his on track woes, that week Piers treated himself to an example of the recently launched Porsche 911 – a surprising move for someone who had just become a dad! The car was probably supplied by Frank Williams. At the time he was importing 911s duty free, using them for a few months, and then re-exporting them without having to get involved in customs paperwork…

Piers now headed off to the Nürburgring for the F2 Eifelrennen, held on the short South Circuit. Snowball fights were the main action on Friday, and the weather only just cleared in time to allow qualifying to take place. Piers lined up in the middle of the pack, but he made a brilliant start to get up to third on the first lap, behind only Rindt and Surtees, and ahead of Clark. In damp conditions, the Dunlops worked well. Clark dropped back with gearbox problems, but Piers eventually lost out to Ickx and local hero Hubert Hahne, who was being cheered on by a freezing cold 100,000-strong crowd.

Top *Piers in Parnell's Lotus in the Spring Trophy F1 race at Oulton Park on 15 April, where he was blighted by engine problems.*

Bottom *Piers hustles the McLaren around a snowy Nürburgring South Circuit in the Eifelrennen on 23 April. He ran a strong third in the early stages, but eventually finished fifth.*

Nevertheless fifth was a morale boosting result, and what's more he finished two places ahead of Irwin. *Autosport* noted that he had "...made up for his porridge in practice at Pau by driving a very smooth race."

It was Irwin's turn to handle Parnell's Lotus at the following week's International Trophy, and once again he had better luck than Piers with reliability, bringing the car home seventh, a couple of laps down on winner Mike Parkes. The competition between BRM's two youngsters was not getting any cooler.

"It wasn't really, the two of them were battling away," says Parnell. "It's just the way it happened. Irwin was a very good lad, no doubt about it. He would have been a top guy. Terrific lot of talent. They were two young lads, moving up the ladder all the time, and one day their day would come, there's no doubt about that."

Their wives were only too aware of the contest, as Sally recalls: "It was very difficult because they were playing Piers and Chris off against each other. It was not a very good situation for either driver. If they had concentrated on one or the other it would have been much better for both of them. They were very competitive against each other, and Piers didn't have a very good time. The car broke a few times, and he crashed, then he got a reputation. You lose your confidence a bit."

Piers under pressure from Chris Amon's Ferrari at Monaco. Later he spun on oil at Ste Devote, and was unable to restart. After that he found himself 'temporarily retired'.

"It got quite difficult in '67," says Loti Irwin. "There was a BRM drive up for grabs, and BRM were being really naughty and playing one off against the other. They were very evenly matched as far as results went. It was not like now where you have test drivers – the only way you could find out who was better was to actually let them race the car. As far as I can remember they never did any testing."

For the Monaco GP Sally flew down late in Irwin's private plane, but was delayed when they landed at San Raphael instead of Cannes, as Sally told the *Daily Mail*: "I knew all along it was the wrong airfield. I had been following the route on my road map!"

Piers had accepted an invitation to share half of a suite of adjoining rooms at the Hotel Hermitage with team mate Jackie Stewart. But unlike JYS, Piers was not yet earning enough to justify a week of five-star accommodation, as he recalled in 1970: "It was hideously expensive and far more than I could possibly afford but Sally was coming with me and I thought she would enjoy it. So I took it, more out of bravado than anything."

"Jackie said take the other room," says Sally. "I thought it was so nice, so lovely. Piers managed to pay the bill, but I'm sure he was broke for months afterwards!"

Piers had finally seen the last of the old Lotus 25/33, and had now been upgraded to a P261, albeit still with V8 engine. Qualifying didn't go very smoothly, for he crashed on Friday and suffered a water pump failure on Saturday. Nevertheless he ended up a respectable 13th, matching Spence's time with the H16 and beating Chris Amon's Ferrari and the Coopers of Jochen Rindt and Pedro Rodriguez. But race day was to be a disaster, and it started to go wrong even before Piers left the Hermitage on Sunday morning.

"That's when I broke my toe," says Sally. "Piers was clowning around throwing wet sponges, and I was throwing them back at him. We were having a sort of water fight and I smashed my foot into the door. I said, 'I can't move, I can't put my shoe on.' He told me, 'Stop complaining, you really are whinging.' It turned out I had broken it. It kept on getting bigger and fatter. I was half-carried, I half-hobbled around. Eventually I got a lift back in somebody's plane!"

Having clipped the hay bales early on in the race, Piers struggled to keep the car in one piece on a very oily track, acutely aware that he was being closely watched by BRM: "The sun was beating down and I was terribly hot. Also I was getting acute cramp in the ball of my foot. This was nothing to do with my accident in the Argentine as it was the other foot. I had to put up with this agonising pain. I began to feel that I really could not go on much longer but I comforted myself with the thought that the race must be almost over. Then they hung out a pit signal announcing that there were 55 laps to go. The race had hardly started."

More oil was dropped, and eventually Piers spun on the exit of Ste Devote on lap 65. Unable to restart due to a flat battery, he made the short trek back to the pits.

In 1969 he explained what happened to author Richard Garrett: "I was completely worn out after about 50 laps. My concentration definitely became very poor. After about 70 laps [sic] I hit some oil and went into a spin which, under normal circumstances, I'm perfectly sure I could have corrected and been perfectly all right. But my concentration wasn't as good as it might have been. I spun and stopped and couldn't get going again. I have always been worried about my physical stamina. I'm not a particularly strong person anyway and physical strength does help a lot."

The fiery accident that befell a similarly tired Lorenzo Bandini at the chicane a few laps later put his problems into perspective. The critically injured Ferrari driver died a few days later, but official festivities went ahead as usual on Sunday evening. At the party Piers "foolishly" told Raymond Mays that he'd been suffering from cramp. The curt response was that he'd better go away and get fit before driving a BRM again. As Piers himself noted, he had been temporarily retired. That left the door wide open for Irwin to establish himself in the Parnell seat.

"You'd have to have been Superman to make one of those wrecks do anything," says Jonathan Williams. "I think Piers was overdriving trying to make a rubbish car perform. Of course he got egg on his shirt. His mistake was he should have stayed on the road. Then they could have said, 'Good lad, slow car, he's doing his best.' But the minute you spin off into the weeds, people say, 'Tut, tut.' After you've done it three times in a row, that's it."

Piers had a couple of free weeks in which to gather his thoughts. He took the opportunity to invite *Autocar* journalist Peter Garnier to his home, the results of their chat appearing in the magazine on 1 June – the day that the release of *Sgt Pepper's Lonely Heart's Club Band* launched the Summer of Love.

Garnier painted an interesting portrait of Piers at that point in his life: "Piers Courage is tallish and slim; loose-limbed and boyish. He has short hair; and his taste in clothes is informal and restrained – modern Savile Row, as distinct from Carnaby Street. He speaks quickly and enthusiastically when becoming immersed in a subject, and with slightly clipped words and using the art of understatement to make his point, so that the occasional 'fantastic' becomes telling; and he smiles a lot. I found it disarming that he should have appeared shy when I took my tape recorder along to Pimlico – usually being the shy party myself on such occasions."

In those days meaningful interviews with racing drivers were still a rarity, but typically Piers was honest and open with Garnier, especially when discussing the problems he'd encountered on his step up to the big time

with BRM. Piers made it clear that he felt a lot of pressure: "Then you get into a car that belongs to a sort of board of directors, somewhere up in the sky, who have given you your big chance. Well…it's just fantastic. I was absolutely staggered when they asked me to drive. You can't help feeling this sense of responsibility – a sort of duty not to let them down."

That clearly had an effect on his driving: "If you're going to have a go early on, you're bound to start making errors – little ones, I hope. But you've obviously got to have a go because of this board of directors who've given you the chance and decided you're good enough to drive their cars. You feel you can't let them down. Except for Jackie Stewart, of course, I was one of the first to move up from F3, and there's always the thought, 'Everybody's watching and criticising.' Also, it's worrying when people come up and say 'You were doing jolly well keeping up with so and so,' when I know perfectly well I could have passed them, but was keeping the speed down because I was frightened of doing something wrong. I find it very difficult to drive like this – sort of striking a happy medium."

Garnier pushed Courage on the subject of accidents, and specifically whether his recent string of shunts had worried him: "No, actually they don't. I think I shall get over them – perhaps when I get used to being where I am. And when I get used to the responsibility."

Piers was able to enjoy an extended stay at Sutherland Street, for the next F2 race was at Crystal Palace on Spring Bank Holiday Monday, just two days after his 26th birthday. With many of the big names busy at Indianapolis Piers finished third in his heat, and then had a solid run to fifth in the final, holding off Jackie Oliver. It was a much-needed boost. The following weekend Piers sat at home while Irwin had his first proper Grand Prix outing in Parnell's Lotus at Zandvoort. He finished a respectable seventh, even beating Spence in the H16.

Having done so well with Roy Pike at Le Mans the previous year, Piers was invited to rejoin the Maranello Concessionaires line-up for the 1967 event. This time he was to share a Ferrari 412P with Richard Attwood, and the pair travelled out to France in Piers's Porsche 911. "It was a rare privilege for me to be in a car like that," says Attwood, who just three years later would give the Stuttgart marque its first outright victory at Le Mans.

Piers had revealed his thoughts on the event to Peter Garnier a couple of weeks earlier: "Le Mans is not one of his favourites – an opinion shared by so many other drivers – but he regards it as well worth doing from the publicity angle as part of the driver's stock-in-trade.

Above Piers shared this Ferrari with Richard Attwood on his second appearance at Le Mans. They formed a good team, but the car retired with engine failure.

Opposite A £300 fee for Le Mans was a welcome boost for the Courage bank account.

He finds it very dangerous, and quite terrifying – but, as he says, it is synonymous with motor racing in the public eye and therefore must continue in its present form."

After the previous year's ill-starred four-car assault, this time Ronnie Hoare had entered only one Ferrari, so there was extra pressure to perform. Attwood was the senior partner in the combination, and Piers was happy to drive to orders.

"He did exactly as I wanted him to do, he was fantastic," says Richard. "I couldn't have asked any more of him. He was a very quick driver and it was a question of slowing him down for this one event, I suppose. He was a perfect team-mate, and we got on hugely well. There was always this little bit of rivalry because I went to Harrow. He had copied my idea of putting the colours on his helmet, which hadn't been done before. He certainly got the idea from me, I do know that!"

The pair were running in ninth place when the engine failed in the 15th hour, while Piers was at the wheel. It had used up all its oil, and a piston popped through the crankcase.

"That year the Ferraris had a very bad set of piston rings," says Attwood. "Most of the engines they had rebuilt had these rings in them, and ours was the last of the batch to fail. We had driven it as well as we could have done. You couldn't replenish oil or water unless you had a 25-lap gap."

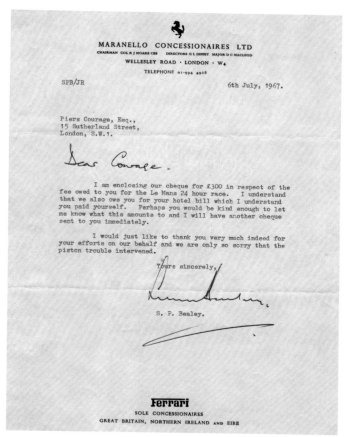

SPB/JR   6th July, 1967.

Piers Courage, Esq.,
15 Sutherland Street,
London, S.W.1.

Dear Courage,

    I am enclosing our cheque for £300 in respect of the
fee owed to you for the Le Mans 24 hour race. I understand
that we also owe you for your hotel bill which I understand
you paid yourself. Perhaps you would be kind enough to let
me know what this amounts to and I will have another cheque
sent to you immediately.

    I would just like to thank you very much indeed for
your efforts on our behalf and we are only so sorry that the
piston trouble intervened.

            Yours sincerely,

            S. P. Bealey.

Sally had come out for the race, and the trip home was not a happy one: "It was let's stay in Paris tonight, because we were so tired. We couldn't afford anywhere decent. So we ended up in a place where the bedroom was so wet I said to Piers I'd rather go and sleep in the car. He was so broke and desperate…" The £300 driving fee he received for Le Mans was most welcome.

An engine problem also claimed Piers in his next F2 outing at Rheims, supporting the 12 Hours, but he had better luck a week later in the Deutschland Trophy at Hockenheim. The clashing non-championship race at Rouen accounted for most of the graded drivers, and Piers missed the chance to link up with Jonathan, who made his F2 debut for Ferrari in France.

But with the big names gone Hockenheim was an opportunity for the lesser lights to bask in some glory. It was a two-heat aggregate event, and in the first slipstreaming affair Piers had a bump with Robin Widdows after Ickx had spun in front of them. He still finished third, behind Gardner and Irwin. In the second Piers again tangled with Widdows, but survived to take fourth place and third overall.

"The biggest problem was when he got near Robin Widdows," says John Coombs. "They were about the same level and they were both about as irresponsible! If they came round on the same lap together you could guarantee that one of them would be missing next time…"

In fact Robin and Piers were both born on 27 May 1942, and that contributed to a friendly rivalry, as they jokingly regarded themselves as twins.

Piers had begun to redeem himself in the eyes of BRM, and he was given another chance at the British GP. However, by now Irwin was well established in the camp, having finished fifth in the French GP on the Le Mans Bugatti track, despite a last lap engine failure. BRM thus entered four cars at Silverstone, with H16s for Stewart, Spence and Irwin, and the older P261 V8 for Piers.

Despite his lack of recent F1 mileage and engine problems on the first day Piers set a respectable time, and had five others behind him. However, he didn't get a chance to race. Stewart's car was a new lightweight machine, and when it suffered a suspension collapse – due to a welding problem – the team decided to park the car for the rest of the weekend. JYS commandeered Irwin's standard H16, and Chris took over the P261. Piers was left without a car for his home race, and in the most humiliating possible circumstances. Irwin eventually finished seventh, and the only good news for Piers was a superb victory for Luke in the F3 support race. There were to be no more invitations to race for BRM in 1967.

Silverstone took place on Saturday, and missing the race did at least give Piers more time to make it over to Austria for Sunday's F2 event. It was held at the Tulln-Langenlebarn military airfield some 20 miles from Vienna, a venue which Jochen Rindt had done much to promote. Piers had an uneventful run to ninth place.

From Austria there was a long trek to another unfamiliar venue in Spain, the new Jarama circuit just outside Madrid. Clark won from Stewart and the increasingly impressive Irwin, while Piers dropped from fifth to eighth after his clutch failed. Indeed, he finished the race with a blistered right hand after 30 laps of clutchless gearchanges. That weekend came chastening news from Jonathan at Mugello. Günther Klass, the man Ferrari had earlier preferred over Piers for the Monza 1000kms drive, had crashed a 206P into a tree during practice. The car had been broken in half, and the German night club owner was killed.

Piers was due for a change of fortune, and it came at Zandvoort on 30 July. The race was reserved for non-graded drivers, so as at Hockenheim, there was much at stake. By now Dunlop had produced some more suitable tyres for the McLaren, and Piers was happier. However, the weekend didn't get off to a good start, as Coombs recalls: "We went to the circuit for practice, came back, and they'd let the room to somebody else – and put all the clothes and suitcases outside the door. Sally went mad, and Piers was scratching his head…"

The grid was to be decided by a qualifying heat, and Piers was slowed by a rear puncture towards the end. As the tyre broke up, he crawled round to fifth. However, the main event was to be much better. Piers passed Rees,

Beltoise and Gardner, and with Irwin dropping back with electrical problems he took a superb second place, behind only the flying Jacky Ickx. Three years earlier Zandvoort had provided his big F3 breakthrough when he finished second to Stewart – now it did the same in F2. But there was a reminder that the sand blown Dutch venue could be dangerous when veteran privateer Ian Raby crashed heavily. He would succumb to his injuries some months later.

Coombs hoped that Zandvoort was to be a turning point, but Piers continued to have adventures. He brushed a barrier at Enna, and then had one of his most embarrassing mishaps to date in the Guards Trophy at Brands Hatch on 28 August.

The weekend started well. Piers qualified a superb third overall, beaten only by John Surtees and Jochen Rindt. The field was split into two qualifying heats, and in his Piers finished third, behind Graham Hill and Jackie Oliver. A slower overall race time put all three well back on the grid for the final, but Piers soon made good progress into third place, behind Rindt and Stewart. But while under pressure from Jo Schlesser he plunged off the road on lap 21, as Simon Taylor noted in *Autosport*: "The McLaren driver missed a gear going into the first part of South Bank and the car went straight on and over a bank. Piers was unhurt, but the car was definitely *hors de combat* – a sad end to one of his best F2 drives to date."

Unfortunately for Piers a quick-witted photographer managed to find an angle from where a Take Courage banner could be seen in the distance behind the battered McLaren. The picture was to be widely used in the press, to the amusement of everyone except poor Piers.

"It was a beautiful photograph!," says Roland Law. "He was as white as a sheet when he came in. He settled down, but it took 10 minutes."

"The car virtually broke its back," says Coombs. "How it got up there, can you imagine? And right in front of everybody."

As London grooved to the summer soundtrack of *All You Need is Love* and *A Whiter Shade of Pale*, Piers was more than a little frustrated with the McLaren. He explained his feelings to Eoin Young the following year: "It was built for Bruce to drive, and Bruce liked it – but I never did find anyone else who liked it as Bruce did. Nobody else could drive it the way Bruce set it up. I went off the road twice with it and bent it reasonably badly, which didn't do me any good psychologically, and it didn't do my entrant any good. John is very nervous anyway, and he was starting to ring me up and tell me to retire and that sort of thing. I was getting very depressed."

"The poor man," says Sally. "He really had a lot on his plate. There was also the fact that he had a wife and

Piers hustles Jackie Oliver's works Lotus during his impressive drive at Brands Hatch on 28 August. Alas, the day was to end in some disappointment...

child and everything else. A huge responsibility. His confidence had obviously been very dented. He was being gunned at, Crasher Courage and everything. But he had faith in himself."

The Brands damage was almost as bad as at Pau, and the Coombs outfit missed the next two races while the car was rebuilt around a new tub. The old one lay unloved at McLaren's Colnbrook works for some time, but was eventually rescued and rebuilt by mechanic Howden Ganley.

Meanwhile the revamped Coombs M4A reappeared at Albi a month after the accident, now sporting a grey colour scheme. He battled with Jacky Ickx but a pit stop to replace a flat battery left Piers way down the order in 10th, although off-track there was fun to be had.

"Sally, Piers and myself came into a restaurant," says Coombs. "There was a big fish tank on the right. And Jo Schlesser was in the tank going 'Glug, glug' like a fish. Jo came out of the tank, took his trousers off and stood there with nothing on!"

The trip to the season finale at Vallelunga on 8 October allowed Piers, Jochen and the rest to check out the latest trends in the boutiques of Rome. "It was hilarious," says Coombs, "setting new fashions with shoes and coats."

Piers was the pacesetter on such occasions, and journalist Heinz Pruller has an interesting insight into how it worked: "Piers and Stewart came up with these flamboyant ties. Jochen basically had three shirts all his life! They were Fred Perry, and one was blue, one was green, and the other was kind of red/brown. Nina also tried to convince him, 'You must be better dressed. Look at Stewart and look at Piers.' He said Piers looked like a parrot – Jochen hated it. But Piers always had an influence on him in dressing."

There was more frustration in the Vallelunga race, as *Autosport* reported: "Piers Courage felt a bump in his back which was a conrod coming out of the engine to finish his day's racing when he was in a very nice sixth position." Ickx won in Italy and thus beat Gardner to the European Championship title, while Piers was a respectable fourth in the final table.

"We had a very depressing year, and it was a very hard year," says Coombs. "The car was most of the time being repaired. But he wasn't hard on engines, just hard on the car. It could have been good if we'd had somebody else in the team, an experienced driver, to help Piers along."

Jonathan wasn't having much better luck. After a year of making odd appearances for Ferrari in F2, sports cars and CanAm, he made his Grand Prix debut with the team in Mexico on 22 October. He had to wait around while Chris Amon decided which chassis he wanted to use, and eventually finished eighth in the one the Kiwi rejected. "I'd never driven that car, I'd never been on

that track, I was propped up with about six inches of foam rubber... I did well not to wreck it!"

Shortly afterwards Jonathan crashed in testing, and his short Ferrari career was over. Meanwhile Piers's own prospects now seemed to be very limited. There was no apparent future at BRM, and no other F1 teams showed any interest. Eoin Young summed up his situation in *Speedworld International* the following June: "The way Courage describes it, at the end of 1967 he was the one bloke nobody wanted to see. 'I was a really bad smell.' He was too. He had a record of crashes and spins that no team manager could possibly ignore. It was true he was fast between accidents, but nobody wanted to foot the sort of repair bills that Piers regularly racked up."

Rather than wait for something to turn up, Piers decided to take the initiative. The Tasman series was fast approaching, and a good showing there might lead to something for the European season. As no paid drive was available, he would have to run his own car, and thus he contacted race organisers and began to assess how much the trip would cost and how much starting money he could generate. But there was also a more immediate chance to salvage his reputation, and it involved Frank Williams.

Frank had not quite given up any aspirations of becoming a top driver, but he'd spent 1967 building up his business. His wheeling and dealing in cars and spares

had become more and more successful, and since April he'd been trading as Frank Williams (Racing Cars) Ltd.

"I'd sold my Brabham and decided to spend the year making some money selling racing cars," he says. "I'd got all those contacts who wanted cars, and would call me and say 'Can you get me a gearbox?' The idea was I'd go back in '68 wealthy, successful, with two cars, spare engines, all that sort of stuff."

In fact the business had taken off. During 1967 he had become an agent for Brabham, and his turnover was an impressive £160,000, although he wasn't making much of a profit on that. Now Frank had got his hands on Brabham's 1968 F3 prototype. He needed a quick driver to showcase it at the high profile season closer, the Motor Show 200 at Brands Hatch, where a good result would generate winter sales. Piers had a lot to lose by stepping back into the category a full year after his last F3 race, and the fact that he was willing to do so showed how desperate he was.

"Piers had all sorts of dramas and mistakes, although I don't know what they were. His future looked very black by the end of the season, and at that point he persuaded me, or I persuaded him, to do an F3 race. The plan was re-establish his confidence and his career, and win the Motor Show race."

Thus for the first time Frank Williams made an appearance as a serious entrant, and the immaculate two-tone green BT21B joined a packed field of 60 cars at Brands on 29 October. Along with the top Brits the cream of Europe's F3 racers were there, including future F1 stars Clay Regazzoni, François Cevert, Henri Pescarolo, Reine Wisell and Jean-Pierre Jabouille.

In a damp practice session Piers managed only six laps, but he still qualified third. He was in the first of two qualifying heats, and having taken the lead from Mike Beckwith, he disappeared into the distance. He won by a ten second margin, and broke Peter Gethin's new F3 lap record by 0.4sec. It was a sublime performance.

His luck ran out in the wet final. Water got into the electrics of the unproven car, and Piers stopped on the warm-up lap. He walked disconsolately back to the pits, only to have to jump for his life when Peter Deal crashed into a marshal's post he was passing. The spinning Brabham clipped Piers's foot, without causing serious injury, but a less fortunate marshal suffered a broken leg and other injuries. An ambulance then pulled into the path of Mike Knight, causing him to crash!

F3 racer Howden Ganley watched the episode unfold from behind the pits: "The spinning car that collected Piers suddenly appeared out of the spray, going straight toward him. I seem to recall that he had the presence of

Opposite Whoops! Piers parked the Coombs M4A on top of the bank at Brands, and the photo opportunity provided by the sign in the background proved too good to miss. The picture was used in Autocar and other publications.

Left Piers and Sally sport the latest fashions while on holiday in France.

mind to jump in the air just as it reached him, but he still got clipped. He also had the presence of mind to realise that there were probably some medical staff sheltering in the little St John's Ambulance hut, and that they were now required on deck, so he hopped over on one leg to fetch them! Amongst all the melée of spinning cars, the ambulance was waved out onto the circuit. I recall one unfortunate driver who found the vehicle bearing down on him just as he came past, and you could almost see the look of horror on his face as he swerved to avoid it, but the thing just kept coming toward him..."

Although it ended early, and very nearly turned into a total disaster, Brands was a fantastic debut for this new combination of Piers and Frank. Both men realised that this could be the start of something special, and before long they had agreed to do an F2 season together in 1968.

"I enjoyed it because we had a good car and a chance of winning," says Frank. "I enjoyed it very much. To have someone like Piers in it, I was very proud, no question about that. Very proud. By that time I must have been becoming a bit of a fan. He was one of us, and we'd grown up in motor racing together, our little group. We all wanted to help him in some way or another. He was a loveable character.

"Certainly he persuaded me to do an F2 programme, although I required no persuasion. I happened to have a Brabham F2 car in stock, or one that a guy didn't want, so we decided to use that. But even by that time the plan was I'd be racing myself the following year."

Not everyone in their circle expected the idea to work, as Sheridan Thynne recalls: "I remember Piers saying to me that he was going to do something with Frank next year, because Frank was such a wonderful organiser. I remember thinking, Frank? Wonderful organiser?"

As Williams set to work putting the pieces together for 1968, Piers focussed on getting to the Tasman series, as the first race at Pukekohe was just two months away. The biggest concern was where he was going to find his proposed budget of £10,000. They lived well, but nevertheless there was little spare cash in the Courage household, and the banks were always politely asking when overdrafts would be taken care of. Piers sold his Porsche 911 the day after the Brands F3 race.

"We had to hock ourselves up to the eyeballs to get him out there," says Sally. "Luckily I could keep working, so I could pay a lot of bills. I did any jobs that I could lay my hands on. I went to work at the Motor Show to sell Britax seatbelts. It was a good job, it paid well."

At first Piers investigated buying a Matra from Ken Tyrrell, but it was too expensive. The answer to his problem lay closer to home. After they bumped into each other at the Motor Show, John Coombs agreed to sell

In August Piers and Sally had a holiday in Italy, and on the way to Enna they stopped at her sister's house in Porto Ercole. This picture was signed as a gift for Lady Watson, Piers's grandmother.

Piers the well-used McLaren M4A for the Tasman campaign. The price would be £4,300, and as a favour, John was willing to wait until 31 March, after the Tasman Series had concluded, to receive full payment: "I was quite happy to have done that. Piers was a helluva nice guy and we got on very well."

"Coombsy was wonderful," says Sally. "He was always very realistic about Piers, but always had great faith in him, even when he was going through his bad crash days."

Piers assumed that any starting and prize money generated down under would go some way to pay for the McLaren. If not, he could sell the car to an Antipodean racer and leave it over there – assuming of course that it was still in one piece...

But he still had to finance everything else, including two engines, spares, transport to New Zealand and the services of a decent mechanic. He calculated that starting money from the eight events would amount to £1,500, and Dunlop helped by chipping in with another £1,500. It still wasn't enough, and as a last resort, Piers went to his father. Commercial sponsorship was still a novelty in motor racing, but Piers knew that Courage was in the process of opening a brewery in Australia, and felt that his presence there – in a Courage-liveried car – would be of great benefit.

Inevitably, Richard was underwhelmed by the idea. He hadn't put any of his own money into Piers' racing since the Merlyn sports car days in 1963, and found the prospect of using company funds for his son's activities extremely uncomfortable. However, again Piers was strongly supported by his mother.

"Mum was pretty vocal," says Andrew Courage. "Dad felt there was a conflict of interests of course. It wasn't so easy, supporting your son. In other people's eyes it would have been quite weird. But it's ludicrous how little the company cashed in on it."

Jean Courage was now fully behind her eldest son's chosen profession.

"There was a lot of moral support once he'd made it," says Charlie Courage. "Once he made it through to F3 with Luke, and started to get his name his print, it gathered force behind him."

After some discussion Richard put his son's proposal to his directors. Matters were confused by the fact that Courage in London was only a minority shareholder in the new Australian venture, but there was tentative support for the idea. Piers would be given A$1,500 – not as much he needed, but welcome nevertheless.

There was no Courage beer link in New Zealand, but there was a company presence in the form of Liquer Cream Whisky and the locally produced Saccone's Gin. The Kiwi management was willing to help out, but they could not offer any hard cash.

A fascinating letter from Courage Ltd to Piers has survived. It is dated 15 December 1968, which was

little second-hand. The car was soon retrieved, and Sheppard set about tidying it up.

The Courage connections paid dividends when Piers received the loan of a Holden estate car in return for putting Saccone's Gin logos on the M4A. Shell helped out with a trailer, and the little *équipe* was complete and ready for the first race. It was a little reminiscent of 1964, but at least this time Piers had a mechanic. And he wasn't planning to sleep in the tow car...

Qualifying kicked off on January 4 at Pukekohe, a horse racing course near Auckland. After those long months of preparation, Piers nearly threw it all away on the first day when he slid into a grass bank. Damage was confined to suspension and a minor ding in the tub, but Les Sheppard was not impressed.

"The McLaren was a fabulous little car," says Sheppard, now a clergyman in his native Australia. "It had been prepared by Roland Law in England, and I just took it out of the box – and Piers bent it straight away. I said. 'I'll build this for you, but if you take it off the road again you can rebuild it yourself!' I just told him outright that I wasn't coming to the Tasman Series to work on rebuilding cars for him. We were edgy together, but he settled down. I think he was more terrified of me than he was the car, because he could see he wasn't going to get anyone else to build it!"

Chastened, Piers qualified seventh, behind all the star names but ahead of the local contenders. He knew that above all, he had to bring the car home. Luck was on his side come the race, as most of the leading contenders fell by the wayside. Clark, Rodriguez and McLaren all suffered mechanical failures, and Hulme had a narrow escape after rolling his Brabham to destruction. Amon scored an easy win in the Ferrari,

with Gardner some way behind. Piers drove a steady race to finish a lap down in third, much to Sheppard's relief. Meanwhile there was plenty to keep the visitors occupied.

"You got to know people a lot better over that series," says Amon. "It was eight weeks, and there was a lot of time to fill in between events. In New Zealand the distances were comparatively small, so you left the last event and took half a day to get to the next one, so you had quite a lot of time to fill in. I ducked out of it a bit because I'd come home for a couple of days, but I still got to know people better than I ever did in Europe. It was a unique little thing for a few years, with water skiing, swimming, golf, meals together, all that sort of thing. And it was the height of summer."

The second race was at Levin, Amon's local track. The circuit consisted mostly of corners, and thus the McLaren's lack of outright bhp was less of a handicap. With Hulme temporarily absent, Piers only had five big boys to beat, and he got ahead of Gardner to finish fifth in the preliminary heat. In the main race he battled hard with McLaren's BRM, and gradually worked his way up the order as once again most of the main contenders retired. He eventually finished in an astonishing second place, some 50 seconds behind Amon.

"We shared accommodation at Levin," says Sheppard. "We stayed in some old woman's house. We put our underwear in a bag and it came back ironed and washed! We started to get to know each other, and I really loved the guy. We knew we couldn't win with that car – that was the secret. It took the pressure off him. We could hang on to them, and if they spun, we were quick enough to keep in front of them. He kept it on the road at Levin, and he started to get some confidence."

The eyes have it! Many saw Piers and Sally as the perfect couple.

Hugely relieved that his gamble already seemed to be paying off, Piers expressed his thoughts in a letter to his parents: "As Sally has probably told you we had a very successful start to the series out here with a second and third. This has been mostly because of others falling by the wayside but still we are now second in the championship (for a while)! Social life is pretty active and I have been skiing a lot. Also I managed to ski on one ski on my first day, much to the amazement of all. My mechanic is turning out very well and the car is absolutely immaculate and so far, touch wood, we have had very little trouble.

"The racing itself has not been too strenuous as I am in a position where I am much faster than all the locals but a little slower than the other overseas drivers who, now that Hulme is temporarily out of it, all have faster cars than me. However at Levin I was about equal to the BRMs which meant we had a fabulous dice with Bruce McLaren for about thirty laps until his car broke. I have already had a lot of people wanting to buy the car so I shouldn't have much difficulty at the end of the series."

The circus then moved to the South Island, Piers making the trip by plane after putting the car on a ferry. At a cocktail party held by the race organisers in Christchurch he was invited to make a speech, an experience that he found "…more unnerving than competing in a race."

At the Lady Wigram airfield track there was a huge controversy as Clark's Lotus appeared in Gold Leaf colours for the first time, and many bemoaned the arrival of a new era of commercialism. No one seemed to have cared too much about the bold Saccone's Gin decals on Piers's humble McLaren in the earlier events! Hulme was now back in action, using a replacement chassis shipped out by none other than Frank Williams.

Clark led Amon home, while in both the preliminary heat and the main race Piers fought hard with World Champion Hulme, the pair eventually finishing third and fourth – ahead of the BRMs. "Denny had Courage doggedly attached to him," *Autosport* noted. "Piers had driven a nicely balanced race and also kept Dunlop in the picture."

McLaren was delighted to see his M4A going so well. "There was a time when you could just about rely on Piers to have some sort of mishap," he noted in *Autosport*. "But his Tasman score of a second, third and a fourth in three races is some indication of the way he's progressing."

By now everyone had taken note of Piers's polished performances, and the domestic press had begun to give his underdog exploits a real push. Meanwhile the word

was getting back to Britain not just through *Autosport* and *Autocar*, but regular reports in the dailies as well.

Richard Courage soon wrote back to Piers, offering a degree of moral support that his eldest son must surely have greatly appreciated: "Obviously you have very wisely decided not to try and run with the fliers but be competitive in your class, and patience has rewarded your efforts. May good fortune, wise judgement, concentration and determination bring you success during the remainder of the tour. *The Daily Telegraph* and *Autosport* have been most complementary… Whether the sales of Saccone's Gin will benefit is another matter, but you have certainly put the name of Courage on the map in NZ. Let's hope it will be the same in Australia."

The last of the New Zealand rounds was at Teretonga, a track Piers knew from his unsuccessful '67 exploits with BRM. McLaren scored a popular win, while once again Piers battled wheel to wheel with Hulme, securing fifth when the local hero pitted with suspension problems.

There was a free weekend to enjoy before action resumed in Australia. Les flew to his home in Melbourne, taking one of the engines with him for servicing, while Piers headed to Sydney. He stayed with

Right Courage Breweries never took any interest in Piers's racing activities, but a subsidiary in New Zealand was quick to take advantage of his successful Tasman campaign.

Opposite top Mechanic Les Sheppard offers Piers advice before the start at Pukekohe. The pair established a good working relationship.

Opposite bottom A delighted Bruce McLaren congratulates Piers after his unexpected second place at Levin.

friend Dennis O'Neil, a successful racing yachtsman and leading light in the local social scene who Piers had met in London. He helped out with the loan of another Holden estate car for the Australian leg, so once again Piers saved some cash.

Piers had already earned more prize money than he had budgeted for, and deciding that there was room for a little extravagance, bought Sally an air ticket. She duly flew out to Sydney, and Piers was there to greet her. The couple were somewhat surprised to find themselves in the middle of an impromptu press call, so great was the interest in the arrival of a top London model with an aristocratic background and racing driver husband. Suddenly the Australian women's weeklies and newspaper fashion columns were full of stories about Lady Sarah. Everyone wanted to know about the latest trends back home.

She revealed her thoughts in *Woman's Day* magazine: "London really does swing, you know. London leads the world today in young fashions and the miniskirt (glancing at her own bare thighs) was an inspired idea. People say 'mini' will give way to the Bonnie and Clyde thing. But I don't believe the miniskirt will ever disappear. It's too comfortable – too symbolic of the young idea."

They were soon off to Queensland for the next race at Surfers' Paradise. Now there was a second Lotus 49T for

Hill, while McLaren's BRM was taken over by Richard Attwood. Now running without the Kiwi gin decals, Piers put in another great performance. He passed Hill and ran second behind Clark, before the FVA engine cut out and caused him to spin. He recovered to finish third, just behind the Lotus pair, despite a recurrent misfire. The points tally continued to grow, as did the interest from the local media, as Piers noted in another letter to his parents:

"We have had the most marvellous tour so far with a great start to Australia at Surfers' Paradise which I am sure you have read about. I am afraid when I last spoke to you on the phone I didn't sound very cheerful but now Sally is here I have too much to think of to be anything but happy, and we are having a simply wonderful time in Sydney. We are getting so much publicity here that it's almost too much. Two TV shows, limitless photographers and newspaper interviews. The phone never seems to stop ringing. I have got a lunch with the Chairman of Shell (Aust) in Melbourne next week and have to appear before 600 employees. All very nerve-wracking!"

Piers and Sally continued to make friends wherever they went, one Sydney paper's social diarist noting that "it would he hard to imagine a more attractive pair of young people, enjoying the sunny life of Australia."

The entry at Warwick Farm, an attractive horse racing venue in the suburbs of Sydney, was boosted by the arrival of Jack Brabham. Dennis O'Neil brought his Rolls-Royce along, and with the aircon going full blast, it provided Piers with a welcome escape from the heat in the paddock.

On the track Piers's remarkable progress continued unabated. In the race he harried Hill and Amon in a three-way battle for second, and gained third spot when the Ferrari driver spun. He had little trouble holding off Amon and Hulme for the remainder of the race. It wasn't just good reliability earning those results. *Autosport* noted: "Once again Courage had shone, and here surely is a driver who must not be allowed to go without a top drive this year."

The penultimate race was the Australian GP at Sandown Park, another four-legged venue near Melbourne and Sheppard's home track. With power more of a factor Piers had less chance to shine, but he still managed a solid fifth, ahead of Attwood's BRM.

The final round involved a trip over to Tasmania and the daunting Longford road course. The journey from Sydney was itself exciting, for Piers and Sally joined Jim Clark in a friend's Piper Aztec, and they landed on a rough field in a heavy crosswind.

For Piers Longford was a reminder of the F3 days and wild places like Caserta, Schleize and Dunboyne, where stone walls and lamp posts were part of the scenery. Frank Gardner remembers it well: "It was over railway lines, onto a bridge with a curve in it, with just well-

spaced wooden railings which you could force a car through. You were coming on to a slippery piece of oily board over a river. That was the safety procedure! It made parts of Nürburgring look quite safe..."

"It was an extraordinarily quick circuit," says Chris Amon. "It was basically a rectangle, and by the time you were halfway down the straight you were absolutely flat out. It was a wonderful circuit in the dry, but in the wet it had the potential to be bloody dangerous."

"Longford was not our circuit," says Sheppard. "I think we could do about 168mph down the straight, and the others were doing 190mph. It was a crazy track. They jumped over railway lines and things like that!"

Piers lost out in qualifying at Longford, and had a minor off in Saturday's heat after hitting oil dropped by Rodriguez. Sunday was free, and as usual there was fun to be had away from the track. While fielding during a game of cricket Piers discovered an elderly bird's egg, and duly bowled it at Tim Parnell. The resulting mess made the pitch unplayable for the rest of the afternoon!

Thanks to the foresight of Les Sheppard, Piers was in good shape for the Monday race.

"On Saturday in practice, it was 102F," Les recalls. "I asked Dunlop where our rain tyres were, and they said, 'They're still in Melbourne.' They didn't think we needed them! And I made a big fuss about it, and said they should be here. Piers had them flown down over night –

he said, 'Just get them down here to appease Les.' And of course it rained on the Monday morning..."

It didn't just rain, it bucketed down, and the course was totally washed out. To make matters worse, vandals set fire to one of the two bridges! Inevitably the start was delayed – not an easy option on a track governed by the train timetable – and there was even talk of cancellation. Piers knew that his lighter, less powerful package could be just the ticket in the conditions, but he was reluctant to vote against his colleagues. After the drivers tried a couple of exploratory warming up laps, the race eventually got underway an hour late, its length reduced from 28 to 15 laps.

Piers was sixth at the start, but as the field tip-toed around the soggy course he soon picked off Hill, Amon (who went up an escape road), Gardner and Rodriguez. And then on the fourth lap he sailed past Clark to take the lead. Back in the pits, nobody could quite believe it.

"They all wanted to stop the race," says Sheppard, "but we knew we had everything going for us. We had a car that didn't have enough power to spin itself off the road, so Piers could drive it flat out down the straight, and we had this magic tyre. He was near the front after the second lap, and

Opposite This posed picture was used over a full page in Australia's Woman's Day magazine, so great was the interest in Sally down under. The maroon and gold Courage colours can be seen on the M4A.

Above Piers chases Graham Hill's works Lotus 49. His giant-killing performances won him a lot of fans.

Indycar – if Jimmy or Graham Hill wouldn't turn up. Colin quite rightly saw the limitations in me, but really he had no choice. Because the season had already started, the drivers he would have preferred had gone off and done something else. He'd not only lost his best driver, he'd also lost his best mate, so he wasn't in very good spirits. All of us were striving to get the best drive at that time, and Piers was a name that was on people's lips, the same as myself."

Piers was convinced he had made the right decision, as Sheridan Thynne recalls: "He actually thought that to do a year in a Grand Prix car which was not a winner was a good thing. He ran that by me and we talked a lot about that. I suppose that he'd had a lot of problems the previous year, and Chris Irwin had moved ahead of him. He saw the sense of a year of consolidation in 1968. He had other alternatives, but he thought it was a good thing to consolidate with Tim. He understood that he had to get rid of the crasher image; he had to put together some finishes. He thought it would be easier to do that with the lower pressure of a semi-private car."

Piers's first appointment with Parnell was the International Trophy, where Lotus was represented by a single 49 for Hill. Attwood drove a second Parnell car, while the twin works entries were handled as usual by Mike Spence and Pedro Rodriguez. Piers had his first ever laps in the ex-Tasman BRM P126 on the Thursday, and found the cockpit ill fitting at first. In the evening Dunlop hosted a party in his honour at The Green Man pub, to celebrate his Tasman success. Competitions boss Dick Jeffreys and PR man Ian Norris presented him with a gold tankard.

Piers qualified a respectable 10th in a 14-car field, and before Saturday's main event commenced he had fun watching Charles Lucas win the supporting historic race in his Maserati 250F. As this was the first F1 race since Hockenheim, there was a minute's silence before the start. A lone piper played, and the drivers stood to attention on the grid. The race itself was effectively a test session for Piers, and his pace improved as the event went on and he learned about the car. When leader Hulme lapped him Piers stayed with the World Champion for the remaining laps, eventually finishing fifth. After five retirements in his five appearances with BRM in 1967, the result came as a huge relief.

"He was very good, and easy to work with," says Parnell mechanic Stan Collier. "He could tell you what was wrong with the car, if it was oversteering, understeering, and we'd sort it, go out and go a bit quicker. He was actually a very nice person, and I had

no problems with him at all. He was very down to earth really. He hadn't got that much experience, but he drove pretty well I thought."

Piers then joined Hill for a dash down to Madrid for Sunday's F2 encounter at Jarama. A special qualifying session was laid on in the morning for the late arrivals, and Piers crashed avoiding a misplaced marker cone, a fate which had previously befallen his 'twin', Robin Widdows. The rear of the car was badly damaged, and despite a frantic effort to repair it, Piers was unable to start. First reserve Max Mosley thus took his place. The journey home was a memorable one, as Frank recalls:

"There was a really tight-fisted promoter who wouldn't pay us any money for going down there! I remember coming back with Graham in his first Piper Aztec. We set off with Graham and got into some very cloudy weather going north as we got towards the Pyrenees. Piers was in the right seat next to Graham. He said, 'Graham, the highest mountain here is 12,000 feet. We're at 7,000 feet.' So Graham said, '12,000?, right…' And up we went. The engines were reverberating away, and then the right wing dropped down. And Graham said, 'Sorry, fuel transfer, I forgot…'"

Next time out at Zolder Piers had another shunt, this time in the race. The consequences could have been worse, as Paul Watson reported in *Autosport*: "Going over the hill behind the pits, which is taken at well in excess of 100mph, a front tyre suddenly went flat. Piers fought desperately to keep the car straight, but it completely failed to respond and flew straight into the countryside at an impossible speed. Thankfully, the Zolder circuit is well-lined with safety fencing, designed to cocoon a car on impact, and so cradle it and reduce its speed. Luckily it worked even at this speed, sending Piers's car rocketing down the fence, writing the chassis off, but not even scratching the driver." It was indeed a lucky escape, and later it was found that Piers had damaged a wheel in an earlier brush with a kerb.

A couple of days after Zolder the racing world was stunned by the death of Mike Spence at Indianapolis. BRM had released him to test a Lotus 56, and he was struck on the head by a front wheel after crashing heavily. The accident came exactly a month after Hockenheim, and once again everyone had to come to terms with an incomprehensible loss.

BRM's truck was already on the continent, and the works team fielded a single car for Rodriguez at the Spanish Grand Prix, a return to Jarama just a fortnight after the F2 event. Piers was the solo Parnell entry, and the P126 had been upgraded with new steering, a new nose and larger front brakes, although it would retain its older, heavier wheels for some time. Piers qualified 11th in a small field of 13, created by poor starting money. After being delayed by a long early stop for overheating, he had a spin on oil before retiring for

Top left *Piers shelters in the Parnell BRM P126. There were to be a lot of wet races in 1968.*

Top right *Piers splashes round Zandvoort on his first appearance in the Dutch GP on 23 June. He ended* the day with an accident, but he wasn't the only one to fall foul of the conditions.

Bottom left *Piers in action at Spa, where he very nearly won the Belgian GP.*

Bottom right Michael Cooper took this wonderful Motor Racing *cover shot of Piers with Sally* and an unidentified model. This was the sort of image that people wanted from their racing drivers.

good with a metering unit failure. Few noticed that he managed to set third fastest lap, behind only Beltoise and Hulme.

Inevitably thoughts soon turned to who would replace Spence in the works BRM. Although he'd turned down Lotus, Piers now felt that he was ideally placed to transfer over from the Parnell car. However, the Bourne management had other ideas, and it was announced that none other than Chris Irwin would return to drive alongside Rodriguez at Monaco. However, longer term Irwin was committed to driving a second works Honda when it appeared, so Piers felt he still had a chance.

After seven straight Sundays of racing Piers finally had some time at home in the middle of May, but his weekend off was to bring yet more dramatic news, this time from the Nürburgring. Irwin had gone to the 1,000kms event to partner Rodriguez in one of Alan Mann's new Ford F3L prototypes, and in a damp Friday practice session he did a back flip near the Flugplatz, possibly as a result of striking a hare. The car came to rest upside down in a ditch with the engine still running, and fuel pumping out. Other drivers stopped to help, but Chris had suffered terrible head injuries, and was lucky to survive.

He spent several weeks in hospital, and it was apparent that his career was over. Once again BRM had to change its plans, and Attwood – who'd driven the sister Ford F3L at the 'Ring – was invited back for a one-off appearance at Monaco.

"I was told that he was going to drive the car at Monaco on a trial basis," says Tony Rudd, "and it struck me as being quite a sensible idea. I'd got all sorts of other problems, so I didn't really argue about it."

Again Piers thought that he would eventually get the works drive, and was determined to show well on the streets of the principality. He qualified an excellent 11th of 18 entries, outpacing Jack Brabham and new Lotus recruit Oliver, among others. However, Sunday was to bring frustration, and after pitting with no rear brakes, he retired early with a broken chassis member. Meanwhile, as Graham Hill eased to his fourth Monaco GP victory, Attwood made astonishing progress in the works BRM. After starting sixth he took advantage of a high attrition rate to work his way up to second, setting fastest lap along the way. It was obvious to all that it would be now be hard for BRM to replace him.

The following day 'Tatty Atty' joined Chris Amon and others to celebrate Piers's 26th birthday on Charles Lucas's chartered boat, *Crin Bleu*. With some free time on their hands Piers and Sally stayed on with Luke for the next three days. When they returned to London they learned that Attwood had been signed for the balance of the season, and Piers would have to stay in the Parnell car.

"I had no idea that Piers reckoned he should have got that drive," says Attwood. "And he would never have said anything about it. Today that would have ended up with fisticuffs in the paddock, but it just wasn't like that. That's something I was not aware of... Politically I was not up to speed. He was hugely enthusiastic about anything, and he was absolutely delighted to see me finish second at Monaco."

"I think the decision was probably made by Sir Alfred Owen," says Tony Rudd. "The Attwood family business was somehow tied up with Rubery Owen, and Sir Alfred thought a lot of him. That's not to say I didn't. But I wouldn't have blamed Piers for thinking he was in with a shout. It would have more or less been explained to him that if he was driving one of Tim's cars, he was first reserve at BRM."

At the time, Piers put a brave face on his situation: "The F1 scene was suddenly confused by Jim's death and then Mike's," he told Barrie Gill that summer. "I was asked to drive one or two cars – including a spot in the Lotus team. But I decided that it was no use going for the best drive or even the most flattering offer. This time I had to choose the car which was right for me. Tim's BRM has a good engine and I like the bloke in charge of the team. I think that the car is good enough to get in the first two rows – whether I'll be able to get out there is another matter. But one thing is certain. I don't intend to jump in with both feet and try to win a lot of races. I just want to do the best I can and finish."

Having damaged the Brabham on his previous two F2 outings Piers was hoping for better luck at Crystal Palace. Frank's little team had soon developed a reputation for smart preparation, and the car arrived at the London track equipped with gold-plated fuel injection trumpets! Piers finished second to Rindt in his wet qualifying heat, and chased the Austrian again in the final. Ironically he was stopped when a badly soldered fuel injection nozzle fell off.

Frank had already expanded into preparing F2 cars for other drivers, but at the Palace a second driver was running as an official Williams entry – Max Mosley. The London lawyer had earlier bought his car and an engine from Frank, but had been run by someone else for the first half of the season, before switching to Williams.

"It was fairly basic, and of course Frank never had any money," he recalls. "We were all struggling along! It was run out of the back of a little in place in Slough, just off that exit from the M4 where you go almost in a complete circle, through 270 degrees. Jochen Rindt was famous for being able to drift it in a complete powerslide for all the 270 degrees coming off the motorway, with one hand!"

It was at this stage that Max got to know the man with whom he would one day change the face of motor racing.

"Rindt was a friend of Piers, so he used to come down to Frank's, because Winkelmann Racing were just up the road underneath the bowling alley. And Bernie Ecclestone was Rindt's financial manager, if not manager full stop."

The following weekend Piers journeyed to the Belgian GP for his first ever appearance at Spa-Francorchamps. The trip allowed him to indulge in one of his lesser known hobbies – exploring military history.

"At Spa he turned up late at the hotel," says Tim Parnell, "And I said, 'Where the hell have you been?' And he said, 'I've been looking round all the World War One trenches round Ypres and all round there.' He was very, very keen on history."

"I remember him being fascinated in the Ardennes, where all the tank battles took place," says Paddy McNally. "He took the time off to go and look at all things like that."

Piers soon got to grips with Spa – it was the sort of high-speed track on which he'd always excelled in his F3 days. He was an impressive seventh in Friday's first qualifying, despite engine problems curtailing his session. When it rained on Saturday he retained that position for the final grid. That day brought tragic news from a far-flung venue; Cooper F1 driver and former Ferrari ace Ludovico Scarfiotti had been killed at a hillclimb in Germany. As an indication that safety was becoming a priority, several teams had followed Jackie Stewart's lead in fitting seat belts for the first time, and Parnell was among them.

Piers heads Henri Pescarolo's Matra in the Hockenheim F2 race on 16 June. He was in the lead group throughout, but just missed the points.

With the Spa race traditionally featuring a high attrition rate, a finish would almost certainly bring some useful points. From the off Piers became involved in a spectacular scrap with Siffert, McLaren and Rodriguez for what was initially sixth place. The order changed by the lap, and on lap nine Piers got to the front of the group just as Amon retired, so the fight was now over fifth. Then leader Surtees retired his Honda and Ickx dropped back into the chasing group, which thus now became a tussle for third place, with only Stewart and Hulme up ahead.

Piers held his own in this distinguished company. With 10 of the 28 laps to run Hulme dropped down the field after a pit stop, leaving only Stewart out in front of the group. Piers was fourth, hustling Bruce and Pedro. But then with just six laps to go the BRM trundled into the pits with an engine failure. At first Piers rued the loss of fourth place, but as the laps ticked away, he realised he'd lost a lot more.

At the start of the last lap leader Stewart dived into the pits for a fuel top-up, and then found he couldn't restart. Then Rodriguez dropped back as he stuttered around on his last dregs of fuel – he'd forgotten the procedure to follow when such a situation occurred. Thus a surprised McLaren coasted across the finish line to score his team's maiden Grand Prix victory. Had Piers kept going he would certainly have deprived Rodriguez

of second, and possibly even done something about the eventual winner.

"If the bloody engine hadn't gone at Spa, I think he would have won there," says Tim Parnell. "He and McLaren and Pedro Rodriguez were dicing away, and as it turned out they were the leading trio."

At least his fighting performance had not gone unnoticed. Paddy McNally gave Piers a glowing report in his *Autosport* column: "His scrap with Bruce McLaren, Pedro Rodriguez and, in the early stages, Jo Siffert showed that the elegant young Englishman is indeed excellent F1 material. It was hard luck indeed to go out so close to the end, and he said to me afterwards, 'Will I never finish a Grand Prix?' I am sure he will, and if he drives as well as he did on Sunday it won't be long before he chalks up his first victory."

By now Piers was regarded favourably at BRM. "I liked him as a human being," says Tony Rudd. "And I was fairly impressed with him as a driver. Once or twice he produced some quite impressive practice times. I think I felt he was better over a short spell than he was in a race, but I never knew if that was fair. I always felt that Tim's cars broke rather sooner than ours. That's not to say he was a car breaker, he just didn't seem to be there at the end of the race."

Louis Stanley, who by now had become more involved with the team's management, was also a supporter: "He had complete youthful enthusiasm," he recalls. "It was so infectious. He had plenty of skill and plenty of courage. His only mistake was that he never complained, which is a virtue sometimes, but not always. In racing engineers are rather dependent on what you report to them, and if you say it's fine, it doesn't help. But he was so conscientious, so hard working, and nothing was too much trouble."

On F2's return to Hockenheim Piers took a frustrating seventh place, just three seconds off the winner after losing out in a race-long slipstreaming battle. The race was notable for a spectacular collision between his team-mate Max Mosley and French veteran Jo Schlesser.

"It was entirely my fault, " says Max. "Afterwards we were sitting having a glass of wine in the evening, and Piers said to me, 'I don't know why you do this, because it is dangerous. You've got a very good career at the bar, but I would only ever have been a very second rate accountant.' He was more or less saying I was quite mad to do it.

"I saw quite a lot of him one way or another, and got on with him well. At least once we went to have dinner with him and Sally. He was just a bloody nice person. He didn't have any side to him. Even if you'd been as quick as him, he wouldn't have tried to psyche you in any way. He was just absolutely straightforward. As a driver he was probably not as good as Jochen or Jackie Stewart, but he was not far off."

Piers travelled to the Dutch GP at Zandvoort hoping to repeat his Spa form. He was sixth fastest on Friday, ahead of Rodriguez in the works car, but fell to 14th on the final grid. Race day was soaking wet, and the track was made even more slippery by oil dropped by saloon cars. Piers spun early on and was tapped by Attwood, forcing him to pit for a new nose. Later he crashed properly, as Paddy McNally reported: "Courage had aquaplaned off round the back of the circuit, tearing a front wheel off the BRM after contacting the retaining fence following an almighty 100 yard slide."

Piers was by no means the only one to fall off, but yet again he had failed to finish a Grand Prix, and that was starting to hurt. The Dutch event clashed with the Monza Lottery F2 event, but Frank found the ideal substitute for Piers – Jonathan Williams. Having fallen out with Abarth earlier in the year, Jonathan had been back in F3 with de Sanctis, and his career was in a sort of limbo.

"My father had loaned Frank the money for the engine earlier in the year, although I didn't know," Jonathan recalls. "Frank was paying him back in instalments! It was a lovely car, beautifully prepared. John Muller was absolutely superb, meticulous. It was the best-prepared car I'd seen; light years better than Ferrari. They were real tatty old things. And it was a lovely car to drive.

"I didn't practise well, I didn't get a good tow, so I was in the middle of the field. But knowing Monza backwards, and how the slipstreaming works, I said to myself, 'I'm going to be in front of this thing as soon as it's humanly possible, because there's going to be a monstrous accident.' It didn't take me long to get in front, and then I looked in my mirrors and there were Ferraris and Tecnos on fire... I remember this great surge of relief. That will make life easier!"

Jonathan went on to score a superb victory, and the first for Frank Williams at F2 level.

"We'd agreed to do it on the basis of half the prize money, if there was any, and if I won Frank would buy me dinner. Which he did, and he didn't smile once... I guess he hadn't expected to have to! Piers was probably perfectly happy; he probably thought he'd have won it if he'd been there."

Sally had resumed modelling at the start of the year, and she was now appearing in the media almost as much as her husband. An interview in the *Daily Express* of July 1 carried her thoughts on fashion and make-up, but also included an interesting insight into the role of a racing driver's wife.

"Sarah and Piers Courage love to entertain, and one of Sarah's favourite hobbies is cooking. Another is reading, and the best time for this, she finds, is at race meetings. How, we wondered, in all that excitement,

could she keep her mind on a book and off the perils of the race track? 'A bad accident to Piers is something I have a complete mental block about,' she replied. 'If I didn't, I think I should literally go mad.'"

The following weekend's French GP at Rouen provided another brutal reminder of the dangers, as for the fourth time in succession there was a tragedy in the first week of the month. Grand Prix debutant Jo Schlesser was running a place behind Piers when he crashed on the third lap. His new Honda contained a lot of magnesium parts, which contributed to the horrific conflagration that followed.

For Piers, the French race did at least bring an improvement in form. He stayed on dry tyres at the start and got away badly, but showing complete mastery of the soaking conditions he got up to seventh by lap 10, and later rose as high as fourth behind Ickx, Surtees and Rodriguez. However, he then had to pit for attention to a strap that held an auxiliary fuel tank in place. The team also took the opportunity to fit full rain tyres.

Sheridan Thynne helped out: "When they changed tyres Tim asked me if I would steady the car on the jack, because there were only two of them. I was at the front of the car looking back. It was much like the old Silverstone – the pitlane and track were separated by a chalk line on the road! It was raining, and I remember looking back and seeing Surtees and Rodriguez coming towards me in a ball of spray…"

After this stop Piers had tumbled down the order to 12th. Unfortunately the track then started to dry, but he recovered in superb style to sixth, claiming his first Grand Prix finish and maiden World Championship point. It could have been so much better.

"He drove bloody brilliantly," says Tim Parnell. "If I'd put the right tyres on it, he could have won that. But I elected not to put the rain tyres on at the start. I could see it was going to rain, but most people on the grid were staying pretty well the same, and I thought it's such a dangerous track, I dare not risk it. He deserved to win."

At Rouen Piers was warned by McLaren's Teddy Mayer that the CanAm team that had promised him a ride did not have the money to go racing. Clearly concerned, Piers wrote to the Canadian operation asking if all was well, and as a back-up contacted other teams, including Chaparral, requesting employment. Nobody else had a vacancy, and he would learn by post the following month that the original deal had indeed floundered through lack of sponsorship. His CanAm

experience would be confined to some testing for McLaren, at Bruce's invitation.

The next F2 outing was at the bleak Tulln-Langenlebarn airfield in Austria, where Piers retired with overheating having run as high as second behind local hero Rindt. Then it was back to Brands Hatch for his first outing in a British GP, exactly a year after he'd had to hand his car to Irwin after qualifying. In fact Chris chose that weekend to make his first appearance at a race meeting since his accident at the Nürburgring two months earlier. He was having terrible problems adjusting to the fact that he wouldn't race again.

"It was the only race we went to after Chris's accident," says Loti Irwin. "He looked awful, awful. It was like parting the Red Sea. You were walking in a straight line and people were suddenly remembering they had something else to do. I was thinking I was just going to lie down and die if somebody doesn't talk to us in a minute. And Jack Brabham walked straight through everybody, straight up to us, 'Nice to see you, chat chat, chat.' I thought, 'My God, you are such a diamond you are.'

"We had an awful lot of problems. When you've been injured in a racing car people are very nice to begin with, and they go off and do their own thing. They would really not think about it, especially when people were being killed left, right and centre. Chris himself wouldn't go to funerals. He didn't go to Jimmy's, although he was right behind him when he crashed. Mike Spence was number two at BRM and I said, 'But he's a mate,' and he said 'No, I don't want to think about it.'"

Piers had high hopes for his home race, but it was to be a disappointing weekend. He struggled with handling problems throughout practice, and couldn't better 16th on the grid. Spots of rain before the start led to some frantic tyre changing up and down the field, but it remained dry for the race. Piers made a good start and passed a couple of cars, but pit stops for overheating and then a misfire left him adrift in a distant eighth place.

After the Saturday race Piers joined many of his colleagues for a riotous party at Graham Hill's country cottage on the Brabourne estate near Ashford, where the guests included Lord Louis Mountbatten. A large marquee was erected in the garden, while bar tending chores were undertaken by the host and his old pal Cliff Davis, in whose backyard so much motor racing history had been made. Fortuitously Graham had won 100 bottles of champagne in Brands qualifying…

On Sunday the survivors turned out at nearby Mersham for a pub lunch and Les Leston's annual charity cricket match, featuring the Grand Prix Drivers against Lord Brabourne's XI. Stirling Moss and Innes Ireland joined a motley crew that included Rindt, McLaren, Rodriguez, Oliver, Amon, Attwood, Hill and, despite his apparent lack of F1 credentials, Charlie Lucas. Piers had not distinguished himself in team games

Top left Piers with Tim Parnell and BRM colleague Richard Attwood on the Thursday prior to the British GP at Brands Hatch. The occasion was the launch of a book about Jim Clark, killed just three months earlier.

Top right Piers was an enthusiastic participant in the charity cricket match held on the day after the British GP. However, he was bowled out by the heir to the throne!

Bottom Pressing on in the P126 in the British GP on 20 July. A misfire ruined the day for Piers, but he struggled home in eighth place.

A reminder of how it used to be in 1964! Wearing his '68 spec Williams team jacket, Piers demonstrates his mechanical aptitude as he sorts out a tricky problem on his E-Type.

at school, but he ended the opposition team's innings at 187 with a catch. Alas, when the drivers came to bat he was bowled out for just two runs by none other than HRH Prince Charles, a fate that also befell captain Denny Hulme! The drivers could manage only 142, Luke achieving a handy top score of 21.

There was more sporting activity at the Zandvoort F2 meeting, where Piers joined the other drivers in a round of mini-golf. "I just couldn't believe how competitive they all were," recalls Max Mosley. "It wasn't done for fun, it was life or death whether you won or not!"

In 1967 the Dutch track had been the scene of Piers's F2 breakthrough, and one year on it provided him with his first victory, albeit in a heat that contained only half the field. After setting equal fastest time with Ferrari's Derek Bell in qualifying, Piers just pipped Henri Pescarolo and Clay Regazzoni to the flag after a spectacular battle.

In the final Bell set the pace, but Piers chased hard and the pair traded the lead. After Derek dropped back Piers once again found himself fighting with Matra twins Beltoise and Pescarolo. He then lost a few spots after a minor off, before stopping for good after a second incident at Tarzan. A year earlier Ian Raby died after an accident at Zandvoort, and once again the track claimed a British driver, young Londoner Chris Lambert losing

his life after being launched off the track following contact with Regazzoni. The wretched 1968 season continued to leave the drivers wondering just who would be next.

"It was completely unsafe in those days," says Beltoise. "When you saw a lot of drivers killed you were sometimes thinking that the week after it was perhaps your turn."

The German GP at the Nürburgring was a soaking wet affair, and saw Jackie Stewart score a famous dominant victory for Matra. Sporting a wing for the first time, Piers qualified a superb eighth, on his first visit to the full track since he drove an F2 car for Ron Harris in the 1966 event. On race day he demonstrated the wet weather skill he'd shown at Longford and Rouen, bringing the car home in a safe eighth place. And as at Rouen, he left works driver Attwood far behind.

By now the works BRM team really missed Spence's input, and the marque was making little progress. Piers would have benefited hugely from having someone like Hill or Stewart in the sister car. "While we were still free wheeling with Mike Spence's setting-up ability, we would have the edge," says Tony Rudd. "After we lost all that Mike contributed, which took two or three races to run out, Dickie Attwood didn't contribute very much. In fact he went to a lot of trouble to keep out of it. And Pedro didn't have a clue! So it went downhill."

A free weekend allowed Piers to take stock. He and Sally had been looking for a new London home, and in early August they acquired 70 Drayton Gardens in South Kensington, for £27,000. The property needed some work, and in addition Piers planned to build a flat over the garage, so it would be over a year before they left 15 Sutherland Street and moved in. Although the purchase gave the impression that they were flush with cash, it was made with funds held in trust for Sally. Paying the day-to-day bills continued to be a juggling act, even if Piers could never resist a flashy road car.

"Things go in swings and roundabouts, don't they?," says Sally. "If I had some money to pay the bills, I could, and if he had some, he could. He was the man of the house, and he made the decisions. He loved his cars. I loved them too, but I was never allowed to get my hands on them. It was absolutely *verboten*. It was, 'No, no darling, here's your Mini.' It was very fast, but it went up the road like a crab. Eventually we found it was two halves stuck together…"

Bubbles Horsley was a useful source of extra revenue, and provides an interesting insight into life Chez Courage: "I actually lodged with Piers and Sal in Pimlico, in Sutherland Street, when I had stopped racing, and was trading in cars and trying to become an actor in TV commercials. They had no money at all – my rent was quite important. It was very nice there, a mixture of racing folk, trading folk and the aristocracy, for want of a better word. In fact it was a mix that worked rather well. There was very much a separate life from racing. Today I'm not sure that anything else comes into their lives.

"[Alexander] Hesketh used to come round to the house, when he was 17 or something, as he knew Antoinette, Luke's wife, quite well. I remember going off to a race at Silverstone and Antoinette saying, 'We must go and have tea at this wonderful house called Easton Neston.' We all looked at her and thought, 'Are you mad? Why would we want to go and have tea at a house?' Who would have believed that a few years later there would be an F1 team based there…"

A sick engine put paid to Piers's prospects in the Oulton Park Gold Cup, and he also had a nasty fright when a front wishbone failed under braking, and he skated to a halt. The F2 season resumed in late August at Enna, and Piers was delighted to meet up with Jonathan, who had landed a Tecno ride. Once again Piers shared fastest practice lap, this time with Pescarolo. Bizarrely the grid was spaced with the rows many metres apart in an attempt to cut down on the sort of suicidal slipstreaming that the lakeside track usually encouraged, but within a handful of laps the lead bunch was as wild as ever. The timekeepers couldn't separate the top four as they crossed the line, but Rindt was a clear nose ahead of Piers. Second was his best result of the season to date.

At around this time Tasman series organiser Ron Frost came to Europe to tie up deals with the leading teams for the 1969 series. He wanted Piers back, so popular had his exploits been the previous winter, and it was logical for him to run in partnership with Frank. Frost could guarantee them £6,000, and to that end a Brabham BT24 was acquired direct from the works. This model had been used in the second half of Denny Hulme's successful 1967 World Championship campaign, and by Brabham and Rindt in early '68, before being superseded by the BT26. Chassis BT24-03 was hardly used, having done just three meetings in the hands of Jochen, Dan Gurney and Kurt Ahrens. The plan was to convert it from Repco spec to take a downsized DFV, known in 2.5-litre form as a DFW. The engines were pukka F1 units and could easily be converted back. As such they were expensive, at £7,500 apiece, but Frank went ahead and ordered two.

Piers went to Monza for his first Italian GP hoping that his slipstreaming expertise would serve him well. There was a new face in the second works BRM, for after disappointing outings in the wet at Rouen and the 'Ring, Attwood had been dropped in favour of USAC star Bobby Unser, whose colleague Mario Andretti had landed a third Lotus seat. Although the Americans practised on Friday they were committed to an event in Indianapolis on Saturday, and thus indulged in an extraordinary round trip that got them back to Monza on race day. Officials were not impressed and refused to let them race. During the discussions BRM's Louis Stanley suggested that Unser should take Piers's seat. To his credit Unser later said that he would not have considered that fair play, and would not have accepted the drive.

Fortunately the saga fizzled out, and the race was to provide Piers with his best finish to date. He qualified a modest 18th, but made good progress in the midfield, spending much of the distance battling with Jack Brabham. A high attrition rate worked in his favour and he rose to an eventual fourth, behind Hulme, Servoz-Gavin and Ickx. He was a lap down, but all that mattered was that Piers had shown once again that he could bring the car home safely, if it held together. Paddy McNally noted that his performance "…should surely earn him a place in the works BRM team."

By co-incidence McNally was in the process of selling Piers a road car: "I managed to sell him my Ferrari 330GTC. I was quite happy to see the back of it; it wasn't the best car in the world!"

While the F1 teams packed their equipment for the North American tour Piers climbed aboard his newly acquired silver Ferrari and headed to Rheims for yet another F2 slipstreamer. This was to be Jackie Stewart's return to the category for the first time since injuring his wrist at Jarama. Practice started badly when Frank's best engine blew up after an oil line came loose, and Piers qualified only eighth.

An early delay for Rindt gave everyone else a chance, and by lap ten Piers had worked his way into the lead battle with the Matras of JYS and Pescarolo, each man taking turns in front. Later, they were also joined by Hill. As the crucial final laps approached Piers had trouble in traffic, lost the tow of Stewart and Pescarolo, and had to settle for third. However, once again he had led an F2 race, and shown he could hold his own in exalted company.

At Rheims Piers met up with his youngest brother Andrew: "In '68 I was doing a wine course, so I drove around in a little Fiat 500, and tried to meet up with Piers at different race circuits. I met up with him at Rheims, and we went to see the battlefields of World War One, and we went to see Waterloo. He was very interested in history generally, and he used to read a lot. His education didn't fail."

However, Piers was still a boy racer at heart, as Andrew recalls: "Just after I got back from this wine course we were at the farmyard behind Fitzwalters, a sort of circular drive. We decided we'd have a race round there. Piers had one of those awful long things – a Zodiac – and the bonnet was so huge we called it the purple table tennis court! We set off, and he was in front, and I was behind in this Fiat 500 trying to keep up with him.

Piers lost his nose early in the US GP at Watkins Glen on 6 October, and later retired with suspension damage.

"We hadn't reckoned on my dad coming out from the house. He was going to investigate what all this noise was, and he was standing just after a blind corner. Piers stopped and began to talk to my father, and I came round going as fast as I could in this little Fiat 500. So it was splat, right into the back of it! And my beautiful Fiat was squished at the front. He was really still very boyish at that stage."

Andrew had seen relatively little of his brother as he grew up, thanks to his spell away at Eton, but now he enjoyed spending time with Piers and his friends.

"They were just fun. They used to play this word game, like charades, where you have to guess the title of the book. They'd got very fertile imaginations. Sally was pregnant at the time. Piers had some grapes, and he held them over her stomach, and we had to guess what that was. It turned out to be 'Grape Expectations!' It was a special kind of humour..."

Piers's first trip to North America was to bring disappointment, thanks to the BRM's poor reliability. In the first Canadian Grand Prix to be held at the spectacular Mont Tremblant track, he qualified 15th, and retired with transmission failure. A fortnight later at Watkins Glen Piers crashed heavily in practice. In the race he lost his nose early on, and later a lost suspension bolt led to his retirement, although he was classified

seventh. He did at least outpace Unser, who returned to the BRM team. Pat McLaren recalls Piers attending a CanAm race at around this time, and even testing a works M8A. It was possibly the Edmonton event that fell neatly between the two Grands Prix.

Just one more European F2 event remained on Piers's schedule, at Albi. He invited old pal Sheridan Thynne to accompany him and Sally on that trip, and Sheridan stayed on a camp bed in Piers's study the night before. Somehow he managed to knock the phone off the hook, which meant that the booked alarm call never came, and thus the party left for Dover late. Thynne's amusing account of their journey, written in 1971, gives a fascinating insight into life with Piers:

"The big Zodiac, driven with plenty of brio, soon made up for the slight delay, and soon we were enjoying a second and more relaxed breakfast on the Dover–Boulogne boat. By then the effortless Courage charm had managed to persuade the chef to keep Sally happy by frying an egg on both sides; this had appeared, for a time, to be against regulations. Custom formalities speedily completed at Boulogne, we were rushing through northern France by noon. By 1pm, Sally and I had ideas about lunch, and I was hopefully perusing M. Michelin's excellent Guide with the aim of discovering somewhere that would satisfy the pangs of hunger. We should have known Piers better! A quick stop, at about 3pm, yielded some exceedingly sticky strawberry *tartes*, washed down with a glass of white wine. This strange little 'low tea' would have to suffice, Piers said, until dinner."

Today Thynne says that Piers's relaxed attitude was often mistaken for a lack of professionalism: "It sounds idyllic, but by '68 he was deeply committed to testing and all the work involved in being a success, and definitely wanted to be a success. He was very fond of Rindt. We spent a long time at Albi with Jochen discussing driving and commitment. We went out for dinner one night. Piers and I were knackered, and quite keen to get back. On the way home we passed one of those places where you can go in and play a series of pub games, including table football. We were there for about an hour and half because Jochen wouldn't leave until he'd played every game and won at it! I remember Piers saying that was an indication of Jochen's commitment, because he was quite unable to look at anything without conquering it."

Frank had sold the regular BT23, but had replaced it with another similar car. Piers put in another solid performance in the Albi race, finishing third behind Pescarolo and Gethin. Sally had an appointment in London so she returned to London in Graham Hill's plane on Monday morning, although there was a panic when she mislaid her passport. Piers and Sheridan then had a leisurely drive back to the Boulogne ferry without her.

"We talked all the way," says Sheridan. "He read a lot and he was a terrific conversationalist. If you travelled from Albi to England with Frank he would have talked 10% about sex and 90% about racing. Perhaps in those days 80–20, now I come to think about it! With Piers we probably talked 25% about racing, and then about the world. He was pretty well informed about lots of different things.

"He was also capable of blushing. We stopped in Limoges and stayed in a hotel called the Royal Limousine. The head waiter happened, by chance, to bear a close resemblance to someone we both knew, coupled with an indefinable air of not speaking English. We therefore interrupted our inspection of the gastronomic delights to discuss him in some detail; we gave careful consideration to his appearance and compared it loudly, and in some cases unfavourably, with our friend.

"When he approached us and said without a trace of an accent, 'Good evening gentlemen, will you permit me to guide you?' we were so covered with confusion that we did just that, meekly accepting all he suggested. Most drivers wouldn't blush, but Piers was able to be embarrassed..."

After catching his breath at home for a few days Piers headed out to Mexico for the last Grand Prix of the season, held just after the conclusion of the Olympic Games. It was a long trip for little reward, for the car jumped out of gear in practice, and in the race stopped

yet again with overheating. Graham Hill won the race and with it the World Championship – most agreed it was a satisfactory end to what had been a terrible season for Lotus.

But while the 1968 F1 season was over, there was still some racing to be done – and at the Williams premises in Slough, Frank and his boys were hard at work. In addition to customer jobs, no fewer than three programmes were now underway. The priority was the revived Temporada series in Argentina, to be held for F2 cars in December. Frank had made a huge four-car commitment to the lucrative event, with one for Piers, and three for locally-sponsored drivers.

Then there was the Tasman Series, due to start on 4 January, just a fortnight after the last South American race. Finally, there was the small matter of Grand Prix racing. As the Tasman machine was being put together, it became apparent that the car was just one step away from being a true F1 contender.

"I had a little flat at Slough, just above the workshops," says Frank. "My secretary was making a bit of toast for me, and I said – or maybe she said, or though I'd never admit this – it would be silly not to do it, now we've got this car..."

From that small germ of an idea, a plan rapidly developed. Piers took little persuading to realise that joining Frank in his entry to the top rank would be both fun and, potentially, very successful. Although the BT24 would have done the job, Frank agreed that they should also consider the latest machinery, and began to look at available options.

Frank wanted the Repco to Cosworth conversion on the BT24 done properly, and by coincidence John Muller knew the model well, having been at the works team in 1967. Although it's been written elsewhere that Frank paid designer Robin Herd £500 to produce proper drawings for the job, his involvement probably extended only to a little informal and free consultation with Muller, with whom he had previously worked at McLaren.

Herd, who was now working on the Cosworth 4WD project, was certainly a familiar face at 361 Bath Road at this time. He knew Muller and Howden Ganley, and had become friendly with Piers during the McLaren M4A F2 days in 1967. The connections were cemented by the fact that Robin was a school friend of Rindt's F2 team mate, Alan Rees. Robin and Alan were talking to Rindt about building an F1 car, and as the Austrian's close pals, Frank and Piers would probably have been aware of such discussions.

It was on one of his appearances at Frank's workshop that Herd became reacquainted with Mosley, who had been a contemporary at Oxford University. As the pair became close friends, the idea of making a car for Rindt progressed, and the seeds of March Engineering were sown...

While Piers was busy in Mexico the Tasman car was given its first proper run at Silverstone by Roy Pike on 1 November. It was a useful opportunity for the American, who had found himself stuck in F3 while his contemporaries had made progress. It wasn't just a case of sticking in a different engine, so the car had be to substantially reworked by Muller, and it incorporated suspension derived from the newer BT26. Indeed the immaculate car was so different that it was given the new designation BT24W.

"We had to shift some of the chassis rails a bit," says Muller, "I remember we had to have bigger water pipes, and we hung them on the outside of the car. When we got to the point where we needed the engines Frank was on the phone for week and a half, ringing round, trying to drum up the money. He was mainly chasing guys who owed him money."

In the end Frank was helped by a loan from a friend, Swiss-based businessman Derek Mackie. "He was a very large Belfast manufacturer of machinery for making textiles of some sort," Williams recalls. "He paid for one engine at the time."

Frank knew the value of good media coverage, and *Autosport*'s Simon Taylor raved about the car when he attended the Pike shakedown. Taylor made it clear where Frank's future lay: "It doesn't take much imagination to realise that here is an *équipe* that could, with just a change of engine capacity, go Grand Prix racing with a considerable hope of success, for they have the car, the driver, the engine and the know-how. Frank makes no secret of the fact that he would dearly love to enter the F1 field, but he isn't saying anything yet; he honestly hasn't decided."

Williams liked the article so much that he ordered reprints for use as PR material. Meanwhile Max Mosley inadvertently became part of Frank's fledgling sponsor hunting activities: "I went in one day and Frank came rushing up all agitated and said, 'Max you've got a physics degree, haven't you? I'm making a proposal to Reynolds Aluminium in the States, and I wanted to take Robin with me. But he can't go because he'd be breaking his contract with Cosworth. I've got to take a designer with me – do you think you could come and pretend to be the designer?' I'd never been to America, so I said, 'If we fly first class, I'll come...'"

Max duly had to bluff his way through a cocktail party, cleverly getting his interrogator – a stress analysis engineer – to talk about the benefits of using aluminium pipes in Alaska oil wells.

"Frank had over-egged the pudding and he'd got Bruce McLaren to come along to make it more impressive. As soon as I found out I said, 'Frank, you're mad, Bruce has got a proper team, he's winning the CanAm series, you won't get Reynolds, he will.' Which was exactly what happened. Frank was 26 then – he wouldn't make that mistake now..."

However, Bruce wasn't there by chance, as a fascinating document reveals. Showing his considerable marketing flair, Frank had gone to the trouble of printing a brochure for use with proposals. It outlined his own history and that of Piers, and explained the benefits of F1 sponsorship. A breakdown of proposed expenditure in 1969 makes interesting reading:

Chassis: £5,000
Spares: £3,000
Transporter: £3,000
Three DFV Engines: £22,500
Mechanic's Salaries: £5,000
Running costs: £10,000
Driver retainer: £3,000

Total: £51,500

As we've seen Frank was already paying exactly £7,500 apiece for his DFVs, so one must assume that the rest of the table was also realistic. The brochure also stated that in 1969 the team would field either a Brabham BT26, as a purely private entry, or a McLaren M7A, which would be run as a third works

car. That presumably explains why Bruce was invited along to Reynolds.

For whatever reason the chassis deal didn't come off, but Frank did at least earn a commission from Bruce for his troubles. He continued his PR assault by inviting former Pinner Road resident Innes Ireland to test the Tasman car at Goodwood, and his extremely positive impressions would form the basis of a three-page article in *Autocar* the following January. Under the headline 'Happiness is Blue and Brabham shaped,' Innes wrote: "Having spent a day with him, I am quite assured in my own mind that Frank Williams is taking his role as entrant in a very serious fashion. There can be little doubt that he put a tremendous amount of thought and hard work into this project, to say nothing of a great deal of money."

In the meantime there was the trip to Argentina to consider. Despite his awful experience in a Buenos Aires hospital at the start of 1966, Piers had enjoyed the country, and saw the series as something of a holiday at the end of a long, hard season. Sally was expecting their second child in February, and thus stayed at home, but Piers would be able to enjoy the company not only of Jochen but also Jonathan, who was to drive a Tecno.

Top Engine failure caused Piers to drop out at San Juan, but his luck was to improve in Buenos Aires a week later.

Bottom Jonathan Williams took this shot of Piers showing off his new straw hat in Argentina. And yes, he's driving the Ford Falcon on a highway...

Jonathan's car was entered by the colourful Alessandro de Tomaso. De Tomaso, who died in May 2003, was the son of a former Argentinian Prime Minister. He had been building racing and road cars in Italy since 1959, although few of his projects had found major success. Now he was planning a return to single-seaters, and with his de Sanctis, Ferrari and Abarth record behind him, it seemed somehow inevitable that Jonathan would get involved.

"He said he was going to make an F2 car," says Jonathan, "but before that and to get some experience he bought a Tecno, and then wrecked it by making it wider and putting a pointy nose on it! It was no bloody good, but at least they had the idea to take all the old bits with them. So after about two races I got it back to standard Tecno."

Fangio's canvassing of the European teams had created a good entry, including Matras for Beltoise and Pescarolo, Ferraris for de Adamich and Brambilla, Tecnos for Siffert, Regazzoni, Rodriguez and local newcomer Carlos Reutemann, Winkelmann Brabhams for Rindt and Rees and a private Lotus for Oliver. Piers was joined in the busy Williams camp by Eduardo Capello, Jean-Manuel Bordeu and Carlos Pairetti, although the last-named didn't even get to start the first two events, after his car burned to the ground in testing.

Frank has fond memories of the series: "It was a big adventure, my first big overseas trip. We flew there on an empty plane, about 50 people on a 707. I just remember it being very hot, and there was lots of enthusiasm around the races. It was paid for mainly by a Buenos Aires publishing house."

Piers's campaign got off to a disappointing start at Buenos Aires. He retired from the opening race while running fourth after his rear wing failed, a fate that had already befallen Rindt's similar car. Brambilla and de Adamich finished one-two, setting up Ferrari's domination of the series. Between events there was plenty of time to relax, as Jonathan recalls: "We had a great time, partying the hell out of it. It was a really nice time."

Inspired by the local efforts, Piers, Jonathan and Frank even commenced a moustache growing competition! Journalist Andrew Marriott was on the trip, and confirms that Piers was always willing to help: "He was amusing, informative, and didn't bullshit. You always got a good tale. The Temporada was very relaxed, and it was a good series. But everyone was well wound up about the Ferraris, because we all thought they were cheating!"

The second round was held some 450 miles inland at the new Oscar Cabelen track near Cordoba, Argentina's second city. The circus stayed in a beautiful

old hotel that showed signs of Britain's influence on the country.

"The Temporada was terrific," says Jackie Oliver. "It was just all the buddies going racing together, on very spectacular circuits. That hotel was built by the English to house the directors of the railway in the early 1900s. It was like going back into old England – green baize bridge tables and grand dining rooms, and the old stables and horses. I remember Piers and I going riding. Cordoba was a big slipstreamer, like racing at Rheims. The visors used to get opaque after each practice session because of the dust!"

"I remember we had a game of charades there," says Marriott. "Piers was very enthusiastic, and brilliant at it. That was a great night…"

With sand constantly blowing over the track conditions were tricky, and in practice race director Fangio stood on the inside of a corner to stop drivers from cutting it and throwing up more muck! In an exciting affair Piers passed Rindt for the lead in the early stages, and was in contention throughout. De Adamich eventually won, while Piers was bundled down to sixth in the closing laps, having set an impressive fastest lap along the way.

From Cordoba it was a 400-mile trip to another new venue at San Juan, near the border with Chile. The journey was made in a fleet of Ford Falcons, thoughtfully provided by the organisers, although Piers and Jochen's chauffeur managed to put their car in a ditch.

"They were pretty beaten up old wrecks, and they all had bald tyres on," says Oliver. "Most of them broke down on the way to Cordoba or San Juan or back to Buenos Aires. It was like a little race off the race track."

When Oliver's car broke down in a remote village, Jonathan and Piers went steaming through with a cheery wave, much to Jackie's frustration. After an appropriate delay they turned back and offered assistance…

The El Zonda track featured an unusual crossover, and the mountain scenery made for a spectacular backdrop, as Jackie recalls: "It had breathtaking views, and Piers said he wanted to go and climb the mountain. I don't think he quite knew how high the Andes were at the back of the circuit!"

The gale force wind after which the circuit was named blew up a sand storm on the Saturday, and second qualifying was abandoned. Come the race Piers bounced between fourth and fifth place, before eventually retiring with a blown engine.

After a few lazy days with Jochen by the swimming pool at the Cordoba hotel, Piers headed back to Buenos Aires for the fourth and final round on 22 December,

held this time on a slightly different track configuration. Piers had new-team mates for this race, as Reutemann moved over from the Ron Harris outfit, while Fangio's son Cacho also joined the line-up.

Piers qualified fifth, but before the race one team member had a strange premonition, as Frank recalls: "I remember at the last race one of the mechanics was sitting on his bottom in the garage at about ten in the morning. He said, 'I don't know Frank, the car's ready, but it feels kind of scary to me, something's bound to go wrong.'"

The race was to be run over two heats with an aggregate result, and in the first Piers overcame a broken steering wheel to finish fourth. The gloomy prediction appeared to come true at the start of the second heat. Pole man de Adamich didn't get away well, and having himself been hit by a third party, Piers rammed the Ferrari. The Italian car struck the pit wall and a group of unfortunate spectators, two of whom suffered broken legs.

"He pushed me into the pits at the start, and I crashed into some people," says de Adamich. "Unfortunately I broke the leg of an Italian person who was a guest of Fangio, and who I knew very well! That put me a little bit against Piers. I was very upset, but he was very nice at the end, so everything was put behind us."

The incident had its funny side: "De Adamich knocked over a couple of people who shouldn't have been there," says Frank. "They put one on a stretcher in the ambulance and shot off in such a hurry that the bloody thing came out of the back…"

"It was like a Fred Karno comedy act!" says Andrew Marriott. Inevitably Piers lost a bit of momentum, but he soon found some inspiration. He quickly passed Oliver and Siffert before homing in on Rindt, eventually passing him with 14 of the 25 laps run. He then pulled away in style to cement an overall win on aggregate, his first proper success of the season since that soggy day in Longford, and his first at F2 level.

Piers was anxious to get home for Christmas, and joined the dash to the airport, where he donated his straw hat to Marriott ("I've still got it!"). The evening's flight home – featuring tinsel decorations in the cabin and Latin American carols on the speakers – was badly delayed. It then made an unscheduled fuel stop in Las Palmas before making it safely to Madrid, where Piers caught a London plane. He finally arrived home at 4pm on Christmas Eve, just in time to spend the festive season with Jason and the pregnant Sally.

Piers had been hard at it since the previous December, and as he reflected on a punishing 36-weekend season, he was probably grateful that his planned CanAm deal hadn't come off and made his schedule even busier. However, there was little time to rest. Within a week he'd have to return to London Airport to commence the long trek to New Zealand.

True grit

Jo Siffert joins
Frank and Piers
for a friendly chat.
The Swiss driver
would battle with
Piers at several
races during 1969.

While Piers enjoyed a brief stop in London, Frank Williams had preferred to stay where the sun was: "I spent a few days in Argentina, doing things a young man does about town! I got rid of Christmas and Boxing Day, then picked up a flight to New York to go to the Tasman series."

With practice commencing at Pukekohe on Thursday 2 January, it was an early start to the season for all concerned. However it would be a shorter stay down under, as the series had been reduced from eight to seven rounds, thanks to the loss of Longford. The site of Piers's fabulous 1968 victory had finally been declared too dangerous for modern machinery.

Only two other teams made the trek from Europe, but they were strong contenders. Ferrari was back again with F2-based cars for Chris Amon and Derek Bell, while Gold Leaf Team Lotus had a pair of 49s for Graham Hill and new signing, Jochen Rindt. After his spell at Brabham the Austrian had joined Colin Chapman still in search of his first Grand Prix victory. The only really serious local car was the unusual Mildren-Alfa, to be handled by Frank Gardner.

John Muller had returned to get married in New Zealand just before Christmas, and met the BT24W when it came off the ship. The Williams Tasman team comprised Frank, John, his new wife Alison, and another Kiwi, ex-Winkelmann mechanic Dewar Thomas. Piers had a good relationship with Dunlop, but as both the opposition teams were on Firestone, there was some concern that he'd be left behind if the American company did a better job. There were even suggestions that he might make a switch, but in any case the opposition was not yet in a position to service him.

At Pukekohe Amon pipped Rindt to pole, while Piers was fourth, a respectable 0.8sec off the Ferrari, having had little time to sort the car as the new front and rear wings did not arrive until final qualifying. Jochen shot off into the lead at the start, and stayed ahead until sliding off on oil and allowing local hero Amon through to his second consecutive New Zealand GP win. Piers passed Hill and thereafter had a steady run to third, albeit some way behind the others. It was a satisfactory debut for the BT24W.

Piers and Jochen had known each other since the early Pinner Road days, but over the past 18 months they'd been drawn closer together. That process continued through the recent Temporada adventure in Argentina, and during the two months downunder, with only Hill as a regular social partner, they would be almost inseparable. For much of their spare time they played gin rummy in what appeared to be a game without end.

Jochen's business partner Bernie Ecclestone saw the friendship with Piers develop over the years: "The drivers were mates and could enjoy each other's company, which is not like it is today. They didn't have these duties to perform, do this and that for the sponsor. It was a bit more relaxing than it is now. Both of them were easy guys to get on with, so it was natural that it was easy for them to get on with each other. Piers was a good guy, a very nice English gentleman."

After Pukekohe the threesome headed to Lake Taupo with the intention of going water skiing, but bad weather meant that the playing cards saw more action than the drivers. However, at one stage Piers and Jochen were able to get a barbecue going. Neither man had much experience in the culinary arts, so the first steak off the coals was tested on an unsuspecting Hill, who'd been sitting inside. They also played around in a little three-wheeled farm vehicle powered by a motorcycle engine and steered by a tiller. Piers managed to flip it over while trying to climb a hill, bruising both himself and passenger Hill!

In the second race at Levin Piers was a much stronger force. He was only sixth in qualifying, and dropped out of the qualifying heat when a bolt – a suspension mount for Lotus but just a plug on the Brabham – came out of the DFW. Fortunately the subsequent loss of oil didn't do any serious harm. Rindt and Amon battled again in the main race, until Jochen had a spin. Later the brakes failed and the Austrian crawled unscathed from a huge accident that destroyed the 49. His faith in Colin Chapman's products took a severe knock…

After Gardner spun and Hill retired Piers worked his way up to second, and began chasing Amon for the lead. When the Ferrari also spun he gratefully accepted the lead, before he too had a moment at the same corner that had claimed everyone else. Amon regained the lead, but Piers began to re-catch him until he had a second

Piers defending his wicket in Chris Amon's garden. There was always fun to be had on the Tasman trip.

moment and ran wide onto the grass. Nevertheless second place was a worthwhile result, and Frank was now confident enough to fly home, leaving Piers in the capable hands of John Muller. There was urgent business to attend to, for Frank's F1 plans were taking shape.

Meanwhile the visitors spent part of their break at Amon's beach house at Paraparamu, north of Wellington. Highlight was the annual Kiwis v Poms cricket match, held next to a shed in the garden. With no BRM this year the English side needed some ringers to make up the numbers, while a still sore Rindt preferred to watch from the sidelines. Eoin Young covered the action for *Autocar*: "As Piers was shaping up to the bowler, Frank Gardner tip-toed up behind him with a huge rock and smashed it into the fruit boxes that formed the wicket. Courage suffered severe palpitations of the heart, and the wicket also took some reviving from the unexpected attack!"

Chapman had another car flown in for Rindt by the third round at the Lady Wigram airfield track, and Jochen managed a Lotus victory at his third attempt, some way clear of Hill and Amon. With Frank now back in England a spectating Rob Walker offered his timekeeping services to Piers, who duly took fourth place.

The last of the New Zealand rounds was at Teretonga Park, where two years earlier Piers blotted his copybook with BRM. This time the outcome was to be very different. Through qualifying Rindt, Amon, Hill and Piers consistently lowered the old lap record, breaking the 100mph for the first time. When officials did their sums at the end of a fraught session, Piers had pipped Rindt to fastest time by 0.1sec. Peter Greenslade told the story in *Autosport*: "There was a look of absolute disbelief on Courage's face. A second check was made and it was found that two of the timekeepers, working quite independently, had the same figure. Piers was still quite unconvinced, but was happy to accept the official decision."

Rindt won the short qualifying race, so he took pole for the final, with Piers and Amon alongside. When the flag dropped, Jochen's car lurched forward and stopped, its driveshaft broken. Amon then held the lead for a couple of laps, but Piers soon found a way past, and continued to pull away. Hill eventually moved into second, but he was 18sec behind at the end, with Amon third. A Williams entry had beaten Lotus and Ferrari, and in his usual style, Piers took a swig from a milk bottle after the flag. He now had 22 points to the 26 of Amon, and a serious shot at series victory.

A delighted Frank heard the news back in Slough. The win followed Jonathan's Monza F2 victory and Piers's

Buenos Aires success, and it meant that the young team had now won races in three major championships. Next step was the biggest of them all, and Frank was hard at work to make it happen. With his McLaren deal having collapsed, he had now decided to follow the Brabham BT26 route. But Jack Brabham and Ron Tauranac would not sell him a car, mainly because of a clash between the respective Goodyear and Dunlop deals.

However, chassis BT26-01 – Jack's car for the full '68 season – had already gone to David Bridges of Red Rose Racing. It was supposed to be converted to F5000 spec, but when Frank rang Bridges, he discovered that the car was now surplus to requirements. He acquired it for just £3,500, some £1,500 less than he had actually budgeted for. With the Tasman engines available for re-conversion, Frank Williams was now a Grand Prix team owner, and the news was revealed in a small story in *Autosport* on 7 February. In the magazine's classified pages it was business as usual; that week Frank was advertising three Cosworth FVA engines, Piers's Temporada BT23C, a 1967 F2 Lola, and "early delivery" on the latest Titan Mk4 Formula Ford car…

Meanwhile the Tasman contenders made their way to the first Australian round at Lakeside, there being only a week's break as opposed to the usual fortnight. Nina Rindt had by now joined the bachelor boys: "They were a bit crazy," she recalls. "Graham had his own aeroplane… he was going along the coast, trying to fly really low, to see if we could see sharks. They were really terrible. I think Piers and Jochen were quite embarrassed because Graham was always at every party doing jokes and things. We understood him, but the Australians were horrified. We went water skiing, we played golf. I have a picture where Jochen is taking one of the sprinklers from the golf course, and spraying us. They were just like six-year-old boys."

The Lotuses were held up in customs and the team didn't quite catch up in practice at Lakeside, so Piers joined pole man Amon on the front row. By now there was a lack of serviceable DFWs, so Piers's spare was loaned to Hill. This was a nice gesture, but come the race the engine and chassis appeared to want a reconciliation. Hill had got into second at the start, and when Piers tried to pass, they touched. Piers plunged off the road and went over a grass bank, much as he had done at the same venue with the BRM in 1967. Fortunately damage was confined to a front suspension link, but the subsequent victory for Amon meant that Piers now had very little chance of winning the series.

The matter was settled at Warwick Farm, where once again Piers got himself into trouble. Race day was soaking wet, and in his urgency to relieve Amon of second place on the first lap, Piers spun. The Ferrari tried to go round the back of him, but didn't make it, and both cars were out with broken suspension. Rindt won the race, and Amon the championship.

After two accidents while trying to overtake established Grand Prix stars, there was a danger that Piers would undo all of the good work of the past 12 months. Frank was more than a little concerned, not least because he was in the final stages of landing a £10,000 F1 contract with Dunlop. Fortunately the lifesaving deal went ahead anyway, and putting the rest of his F1 preparations on hold, Frank and a friend headed to the final Tasman round at Sandown Park on 16 February.

"I decided to stop all the crashing by going out and giving the boy a talking to at the last race," he recalls. "We did London-Zurich, Zurich-Rome, Rome-Delhi, four hours on the ground waiting for a crew, Delhi-Singapore, Singapore-somewhere… then Sydney and a connection to Melbourne. We arrived in a taxi in the paddock at Sandown after qualifying on Saturday. It was, 'Hello Frank, what the devil are you doing here?' I don't know why I didn't just phone! It would have saved myself a lot of aggravation. I couldn't really afford the ticket…"

Meanwhile there had been much amusement at Piers's expense. The running joke was that after his clashes with Hill and Amon, now only Rindt and Bell were left on his target list, and Jochen made his point in style by tying the BT24W to a tent post in the paddock! In fact there was a third possibility, as Jack Brabham joined the fray at this race in the new BT31. As it turned out the opposition had no need to worry, for Piers lasted just two laps in the race before his driveshaft broke. Despite retiring in all three Aussie races Piers still finished third in the series, behind Amon and Rindt. The holiday in the sun was over, not just for 1969, but forever. From 1970 the much-loved Tasman was contested only by local drivers. It truly was the end of an era.

After Sandown Piers flew back to London as fast as the tortuous connections would allow him. Sally was expecting their second child, and Amos arrived on 26 February, ten days after the last Tasman race. A *Daily Express* cutting suggests that he made it back: "I came back especially in time for Amos's birth," he told the paper. "Two years ago I was stuck racing on the other side of the world when Jason was born, but I was determined to be here this time."

However, Sally remains convinced that Piers missed the birth of both their sons: "I promise you he wasn't there at the birth! He came in late the following day, because he had to go and do something else first."

Godparents included Frank, Piers's younger brother Andrew and Australian friend Dennis O'Neil. Once again, there was no special story behind the chosen name, and in fact the original choice was a far better

one: "I was going to call him Adam," says Sally, "but a great girlfriend of mine had just called her son Adam, so it changed to Amos. My brother-in-law said Amos is such a lovely name."

Meanwhile work had progressed on the conversion of the BT26 from Repco to DFV spec. Having offered advice to John Muller on the Tasman project, Robin Herd was formally hired by Frank to oversee an even more complex job than the previous one, although he had to keep his involvement low-key.

"At the time I was still working at Cosworth on their four-wheel drive F1 car," says Robin. "The BT26 was literally done in a cellar of a petrol station between Northampton and Wellingborough. It was Keith Leighton's father's garage; Keith was a very good mechanic who was also working with me at Cosworth. I was doing traditional drawings on the back of cigarette packets, John Thompson was doing the fabricating, and a few bits were made in Cosworth. We literally took the Brabham, sawed off the back of the frame, and bolted the engine on."

"Robin sort of sketched things out," says Thompson, long regarded as one of the best in the business. "We were doing it in the evenings and at weekends because we were all working at Cosworth. There was a lot of work involved in it, and I remember a lot of cold nights!"

Herd confirms that he only did one paid job for Frank, although his fee took some time to arrive.

"I only got one lot of £500. Frank wasn't exactly flush in those days. It took a whole time coming, and I thought, 'Well, I'll put it down to experience.' Then one day he arrived at the house, thumbs up as he was coming up the drive, and out came £500 in oncers. Remember those big orange balls with horns on and a face? He took one off my son Mark, and bounced around the garden!"

John Muller was not coming back from the Tasman Series, so the team had a new chief mechanic in former Lotus man Bob Sparshott. He recalls converting the BT26 on his own at 361 Bath Road, but what seems more likely is that he actually took over the chassis for final race preparation after the basic metalwork was completed by Herd, Leighton and Thompson in Northants.

"I was at a loose end, so I went to do it at Slough," says Sparshott. "There were no drawings, but perhaps there was a bit of input from Frank on what they'd done on the Tasman car, although I never saw it. It was a massive job, as everything backed into everything else. I spent quite a lot of time on my own! I was commuting from Harpenden, where I lived. I was working long hours, and after a while Frank said, 'Why don't you move into the flat upstairs, and I'll move in with my girlfriend in London.' So I did that for a while. Meanwhile my money wasn't forthcoming, so I tackled Frank about it one day, and he said, 'You know that

wardrobe in the flat? If you have a look in there you'll see there are some very nice suits. Why don't you take a couple?' I didn't think my missus would be very pleased with that – I wanted cash! He came the next night and paid me up to date..."

The original plan was to keep the BT24W as a spare, but instead it was sold to Swiss privateer Silvio Moser. There was never any realistic chance of getting the new car to the South African GP on 1 March, so the target was the Race of Champions a fortnight later. The car was finally ready to run on 14 March, first practice day at Brands, but the team went to Silverstone for a very brief shakedown, before heading down to Kent. The organisers had introduced a novel Indianapolis-style qualifying format, with the cars running one at time, but poor weather and a wave of unreliability spoiled it. Piers managed only a few laps during free practice after a day of hanging about waiting for the fog to lift.

With no time in qualifying proper, he was put on the back row, alongside none other than Roy Pike – for some reason the American had been allowed to run a Brabham F2 car. Piers had gear selection problems on the warming up lap, but was able to take his place at the start. However, he was soon back into the pits for more attention to the problem. Later he had to pit when his goggles were coated with leaking fuel from Brabham's car; the team found that Piers had a similar leak, due to

a split weld, and he was retired. It was not a great debut, but with no testing it was inevitable that such problems would surface. By way of small consolation for Frank, Tony Trimmer won the FF1600 event in a Williams-entered Titan. A newcomer called James Hunt finished fourth in one of Selwyn Hayward's Merlyns – the youngster had copied Richard Attwood and Piers by putting his school colours on his helmet.

"That was the first time I remember thinking, 'Crikey, Piers was right, Frank does know what he's doing,'" says Thynne. "The presentation was terrific. Frank was very good at getting the car to look good. They had that mutual respect which is terribly important in motor racing, and very often teams go wrong because the team principal and driver don't have enough respect for each other. They had that very early on."

The team now had two weeks to prepare the car properly for the International Trophy on 30 March. Piers's parents were touring Australia at the time, and he kept them up to date by letter in typical style: "Motor racing news is not very spectacular as yet, as the new car was only just ready for Brands and was really too new to be raced. However we started and found out many faults in the car which have since been put right and I am sure that for Silverstone next week we shall be up with the leaders. We have had a very social week since Brands having the Rindts to stay and out at Annabel's every

Above The Williams F1 team makes its first appearance in the Race of Champions at Brands Hatch on 16 March. The BT26 had only just been completed, and inevitably suffered teething problems.

Opposite On the grid with Jackie Stewart at the Thruxton F2 event on Easter Monday. The pair had become good friends.

night, so now I have signed the pledge (under duress) until the end of the season!"

Of greater interest to the Courages no doubt was the progress of their grandchildren: "Jason is getting chattier every day now and he can carry on quite a long conversation with no prompting. Amos is much the same as before only a little more so – not a very exciting age for the father yet!"

By now Piers and Jochen had become almost inseparable, and Sally and Nina were also drawing closer. With Jochen's fellow Swiss residents Jackie and Helen Stewart, they formed a closely-knit group of bright young things, a private club that others could only view from the outside. It was a little like the F3 days, when Piers was at the core of a bunch of like-minded pals.

"Jochen and Piers had always been friendly," says Sally, "And then they became great, great friends. They'd known each other a long time, but they got very close in the Tasman series. We went on holiday together, we were always around each other, we tried to stay in the same hotels, things like that. Nina and I also became very good friends. We always sat next door to each other in the pits even though we were with different teams. We always had to be split up!"

"We were all good friends," says Stewart. "Jochen and Nina, Piers and Sally, Helen and I. Sally was nice,

she was coy. I don't know if she knew how to take all this bunch, but she fitted in very well. Sally, Helen and Nina were all the same age, and they were all the stopwatch merchants."

"We always used to hang out together in London or wherever it might have been," says Helen Stewart. "Piers and Sally came over to Switzerland from time to time. They mainly stayed with Nina, but they might come down to us for dinner, or we'd all go out to lunch. We were just a young bunch together, It was a fun period in our lives. I suppose people could have been envious or want to be like us."

Jochen's friend and biographer Heinz Pruller had a close-up view of their relationship: "They were like two students looking for girls! It was also a very nice combination because Sally and Nina got on well together, so there was a really nice harmony."

The second outing for the Brabham was to prove altogether more satisfactory than the first. Helped by a newer spec DFV, Piers qualified an excellent fifth in the 14-car Silverstone field. When it rained on race day pole man Jackie Stewart opted to start his proven 1968 Matra, and not having qualified it, he had to go to the back of the grid. That effectively promoted Piers to fourth.

When the flag dropped Brabham emerged from the cloud of spray in front of new team-mate Jacky Ickx, and Piers slotted into third place to establish a one-two-three for the BT26. Piers focussed on finding a way past the Belgian, an acknowledged wet weather ace. Later traffic problems allowed a delayed Rindt to catch and pass both of them, so it became a battle for third. By now Piers was struggling with burned feet, thanks to heat from the radiator – the sort of thing that would only come to light during extended running. The flying Stewart demoted him to fifth and despite losing fifth gear, Piers stayed there to the flag. The little Williams team had really made its mark, and the relationship between the two principals worked as well as it had in F2.

"There wasn't a lot of chat," says Frank. "I was always worried about him having an accident – not hurting himself, but crashing or spinning and throwing away a good position. I'd give him a 30 second lecture on that, and that was it really. Not a finger wagging as such, but I'd tell him to try and be sensible at the start and first corner.

"The car always had lots of little technical problems, like this pipe would crack or a water leak from here, or the clutch didn't work very well, or the gearchange. It's not that the car wasn't well made, the engineering standards just weren't what they are now."

Piers and Frank had decided to continue their F2 collaboration into 1969, and there were no fewer than four major races to fill the gap before the team's planned Grand Prix debut. Having scored F1 points with Parnell, Piers was now a graded driver. As such he was one of the stars that the new generation wanted to shoot at, along with Rindt, Stewart and Hill.

With so many ex-Temporada cars around the Williams entry had expanded to four, and Frank also prepared the Brabham owned by pint-sized 500cc motorcycle ace Bill Ivy, who was attempting the tricky transition to four wheels. Incredibly Ivy qualified second at Thruxton, his time bettered only by Rindt. It would be hard to imagine anyone less like Piers than the down-to-earth Londoner, who made quite an impression in the paddock with his flowing locks and colourful language. However, they shared a sense of fun, and Ivy established an unlikely rapport with Piers and Sally.

"That was quite funny, his relationship with Bill Ivy," says Stewart. "They were an odd couple really, but they did get on really well, and so did Sally. There was Lady Sarah Curzon and here was a little cockney wheeler-dealer. Bill had such a lot of charm, so the three of them got on so well together."

Coombs mechanic Roland Law recalls Thruxton well: "Ivy asked Stewart what revs he dropped the clutch at. Never made a start before! All the ladies were standing around, and Piers asked him, 'Tell me Billy, when you come off and slide alongside on your backside like that, does it hurt?' Billy looked at him and said, 'Course it

fucking hurts!' Piers went pink... What a little spark that guy was."

The field was divided into two qualifying heats, and in his Piers relieved Pescarolo of second place at the chicane, and then inherited victory when Rindt stopped with a puncture. In the final Piers had just passed Beltoise for third when a left rear tyre punctured, and he dropped down the order. He eventually finished eighth, while Ivy's debut ended with an engine failure.

A week later Piers was at Hockenheim for what was now known as the Jim Clark Memorial Trophy. He'd battled for the lead in the fateful 1968 race, and did the same this time. This was an aggregate affair, and with the lead changing every lap Piers took a turn in front on several occasions in the first race, although he lost out in the final sprint and finished fifth. In the second he traded the lead with Beltoise and Hubert Hahne before a late spin saw him stranded in third. Winner Beltoise received his trophy from James Clark Snr, an honour that Piers would surely have appreciated. At Pau on 20 April he finished third again, this time behind Rindt and Beltoise. The next stop should have been the Nürburgring, but the organisers rejected the Williams entry after the limit of six graded drivers was reached.

After a long break since Kyalami the Grand Prix season resumed on 5 May with the Spanish GP, the first to be held on the wonderful Montjuich Park track. It was also the first time that the Williams team appeared on the entry list for a World Championship race. Meanwhile Piers's old Tasman mechanic, Les Sheppard, had been persuaded to return to Europe and join the outfit. Robin Herd took time off from his day job at Cosworth to act as engineer on the BT26, although the fuel leak problem from Brands had been addressed not by science, but by liberal coats of Araldite!

Piers holds off Henri Pescarolo's Matra at the Thruxton chicane. He won his heat, but was delayed by a puncture in the main event.

"In those days the engineering was really done by the chief mechanic," says Herd, "So Tony Fox was really the senior guy. I remember going shopping with Sally in Barcelona! But it was great fun. Frank had a very tight budget, and considering everything, they put up a super performance. Everything was done as cheaply as possible. In terms of personnel it was probably the smallest team in F1. But it seemed to work reasonably well."

Andrew Duncan of *The Daily Telegraph* attended the race, and wrote a piece in the Saturday colour supplement based on the privateer exploits of Williams and Rob Walker, who was running Jo Siffert. "Piers Courage strides by in a light suede cowboy jacket, looking young and unruffled," wrote Duncan. "Frank Williams, in a blue blazer, looks worried and is beginning to lose his hair. He smiles now and again."

Duncan had the good fortune to capture Frank's mood on the very eve of his Grand Prix baptism: "Of

course, in this life, everyone in life's got problems. I suppose I'm a bit irresponsible in that I'm not frightened of big money. I'm very good at the chat when talking to people about it. My ambition is to win. I have terrific faith in Piers, and we have a fabulous relationship. The racing has strangled my business because I've put all my money into it. But I want to do it better than anyone else. I'm not sure what I'll be doing in two years' time, but whatever it is, I'll be trying to make money. I need money to succeed."

Practice was stretched out over three days. Having missed the first day's running, Piers eventually qualified 11th in a small field of 14 cars. But that position meant nothing when his engine refused to fire up on the grid, as the starter motor had seized. The car was stranded on a blind brow, and with the pack well into the first lap, there were farcical scenes as the Williams mechanics and others attempted to go to Piers's aid.

"We had an almighty battle with the police," mechanic Bob Sparshott recalls. "I remember even Tim Parnell got involved, and we got severely hit with truncheons. We did get him away, but it was an accident about to happen any second. We hadn't got long to do it in. He was in a fearful state old Piers –

Above Piers on the first World Championship outing for the BT26 at Montjuich Park. He got away late and retired with engine problems.

Right Eoin Young captured Piers and Sally together in the pits at Monaco. It was to be the greatest race of his career to date.

his arm was going up and down like a yo-yo. He'd pushed every switch and button in the cockpit."

Piers made it away late in last place, but pitted after 19 laps because the engine wouldn't pull more than 8,000rpm. "He got going and then came in," says Herd. "I remember Frank saying to me what should I do? I said he should jack it in or the engine's going to blow up." After the promise of the International Trophy, it was a huge disappointment.

Piers's more immediate concern was for his friend Rindt. Jochen ended the day in a Barcelona hospital after crashing heavily when his rear wing failed, a fate that earlier befell Hill but with less serious consequences. At least Piers was able to visit Jochen, for he was in no hurry to leave Spain, as the next F2 race was the following weekend at Jarama. There he fought with the Matras of Stewart and Beltoise, but when third gear broke he faded to a distant third place.

Rindt was to be out of action for a couple of weeks, and during that time safety was in everyone's minds, as it had been during that awful period in mid-1968. Jochen, who would certainly have shared his thoughts with Piers, wrote letters to magazines asking for wings to be banned. When the circus reconvened at Monaco, there was a lot of tension in the air.

Piers and Frank travelled to the race in relative luxury. Having retired from driving at the start of 1967,

following his marriage to Shirley Ann Field, Charlie Crichton-Stuart was now making a living as personal pilot to businessman Hugh Fraser. The old Pinner Road crowd hadn't seen much of him of late, but that weekend was free to give his pals a ride.

"It was a little twin Piper Commanche, a small plane with two propellers," he recalled. "It was Frank, Piers, Sally, myself, probably one other. We stuffed everybody in that, and went down to Nice – probably grossly overloaded!"

By now Bob Sparshott had moved on, and there was no sign either of Robin Herd: "I think I was warned off by Cosworth." Frank would complete the season without proper engineering support, and that would prove costly.

The BT26 now had properly reinforced fuel tanks, and had been fitted with unbreakable Ford GT40 driveshafts for the punishing street track. Piers set the pace early in the first session on Thursday, and was still a very promising fifth at its conclusion. But at that point the CSI announced an immediate and very controversial ban on high wings; all the times were annulled, and set-up work had to start anew on Friday. Piers was sixth in this session, but didn't improve his time on Saturday, and slipped to ninth on the final grid, immediately behind the two works Brabhams. It was going to be a long hard, Sunday afternoon, and Frank allowed himself a smile when he heard that both works BT26s had suffered broken driveshafts in practice.

After Prince Rainier had opened the circuit in a Lamborghini Espada, race director Paul Frère waved the Monagasque flag to get the event underway. Frank recalls that the location of the garage caused a panic: "The established teams had one opposite the present pits, but we were up the bloody hill, and nearly missed the start of the race trying to get down!"

Poleman Stewart led Amon, Beltoise, Hill, Siffert and Ickx away, while Piers passed Brabham on the first lap and Surtees on the second to claim seventh. On lap four he took Siffert's Lotus 49 to claim sixth place and put himself in the points. He was now chasing Ickx in the works BT26, and the pair began a battle that was to rage for over 40 laps.

Initially it was for fifth place, but it soon took on a far greater significance. On lap 18 Amon dropped out of second place with a diff failure, leaving JYS so far ahead of Hill and Beltoise that he was able to drop his revs and try to preserve the car. Then it all went wrong for Matra. Beltoise suffered a broken driveshaft on lap 22, and on the very next lap Stewart suffered a repeat, despite his careful pace. Ickx and Piers were now contesting second place, with only Hill left between them and a possible victory.

On lap 27 the Belgian missed a gear and Piers stuck his nose in front for four laps, before Ickx reclaimed the place. It was terrific stuff, as Denis Jenkinson explained in *Motor Sport*: "These two young lads were putting on a splendid show, driving right on their limits and giving nothing away to each other. A hopeful flag marshal at the Gasworks hairpin kept showing Ickx a blue flag, but he was wasting his time, neither of them was giving an inch and neither of them expected it. It was first class racing."

The recuperating Rindt, watching the race on TV in Switzerland, cheered his progress. Frank was only too aware that third place was more than anyone could have hoped for, and he gave Piers a 'P3 – OK' sign, suggesting that he hold back. "The race developed, and we got patient," says Frank. "We didn't want to mix it and crash. We wanted to get good solid results and points."

But then on lap 48 Ickx suffered a spectacular rear upright failure just before the tunnel, and speared off the road just in front of the Williams entry. So Piers now found himself in a safe second place, some 23 seconds behind Hill. He was well clear of Siffert, McLaren and Attwood, the last-named deputising for Rindt at Lotus, but there were still 31 laps to run. He just had to stay out of trouble.

"Piers had finesse," says Sheppard. "He could be quite gentle on a car, and he didn't tear the gearboxes apart or anything like that."

However, every lap must have brought back memories of past misadventures. So much had happened to him at Monaco over the years. There was the embarrassing first

lap crash at Mirabeau in F3 practice in 1964, and the off at Tabac while leading the final two years later. In 1967 he'd spun to a frustrating halt at Ste Devote on his debut in the Grand Prix itself. On that occasion he blamed tiredness and cramp. He was fitter and more experienced now, but his feet remained a perennial problem.

"Piers had such cramp, poor man," says Sally. "He used to have a terrible time with his feet, and it had always been a problem with him. He had to make his own shoes to take the pressure off a certain part of his foot. He suffered unbelievable pain in the race, and had gone through the pain barrier."

Frank again signalled Piers to hold station and not to try to catch Hill who, feeling no threat from behind, had eased off. After what seemed like an age the chequered flag finally came with Piers some 17.6 seconds behind Graham, who logged his fifth win in the principality.

Later that year Piers gave his views on the race to journalist Richard Garrett: "I think we had 24 laps to go, or something like that. I was holding Siffert fairly comfortably. He had reduced my lead to 15 seconds and I instantly got it back to 23 seconds – quite easily. But what I didn't know was that Graham was only 17 seconds in front of me. Frank Williams made the decision that it was better for the *équipe* as a whole to have the prestige of coming second. This he decided was much more important than the chance of being first.

Above *Piers on his way to second place at Monaco. The BT26 looks a little naked, for after first practice the FIA announced that wings were banned with immediate effect.*

Opposite top *Party time! Piers joins Frank, Sally and Charlie Crichton-*

Stuart *on Sunday night to celebrate the amazing Monaco second place.*

Opposite middle *Piers and Sally at Monaco with close friends Bruce and Pat McLaren. The Kiwi had long been a supporter of Piers.*

Opposite bottom *Piers at the wheel of Frank's new Brabham BT30 at the Zolder F2 race on 8 June, in which he finished third. Graham Hill follows here.*

"I think the way he played it was right. If he'd put up a sign saying 'Hill 17 seconds,' or something like that, I would perhaps have had a go. But, late in the race one is tired and one's concentration isn't so good. The cars aren't handling so well because the road is greasy, you know, and there's a good chance that you might clip a kerb. You'd feel an awful fool if you ruined your chances of a good place with so few laps to go."

Piers had a huge grin on his face as he toured round to the pits, acknowledging the crowd, his pleasure even overcoming the pain from his feet. "They were absolutely rigid," says Sally. "When he stopped, he couldn't get out of the car. He had to wait, with us pouring water over him, and eventually they lifted him out of the car and we tried to get the circulation back."

Piers was soon feeling fine, and the celebrations got underway: "We thought this is unreal," says Frank. "It was clearly a wonderful result."

"It was just brilliant," Sally recalls. "We all went out for dinner that night. Everyone was very tired, and emotionally exhausted. But it was such euphoria. I remember we were staying outside Monaco in a very downmarket Holiday Inn type place."

Autosport's editorial summed up the general feeling: "Piers Courage drove the race of his life on Sunday, thoroughly justifying the faith Frank Williams has in him."

After a busy start to the season, Piers now had a couple of free weekends. Life at 15 Sutherland Street continued to be hectic, with visitors coming and going and the likes of Bubbles Horsley living there on a more or less permanent basis. Another long-term tenant was Arabella von Westenholz, a former school friend of Sally's. She provides a fascinating insight into life with the Courages.

"I always made the joke that I was invited for a weekend and stayed for five years! When my marriage broke up they invited me to stay at Sutherland Street, where Sally helped me through a difficult period in my life, and they both made me feel very welcome. I became great friends with Piers and got to know many of his friends as well. In fact he appeared quite protective towards me and was very critical of people I went out with – a sort of older brother attitude. At the time I was a fashion editor at *Vogue*, but I doubt whether the rent I paid would have covered the cost of my supper. Not only were they my best friends, they were also incredibly generous.

"The combination of Sally's stunning looks and her modelling career, at a time when Britain led the field in a fashion revolution, and Piers's daredevil lifestyle made them an extremely glamorous and popular couple. When it came to motor racing they were a close team in which Sally played an active part, helping in every possible way,

devoting most of her time and energy to furthering Piers's career.

"I remember Piers as an incredibly attractive man, with an attractive personality. He also had a wonderful sense of humour – I think that kept him going when things got tough. Unlike some of the other racers he had an interest in things like music, poetry, literature and politics. On quiet evenings we'd have supper and chat, even argue, but very seldom about motor racing. He was horrified if I ever asked him anything about cars or racing.

"I also remember there were these terrible goldfish – I think he won them at a fair and brought them back. He said he didn't know what to do with them, and I said well I'll take them and look after them… he said I don't want to see them again unless they're on toast!"

Meanwhile her fellow lodger Horsley used the Courage house as a base for his car dealing. Not all customers were satisfied, as Sally recalls: "Bubbles was running his second-hand car business and outside Sutherland Street all these old bangers were lined up. There was a wonderful old-fashioned nanny who was an absolute saint to my children. They'd say, 'I want my money back!' 'I have no idea who you are talking about. Lady Sarah has just gone out.' They used to be completely flummoxed by this incredibly imperious nanny who wouldn't let them cross the threshold – meanwhile Bubbles would be shaking like a jelly in the dining room…"

Action resumed for Piers with the F2 race at Zolder on 8 June, which should have been the date of the Belgian GP at Spa, until a debate over safety led to its cancellation. Frank had acquired a brand new Brabham BT30, and Piers finished third, behind Rindt and local hero Ickx. From Belgium he drove straight to Le Mans. Having contested the 24 Hours with Maranello Concessionaires in 1966 and '67, Piers was invited back to the Sarthe for a works drive with Matra Sport, who had a serious shot at outright victory. The French marque knew Piers well from F1, F2 and even F3, and as a sign of the high regard in which he was held, he was paired with Beltoise, the undoubted star of the four-car team.

"I was quite friendly with Piers," says Beltoise. "We had a very good relationship, and we were often competing close together in F3 and F2. I remember one or two times our wheels were too close, and we jumped!"

Piers was effectively replacing Henri Pescarolo, who'd been injured in a testing crash, one of three that had seriously hampered Matra's Le Mans preparations. He and Beltoise were to share a brand new 650 Spyder, the only new car in Matra's line-up, which itself had already been badly crunched in testing.

Left Piers in the Matra he shared with Jean-Pierre Beltoise at Le Mans. He had acquired a new full-face Bell helmet, but had not yet had time to paint it in the familiar Eton colours.

Right Piers pushes on in the Matra at Le Mans. He and Beltoise finished fourth, but they could well have won the race.

There was serious opposition in the form of works Ferraris, Ford GT40s, Porsches in 908 and 917 guise, and it promised to be a classic encounter. The German cars dominated qualifying, but Matra hoped that a steady run in the race with its V12 machines would pay dividends.

Piers and Sally spent most of the week before the race staying with the other Matra drivers at an impressive chateau, complete with swimming pool. "It was fantastic," says Jacqueline Beltoise. "A good life! Piers was always very friendly, very kind. I never saw him unhappy or angry, he always had a smile. We knew him before, but I was very happy to get to know him better that week."

At Le Mans Piers was using a new Bell helmet, and not having had time to paint it, ran in unfamiliar white colours. In order to give Beltoise more options, Piers was in the car for the start, which was notable for an horrific first lap crash that claimed the life of Porsche privateer John Woolfe. After a couple of hours the Matra was seventh, and by the sixth hour it was third, until as darkness fell precious time was lost in the pits for attention to a defective rear light. By 10pm the car was

sixth, well behind the leading Porsches, but on the same lap as the JWA/Gulf Ford GT40 of Jacky Ickx/Jackie Oliver, and four laps ahead of the Porsche of Hans Herrmann/Gerard Larrousse.

Sometime after midnight Piers had a lucky escape, as *Autosport* reported: "Courage had a nasty moment; he was following the leading 917 down the Mulsanne Straight and, as the big Porsche blasted past a 911, the 911 veered across the road and into the Matra's front wing."

He got safely back to the pits and the tattered bodywork was taped up. The Matra still ran seventh, but a couple of laps were lost, and then just before dawn there was a costly nine minute stop for work on the brakes and more attention to the nose. The Ickx/Oliver GT40 had been on the same lap, but now the Matra was five laps behind it. For the rest of the race the blue car ran without major dramas, although pit work was a little scrappy.

At 4pm on Sunday all eyes were on the sensational battle to the line between Ickx and Herrmann, which the Belgian won by just 100 metres. The Matra rose up to fourth place by the flag, nearly catching the second

JWA/Gulf GT40 of Hailwood/Hobbs. It was a good result, but before Piers was struck by that errant 911, he and Beltoise had been five laps clear of the car that eventually finished second by a tiny margin. Of course many others had hard luck stories, and brake disc problems had also delayed the Matra, but it was obvious that a great opportunity had been missed. Piers had at least established his credentials as an endurance driver.

"I think we were not lucky," says Beltoise, "because we stopped for something like ten minutes more than usual. If we had not stopped, perhaps we could have won that race. In fact we should have won! But Piers was very quick and very reliable, and also *sympathetique*. I developed a lot of respect for him."

Piers must have picked up a cold at Le Mans, for he was feeling a little under the weather at the Dutch GP at Zandvoort. After the joy of Monaco the meeting was to prove a huge disappointment. Piers qualified ninth, once again just behind the works BT26 of Jack Brabham, but on the fourth lap he was in the pits with clutch dramas. A few laps after that, he stopped for good.

In February 1970 Frank explained the problems to Doug Nye in *Autosport*: "Our trouble was lack of an engineer. You can't expect even the best mechanics to prevent rather than cure trouble, however good their general preparation may be. We were plagued all season with fuel pressure problems which with a good engineer on hand, we could have beaten."

Below Piers leads Jo Siffert, Jackie Stewart and the rest of the field at Rheims on 29 June. He set a new lap record, but lost out in a last corner shuffle, and finished third.

Opposite Piers sharing a joke with Jochen Rindt and Denny Hulme in the Gulf caravan at Clermont-Ferrand.

Zandvoort clashed with the F2 race at Monza, where an interesting new car made its debut. After driving the de Tomaso-entered Tecno in December's Temporada series, Jonathan Williams had waited patiently for the marque's own car to be readied, and now it was. The red car used a Cosworth engine supplied by none other than Frank Williams. Although Alessandro de Tomaso didn't actually go on the Temporada trip with Jonathan, he had probably first met Frank three or four years earlier, when he was dabbling in F3. Their renewed contact was to lead to bigger things.

"De Tomaso was a complete madman," says Jonathan. "Insane, but nice. Trouble was he had this thing about cast magnesium. But his early F3 cars were gems to look at, all radically different, and he never copied anybody. I reckon he thought he could get up there with Ferrari. And he would have. He was a visionary, but he got bored. He never did any fine tuning, and would

always move onto the next thing. He married an American lady from a very wealthy family. He didn't have to make a profit on anything he did."

Designed by Gianpaulo Dallara, the new F2 car attracted a lot of favourable comment, and it was clearly very well made. However, even the slightly-built Jonathan could only just squeeze into it. Unable to use the team's best engine or nose, he qualified near the back of the field, and finished ninth, after a pit stop.

Piers had always excelled on slipstreaming tracks, and in the F2 race at Rheims on 29 June he was in the thick of some sensational action. He qualified second and was in the leading pack throughout, taking a turn in front on several occasions. Piers led across the line at the start of the last lap, but didn't want to be in front at the crucial Thillois corner; but when like Stewart and others he hung back, François Cevert nipped through. The cheeky newcomer just managed to stay ahead in a seven-car dash to the line, while Piers had to settle for third, convinced that he'd beaten Robin Widdows to second in the blanket finish. He did at least have a new F2 lap record as a consolation, and headed off to play golf with JYS. Rheims would never again host a major event.

Piers had not been to the challenging Clermont-Ferrand road course until the French GP the following weekend. There was a peculiar sight in practice when he

suddenly appeared in a works Lotus 49, but it turned out that Rindt had borrowed Piers's spare open helmet, as he was feeling sick when using his own enclosed version. Like Zandvoort, race day was to be a disappointment. The team had made detailed modifications to the car, including changing the one-piece bodywork for a more convenient separate nose arrangement. During the race the nosebox began to collapse and the cockpit section came adrift, even making it hard to change gear. Following several stops, Piers was eventually forced to retire.

The previous year Piers had failed in his attempt to land a CanAm drive, and once again he tried to put a deal together, this time with Frank. They had intended to use a McLaren M6B previously owned by the late John Woolfe, but in mid-July the proposed sponsorship package fell through, and Frank dropped the plan.

"He never had any money," says Sheppard. "I'd say, 'Frank, I want to go and pick up the engines,' and he'd sell his Ferrari to pay for them. We were on cash with everybody. Frank used to go out and buy clothes and throw them in through the window, so the operations manager wouldn't see them! But he always paid us our money."

July brought some tragic news, this time from a far away motorcycle event. Bill Ivy had really made a name for himself in F2, but continued to ride bikes to earn a living. At the Sachsenring the engine of his works 350c Jawa had seized, pitching him into a wall. He was killed instantly.

After two disappointments Monaco suddenly seemed like a long time ago, but Piers got his season back on track at Silverstone on 19 July. That weekend he and Sally stayed with the Rindts and the Stewarts at Alexander Hesketh's house, and the hospitable teenager even arranged for everyone to commute by helicopter, and make the short hop to the paddock in his Aston Martin. Pretty flash for 1969.

After yet more trouble with fuel leaks in practice, Piers qualified 10th. He made a good start in Saturday's race, and immediately passed Siffert, Ickx and a slowing Surtees to get up to seventh. Ickx soon got back ahead, but as Stewart and Rindt pulled away in front, Piers becoming involved in a superb scrap that included Siffert, Hill and the Ferraris of Amon and Rodriguez. Piers fought his way past the latter pair to claim sixth on lap 13, which became fifth when Hulme pitted on lap 27.

Under pressure from behind, Piers then ran wide at Copse, dropping to seventh as Hill and Siffert went past. For the next 40 laps Piers traded places with the two Lotus 49s, at one point passing the World Champion in a splendid move down the inside of Woodcote. When Hill pitted for a late fuel stop Piers was secure in fifth,

but that became fourth when he passed Rindt, who had
dropped out of the lead with a fuel stop of his own and
had now lost interest. The Austrian suddenly woke up
when he learned Piers was on the same lap, and nipped
back by. Piers was furious with Frank when he found
out that he'd given up a position so easily and had not
been kept informed – it was the only time they had a
major disagreement, but it was soon put down to
experience. Fifth was a fine result for Piers and the team,
and he'd shown a home crowd that he could run with
some of the biggest names of the day.

At the time the world had its eyes on rather more
important matters than motor racing, and like everyone
else Piers was fascinated by the Apollo 11 mission. On
the Tuesday after Silverstone he and Sally dashed back
from a friend's house to catch the moon landings on TV.

In the next Grand Prix at the Nürburgring on 3 August
Piers was to have a flight of his own, but the landing was
not as successful as that of Armstrong and Aldrin. For the
first time Frank had entered a second car, albeit only in
the F2 class that made up the numbers. He wanted an
experienced hand to drive Piers's regular BT30, and in a
reversal of what had previously happened with BRM and
with Maranello Concessionaires at Le Mans in
1967, Richard Attwood found himself playing a
supporting role.

Piers put on a great show in the British GP, and eventually finished fifth. Here he leads Graham Hill's works Lotus.

"They were very loathe to let another driver
go out in Piers's car," he recalls. "Being the
'Ring, if you make a mistake it's going to be
bad. But I think I was on a short list of
probably one, and it worked out well. We all
got on very well, Piers, Sally, myself and my wife
Veronica. Piers was happy with the way the car was so I
wasn't about to alter it, so the input from me was just to
get in and drive the thing."

Practice was marred by the death of local hero
Gerhard Mitter, who had briefly been Piers's team-mate
when he drove for Ron Harris at the same race three
years earlier.

The BT26 now featured the logos of Ward Machine
Tools, Frank's first proper sponsor. Company boss Ted
Williams would be a loyal supporter through difficult
times. Meanwhile the car now had new rubber bag tanks
in an attempt to solve its ongoing problems with leaks,
but fuel system bothers would continue to hamper Piers
throughout the weekend. Nevertheless he qualified
seventh, ahead of veteran 'Ring campaigners like
McLaren and Hill.

After a display by the Red Arrows, the race got
underway. Piers banged wheels with Beltoise, losing a
few places, and later in the lap he was extremely lucky
not to get involved in an accident involving Mario
Andretti and Vic Elford, that left the latter in hospital.
Piers himself failed to complete the second lap. He
explained what happened to author Richard Garrett:

"I jumped a considerable distance. When the car came down, instead of just landing and going on down the hill, it hit the ground very hard on the chassis. There was a lot of right hand lock on, and a chassis doesn't have so much adhesion as the tyres. Consequently it just slid sideways. The moment this happened, I knew that I was in for trouble, because the hedge was very, very close. So I put on opposite lock and I had the brakes on. But my left hand rear wheel was too close to the hedge, which was a fairly stiff one.

"It knocked the wheel off. I had my foot hard down on the brake pedal but nothing happened. Luckily the car just slid down the road as I watched the bank coming up. Normally, you can judge your speed of impact, and I thought, 'Ah, obviously the car is going to reach the bank, but it won't be going very fast.' It all happened very quickly but your brain accelerates enormously. In fact the car landed just against the bank. The nose was damaged but it didn't bend the radiator or anything."

Piers's fire extinguisher went off on impact and "…made me feel very fuzzy. I sat down and I felt, well, not quite dizzy exactly, though I did feel rather groggy for a few moments. I think that as the accident's happening your brain is working overtime, trying to cope with the situation. When it all stops and your brain relaxes, there is a sort of reaction; you're a bit shaky for perhaps thirty seconds."

He'd had some major shunts earlier in his career, but this was the biggest fright Piers had yet experienced in an F1 car.

"You feel slightly apprehensive. I don't think you really feel scared, because there is absolutely nothing you can do about it. The actual accident is sort of continuous, you know – and so you are working all the time. It is not something you are waiting for, but sometimes you are trying to prevent."

Inevitably many took the view that Piers had simply overdone it, but Les Sheppard says it was a set-up problem: "I was sick and I didn't go, and I'd told them, whatever you do don't take those bump rubbers out because the car will hit the deck. And they took the bump rubbers out and filled the car up with fuel! To me that was bloody stupid. Frank and I parted company after that, and I never went back to motor racing…"

Frank admits that it was probably a team error: "The car bottomed out and got away from him. We were a bunch of amateurs looking back; the car just bottomed out on its suspension and went off the road. At least we ended up with the latest factory parts after that, new nose and so on. It was a very much rebuilt car – the

Top left *With Johnny Servoz-Gavins's Matra alongside, Piers awaits the start at Enna on 24 August. The nose of the Brabham is taped up in an effort to minimise stone damage.* Bottom left *A delighted Frank Williams watches the celebrations at Enna, where Piers scored the first – and only – European F2 victory of his career.* Above *Piers and Frank look a little serious during practice for the Italian GP at Monza. Sally sees the funny side, and ensures that her husband is well groomed....*

chassis went off to Arch Motors, who did the chassis for Brabham."

While the BT26 was being repaired Piers bounced back by finally scoring his first F2 victory in Europe, after three years of trying. Since his frustrating first appearance in the Mediterranean GP with Bob Gerard in 1965, Piers had always liked Enna and its wild slipstreaming battles. This time the team came prepared for the Sicilian track's abrasive dust, equipping the nose and suspension parts with plastic shields to minimise the effects of sand blasting. Jonathan was supposed to give the de Tomaso its second outing, but he'd been dropped in favour of none other than Jacky Ickx.

Although he'd lost out earlier in the year in a last corner fumble at Rheims, Piers was by now an absolute master of slipstreaming. He explained the technique to Richard Garrett: "On circuits where there's a lot of slipstreaming, you can feint, as if you're going up one side, and then go up the other. You just have to turn the wheel a bit and he'll notice. People are so in tune with what the other person is doing that you only have to make a little show of it, and he'll move slightly across – or something like that. If it doesn't work you can always have another go."

Enna was a two-heat, aggregate affair, and both races saw a fantastic dice for the lead. Piers showed what he'd learned by heading Johnny Servoz-Gavin, Beltoise, Cevert and Regazzoni across the line in the first heat, and then Hill, Pescarolo, Cevert et al in the second. He'd beaten some established names and the best of the young lions, and picked up five trophies and a gold medal for his troubles.

He'd also caught the eye of Gianpaulo Dallara, the talented designer of the de Tomaso: "We were all staying in the Hotel de la Regione, in the village. We had a very good time, because the atmosphere was very relaxed. I remember Frank was putting a lot of tape in the nose of his car because there were a lot of stones! We realised immediately how fast the driver was, so when I went home I suggested to Mr de Tomaso, 'Why don't you ask Piers Courage to drive our car?'"

At Enna Ickx had qualified the red car an impressive fifth, and had run with the leading group until his engine failed. During the Italian trip Jacky paid a visit to Enzo Ferrari, sparking rumours that he might leave Brabham and return to the team he'd driven for in 1968. The driver market was getting interesting.

For Piers the timing of the Enna win was handy, for the next race was the Italian GP. He went there bursting with confidence and in full slipstreaming mode, sure that he could run with the leaders and hopefully get himself into the right position on the last lap. In qualifying he and Jochen worked out a careful strategy that towed them both to good times, the Austrian taking pole and Piers a splendid fourth, by far his best Grand Prix grid

position to date. He set the same time as McLaren, and not knowing who had recorded it first, the organisers asked Bruce and Frank to draw lots. Williams won! However, as usual the car was plagued by fuel system bothers.

Any lingering doubts about Piers's ability to mix with the very best were surely shattered at Monza. From the off he ran in the thick of a leading group that included the biggest names of the day, and in 68 laps his position across the start/finish line changed 22 times. Piers was fifth on the first lap, and by lap nine crossed the line in third, behind only Stewart and Hulme. He subsequently bounced between third and fourth before slotting behind Stewart in second on lap 16. Two laps later he snuck in front of the Matra, and led a Grand Prix for the first time. JYS was back past him on the very next lap, and for the next 20 laps or so the blue Brabham traded places with Stewart and Rindt, before taking another brief turn in front on lap 32. Hulme and Siffert eventually dropped out of the leading battle, leaving a group of six that comprised Stewart, Rindt, Piers, Hill, Beltoise and McLaren.

Bruce described the fun in his *Autosport* column: "A couple of times during the race I almost found myself in the role of excited spectator. There I was, at 180mph on the straight, with four or five cars in front of me all having such an enormous race that it was hard to remember that you were supposed to be in it instead of just sitting back and watching…"

Piers stayed in third or fourth, biding his time and counting the laps down to that crucial 68th and last lap. But lap 55 signalled the return of the gremlins that had blighted his season, as Frank explains: "We had a fuel system problem on the car, and as the fuel got hot it would give a misfire."

Paddy McNally told the story in *Autosport*: "Only 13 laps before the end Piers suddenly slowed; low fuel pressure was making the engine cough and bang as if it were about to die at any moment. This was really a shame, as Piers had driven a splendid race – in many people's opinion even more creditable than his epic at Monaco. However, he gamely struggled on, never giving up, and surprisingly was only 13sec behind with seven laps still to go."

Hill's late retirement promoted him to fifth, and with no pressure from behind he toured round to finish 33sec behind a four-car blur in which Stewart pipped Rindt by a matter of feet. Piers deserved better. Intriguingly along with Beltoise he was one of only two drivers in the top group running wings, and on a last-lap plunge into the Parabolica that might just have given him an edge as the opposition scrabbled for grip. At least new World Champion Stewart paid him a glowing tribute at Dunlop's celebratory party at the Hotel de la Ville that evening.

However, even today JYS gives the impression that he never truly accepted Piers as a rival in the same way that he considered Rindt: "I think of Piers more as a kind of nice friend rather than a racing driver. The only time I remember was at Monza '69, when he was using wings and we weren't and he was very quick through Curva Grande. We always thought he was good, but it was just a question of him coming of age in a way."

Jackie admits that Piers's public schoolboy image often worked against him: "I never had a tough job convincing anybody that I was a serious contender. Piers had a problem. He had that look about him, that style about him, that suaveness about him, that worldliness about him in comparison to a bunch of us who were much more basic people. He had privileges and was born with a silver spoon. He would always say he had no money, but he drove a Ferrari!"

According to Heinz Pruller, Rindt was always quick to support his friend: "Whenever there was talk about Piers being a hobby racer, Jochen always defended him, and said, 'No, no, Piers is not any less professional than all of you.'"

It was at Monza that Frank began serious discussions with Alessandro de Tomaso about a possible collaboration in 1970. Although his F2 car had made only a couple of appearances, the ambitious Argentinian already wanted to make the big step up to Grand Prix racing. He saw it as the ideal promotion for his roadgoing supercars, which were about to progress to another level. He had established a friendship with Ford boss Lee Iacocca, who just the previous month had agreed to support the forthcoming Pantera model, a development of the existing Mangusta.

The sensational lead battle at Monza on 7 September. Here Jackie Stewart leads Piers, Jo Siffert, Denny Hulme, Jochen Rindt, Bruce McLaren and Jean-Pierre Beltoise. It was the only time Piers led a Grand Prix.

Still making a quick buck selling old car parts, Frank couldn't fail to be impressed by such lofty connections. The factory in Modena, not far from Ferrari, looked good. Equally impressive was Gianpaulo Dallara, the 33-year-old designer of the F2 car. It was still early days, but the basic idea was that de Tomaso would build a chassis, and Frank would run it from Slough. There was never any question about who would drive it.

"Mr de Tomaso wanted to enter the F1 arena," says Dallara, "and knowing Frank Williams and Piers, the best opportunity was to try to have an agreement with these people. The condition was that de Tomaso would supply a car, and Frank would support the costs of running a team."

Piers had a disappointing retirement in the F2 race at Albi before boarding a plane to Toronto for the Canadian GP at Mosport. The familiar fuel system problems resurfaced again, and he qualified 10th. In the race he was running at the back of a six-car battle for fourth place when the fuel tank split yet again, and he found himself doused in petrol. At the time he was right with Jack Brabham, who went on to finish second behind team-mate Ickx.

Below *Piers in action at Monza. Had he not hit problems, he would have been in the middle of the final dash to the line.*

Opposite *Piers heads the similar works BT26s of Jacky Ickx and Jack Brabham at Watkins Glen on 5 October. His determined performance earned a $20,000 windfall for Frank Williams.*

Frank recalled the race to Doug Nye: "In Canada we just ran uncompetitively – it was depressing. The car had an oversteer problem, but we lost out on the communication between driver and manager which I prize so highly."

A fortnight later at Watkins Glen Piers again ran in company with Jack, but in rather more enjoyable circumstances. The US GP was the richest race of the year, and everyone was always keen to get a share of the huge prize fund. Piers *had* to finish this one.

He qualified ninth, splitting the two works BT26s. At the start he snuck ahead of Ickx, and with McLaren non-starting and Hulme in immediate trouble, the Williams car was straight into sixth place. By lap six Siffert had retired and Piers passed both Hill and Beltoise to take third. Now only the battling Rindt and Stewart lay ahead.

As they pulled away, Piers was more than occupied by looking in his mirrors. Ickx and Brabham were right on his tail and pushing hard, but Piers held them off in confident style until Ickx got ahead on lap 22. Four laps after that he re-passed the Belgian,

and the battle continued. It took on a greater significance when JYS stopped on lap 36, and Piers moved up to second. Now only Rindt lay ahead, and with 72 laps to go, there seemed like more than enough time for the Austrian's legendary bad luck to rob him of a maiden victory. Piers drove superbly, holding off first Ickx and then, after they traded places on lap 63, triple World Champion Brabham.

Andrew Marriott described their epic fight in *Motor Sport*: "Brabham tried all the tricks, such as rushing up the inside under late braking in an attempt to force Courage over. But Courage would have none of it and retaliated by occasionally dropping a wheel into the dirt and flinging up a stone or two at Brabham."

A gentleman off the track, Piers could scrap with the best of them when he had to, and in those days a little stone throwing was part of the driver's art. Then with a few laps to go Jack dropped back with fuel starvation, and Piers was able to enjoy an easy run to second and a $20,000 windfall for the team, recent testing at Silverstone having cured the team's own fuel pick-up problems. Brabham was not overjoyed with his fourth place, and made his feelings about Piers's forceful driving known when he swung into the pits, clipping the front wing of the parked Williams car.

"His nickname was Black Jack," says Frank, "and I understood why when he revved up in the pit to go back

up to the garage. Piers blew him away. Anyway, it was just a little bit of dust really…"

For once Jochen had an untroubled day and was delighted to have Piers join in the celebrations for his long-awaited first Grand Prix win. Piers won the BOAC Driver of the Day trophy, made in the shape of a Boeing 707, and picked up a bonus of $5,000 to go with it. However, like everyone else he was concerned about the fate of Graham Hill, who broke both his legs in a spectacular crash during the closing stages.

Piers and Frank dashed back from New York to Rome for the final F2 race at Vallelunga on 12 October. The de Tomaso deal was progressing well, and as a taster Piers was invited to drive the Italian car at Vallelunga, fitted with Frank's engine.

"De Tomaso was obviously a good businessman," says Frank, "And he ran a couple of large companies. He kept saying, 'You should be doing F1 with me.' I thought about it and discussed it with Piers, and we thought we'd have a go at it. The guy was going to do the car, the basic chassis, and we were going to provide the engines and gearboxes and anything required to run the team."

Above Piers joins Jochen Rindt as the Austrian celebrates his first GP victory at Watkins Glen.

Opposite Charlie Courage offers encouragement as Piers and Sally set off in their Isetta bubble car. The special dark blue and gold pinstripe paint job was done by a Rolls-Royce dealer!

The Dunlop tyres worked well at Vallelunga, and Piers qualified second to European champion elect Servoz-Gavin. However, he was extremely cramped in the car, unable to change gear comfortably and struggling even to steer. Even the safety belts had to be discarded. "I don't know how Piers got in it, as it was tight for me!," says Jonathan. "Dallara had really made it small."

A spin dropped Piers from second to third in the first heat, and then he retired from the second with electrical problems. However, he had made his mark on Dallara: "The personality of Piers Courage was really very nice, and he was also a very good driver. He impressed everybody. The cockpit was very small and he had very little room. We managed to slide him inside, but it was not really good for him."

Despite the problems the new car had again shown that it could compete with the established marques, and that gave cause for optimism. Meanwhile the F1 market had been turned on its head by the arrival of a new constructor. Since meeting up at Frank's place a year earlier, Robin Herd and Max Mosley had pushed ahead with the proposed F1 car for Jochen Rindt. When he dropped out of the picture March Engineering was born. They planned to run a works team, and had managed to tempt Amon away from Ferrari, although the news had yet to be confirmed. They were also busy touting customer cars. Ken Tyrrell would eventually sign up, and Frank was an obvious candidate, although he wasn't interested:

"They were asking a lot of money, but they'd got a lot of cars out there already, and there was a limit to how many people they could develop with. But the 'Tomato' was free. Big difference."

Williams was convinced of the merits of the de Tomaso deal, but there remained a tantalising alternative for Piers. Perhaps on the strength of his televised drive in the Italian GP, Enzo Ferrari had taken a close interest in him. The *Commendatore* had known Sally's father Earl Howe and, always impressed by aristocratic connections, not to mention pretty faces, he had been delighted to meet her during an earlier visit to practice at Monza.

At some stage – probably during the Vallelunga trip – Piers visited Maranello, and he was offered Amon's seat alongside the returning Jacky Ickx. It says a lot for Piers's character that he didn't think twice about taking Frank along in the role of manager, despite the obvious clash of interests. Fluent in Italian, Williams was not overawed.

"We went to see Mr Ferrari, and he was a little bit disdainful of my being there," says Frank. "But I was there as Piers's manager. He was just another bloke as far as I was concerned, always was…"

Frank admits that he was desperate to hang on to Piers: "Sure, it wouldn't have been easy without him. I was very open with Piers about it. I said to him, 'It's up to you exactly what you want to do.'"

Piers faced an excruciatingly hard decision. In April 1968 he'd turned down Jim Clark's seat at Lotus, partly out of loyalty to Tim Parnell, but this was an even tougher choice. The difference was this time he knew he was ready to drive for a front running team.

"Ferrari asked him to come and race for him," says Sally. "Piers was in two minds whether to leave Frank. I think it was Jacky Ickx who said, 'Don't go, you won't be able to cope with the politics.' I said, 'Piers, you *can* cope with it.' Frank was seriously underfunded, and I just wanted, I suppose, my husband to have a bit of security. You do need something to pay the bills with!

"He wouldn't leave Frank. He said, 'Frank knows me, Frank understands me. I have faith in Frank, Frank has faith in me.' But Frank had to find the money to pay Piers, get sponsors in. He had to give Piers a proper wage, to keep him, and at the same time have enough money to run the team. Frank was living hand to mouth, but he was determined to have it really well organised, and well run. How he juggled the books, you've got to admire him for it."

Meanwhile in the middle of October the Courages were finally able to move from 15 Sutherland Street to their new home at 70 Drayton Gardens, a busy connection between Fulham Road and Cromwell Road. It was just round the corner from Sally's old flat in Roland Gardens, where they had lived for the first few months of their marriage.

Their new base was a smart three-storey house that opened straight out onto the street, Victorian paving stones and chains and wooden posts outside adding a touch of class. They'd owned the property for a year, but it had taken time to remodel it and build a studio flat over the mews garage at the back, which Piers would use as an office.

Just one more race remained on the 1969 schedule, and after Vallelunga Piers and Frank dashed back across the Atlantic for the Mexican GP on 19 October. Piers struggled with oversteer on the bumpy track, and even an exploratory test by Jack Brabham couldn't sort the set-up properly. In the race Piers was bumped into a spin by Siffert, and after a pit stop, he finished 10th. It was an extremely disappointing end to a season that saw Piers finish eighth in the World Championship, with 16 points to his name.

Once back in Europe, he had to make his mind up quickly. Ferrari was offering him £25,000 for a season of F1 and sports car racing, and Frank could only guarantee a little more than a tenth of that. However, Piers could make up the balance by racing sports cars for somebody else. Porsche had recently announced that Gulf and John Wyer were to run its works 917 programme in 1970 from its base in Slough. With Wyer star Ickx now departed for Ferrari, Piers was one of several drivers invited to try the car at the new Österreichring circuit in October.

Then Alfa Romeo came into the picture. The Italian company was prepared to offer serious money to get a top line Grand Prix driver, and Piers fitted the bill perfectly. Although it had long been in the second

division of sports car racing, the works Autodelta team was ambitious, and Piers was happy with the V8-powered Tipo 33 when he tested it at Vallelunga. Alfa were prepared to pay a generous salary of £20,000, which would go some way to making up for the modest £3,000 that Frank could offer. Eventually, the pieces fell into place. Piers turned down Ferrari.

"Piers said he'd far rather drive the 'Tomato,' and Alfa with the sporty cars, for the same money," says Frank.

The arrangements were officially announced in early November, and the news garnered a lot of coverage in the national press. As one of the perks of the sports car job Alfa Romeo GB handed Piers the keys of a new 1750 GTV, while de Tomaso promised a Mangusta that he and Frank would share.

In retrospect it's easy to say that turning down Ferrari was a mistake, and even at the time some of his friends had their doubts.

"He should have taken it," said Crichton-Stuart. "I don't know why he did stay with Frank. He was a Ferrari-type driver; he was mercurial, he was good with people, the press would have loved him. And he was British, which was very popular at that time."

However, Piers had justifiable concerns about being in the team alongside Ickx, who knew how to play the Ferrari system from his season there in 1968. He also remembered what a frustrating time Jonathan had endured at Maranello in '67, although Williams himself says he had no direct influence on Piers's thinking: "Not at all. I wasn't consulted. He was just happy with Frank, and the money side was pretty much eased by Alfa Romeo giving what was a load of money in those days. He could stick with his buddy Frank, and wouldn't have any stress. He wouldn't have done well at Ferrari – they would have eaten him alive. You've got to have a very special outlook to survive there. With de Tomaso they'd got the DFV, the engine that you had to have. I was sure that they were doing a good thing, and they would be on the pace. I would have backed it. I thought Dallara was an exceptionally gifted guy."

But what really mattered was his loyalty to his friend, as Sally confirms: "Piers didn't want to leave him, because he knew Frank would make it. He said, 'I just know this man is going to have a top team, and I know if I stay with him, I can work with him.' And he was going to be number one, he was the only driver, which was another plus sign, so all efforts were concentrated on Piers. And Frank was as ambitious as Piers was, and that's also a very good combination

"If you know there's a formula there, and you've got a good communication going, there's something about it. Other offers were very tempting. But if Frank could get the money together after he'd done so well with absolutely nothing, he'd have a winning formula. Piers was absolutely right, because look what happened…"

With a works sports car contract in his pocket, and the de Tomaso project looking good on paper, Piers could justifiably think that he had finally made it. That winter he talked to author Richard Garrett, who was writing *Anatomy of a Grand Prix Driver*, due to come out the following summer. Typically Piers was very open and honest, and was keen to make it clear that he wasn't happy with the way he was often perceived by the outside world.

"It doesn't matter a damn what you're like off the circuit, so long as you keep yourself in good condition physically. But if you are not serious, and walking about with a long face all the time, people think you're a sort of playboy. I've had this right the way through my whole career in racing – this business of having a playboy image.

"It matters because people don't take you seriously. A year ago Colin Chapman said to me, 'Are you really serious about motor racing?' I've been racing now for about eight years and it's been my only real means of support since 1964, so I'm obviously serious about it. It's just that I happen to have a fairly lighthearted appearance. I mean, I'm a fairly volatile sort of person. I don't get depressed easily and I'm not particularly nervy. I'm never nervous before a race, or anything like that. Consequently people think that I'm lacking in professionalism.

"I think that very few people who write about motor racing try to look beyond the external things. They'll say a chap is immature in his driving outlook simply because he has a kind of jovial outlook in the pits. In fact, this needn't be so at all. One of the reasons why you no longer get what they call 'characters' in motor racing is because they're frightened of making an impression that they're not serious about it. People no longer ever let themselves go."

The Christmas edition of *Autosport* provided a reminder of the days when racing was all about fun, for under the title 'That flat' Charles Lucas wrote a two-page article about Pinner Road and the wayward antics of its many inhabitants. He revealed a few anecdotes that Frank – now keen to be seen as serious team owner – would probably have preferred to keep quiet. It was only four or five years earlier, but already those days seemed like another age. Everyone was growing up.

Luke made no secret of his admiration for Piers: "The thing that always amazed me was his fantastic confidence. No matter if the car would hardly drag itself along and was on the back row of the grid, Piers was always sure that he had more than a fair chance of winning. To somebody like myself, who suffers from exactly the opposite attitude, this was quite astonishing. I have only just begun to realise the importance of this approach."

It remained to be seen just how good – or bad – the new de Tomaso would be.

Top Frank oversees Piers's first and only appearance in the de Tomaso F2 car at Vallelunga on 12 October. It was the start of Frank's biggest commercial deal to date.

Bottom Piers could barely fit into the de Tomaso, but at Vallelunga he qualified second and showed well until retiring.

Les choses de la vie

Piers in the Alfa Romeo T33/3 on his final visit to Le Mans, just a week before he died. The car retired on Sunday morning after he and Andrea de Adamich had endured a hard slog through the night on seven cylinders.

For the previous three years Piers had been on the way to South Africa or New Zealand even before New Year's Eve, but at the turn of the decade he was able to enjoy a slightly more relaxed Christmas with Sally, Jason and Amos. At some point that winter they also fitted in a seasonal visit to the Rindts in Switzerland, where Jochen noted that Piers "…skied like a girl!"

Jochen's friend Heinz Pruller recalls the visit: "We were in one of the drinking places. We drank a lot, and we had to pee a lot! Suddenly there was a discussion. It was the kind of philosophical moment that you have when you drink sometimes. Jochen said, 'None of us knows how long we are living, and we have a duty just to put in our lives as much as possible, and use our time. This year I want to be World Champion and then retire, because I don't want to be burned out like others at 30. Then you see, I will become the biggest name in motor racing.' I said, 'Well, you have to pass the biggest name and beat the all-time record of Jimmy Clark,' who had 25 wins, and was a two-time World Champion. He said, 'No, look where Jimmy is...'"

Although there was no Tasman trip in 1970, Piers only had a week longer than usual in Europe, for he was soon on a plane to Argentina for his first appearance as a works Alfa Romeo driver. After being run for F3 racing at the start of 1966, and F2 at the end of 1968, the Temporada Series now had yet another format. Two sports car races were to be held in Buenos Aires, with a 1,000kms event on 11 January and a two-heat, 200-mile race a week later. Piers joined up with Andrea de Adamich, who was to be his regular Alfa team-mate. The pair had first come across each other in F3 days, and had always got on well.

"We were together because of our size," says de Adamich. "I was tall, and he was tall as well, so we could do long distance races with just adapting the seat. He was young, but very professional. As a person he was nice to talk with, and he had other interests, not only racing. He was a professional driver, but he wasn't rough. Racing was number one, but not a number one cancelling any other thing like was happening with other drivers. He didn't need F1 alone to be somebody."

There was a respectable entry for the South American double header, including a second Alfa for Rolf Stommelen and Nanni Galli, a works Matra for Jean-Pierre Beltoise and Henri Pescarolo, and a Porsche 908 for Jochen Rindt and sometime Lotus F1 driver Alex Soler-Roig. Jonathan Williams came along to drive the unloved Serenissima.

Piers and de Adamich qualified second, beaten only by Brian Redman's Porsche 917. After Redman retired, they spent the early part of the race trading the lead with the sole Matra, until the Italian car picked up a

misfire and lost time in the pits. When it emerged Piers and Andrea chugged round to the finish on seven cylinders, eventually taking sixth, 11 laps down on the winning Matra.

Piers had a week to kill in Buenos Aires before the next race. Rindt went home, but with Jonathan still around, finding something to do was never going to be difficult. Jackie Stewart was a surprise guest at the second event, but only in the rather unusual role of journalist.

The shorter race proved to be rather more productive for Alfa. It was split into two 26-lap heats, with one race for each driver, and having qualified on pole Piers went first. Veteran Masten Gregory grabbed the early initiative with his Porsche 908, but Piers was soon in front and pulled ahead of the American to win with ease. De Adamich repeated the performance in the second part, and thus the pair scored a comfortable victory on aggregate.

Delighted by a great start to his relationship with Alfa, Piers returned home in plenty of time for Sally's 25th birthday on 25 January. Thanks to his busy racing schedule, it was the first time they had actually been together on that date, and he was happy to spend some time at 70 Drayton Gardens, their home since October. The house was handily placed just two minutes' walk from a cinema, so since moving Piers had renewed his old passion for the movies, popping down the road with various members of the old Pinner Road set. That winter he and Luke saw a re-release of *The Jazz Singer* three times, but his more regular partner was Bubbles Horsley, who by now had progressed to sharing a proper car lot. Arabella von Westenholz, still living with the Courages, recalls the code word: "They used to slope off in the

Piers soon formed a close bond with Andrea de Adamich, his regular co-driver at Alfa.

afternoon, and in order to tell Sally what they were doing it was called afternoon drama classes."

"Ah, the afternoon drama class!" Bubbles confirms. "Obviously midweek he didn't have a lot to do, and if things were quiet on the car lot, he'd ring up and say, 'Are you busy?' and I'd say, 'It's a quiet moment, how about a drama class?' 'I'd say, 'That sounds like a good idea, what's on?' And we go off to the Odeon..."

Sally wasn't fooled for long: "Bubbles and Piers used to go off to drama classes. I used to think in my naivety perhaps he's adding another string to his bow. Get another job on the side! Then I found out they were going off to the movies. He used to escape."

Piers was supposed to join Bruce McLaren, Jo Siffert and others for a drivers' winter sports festival in Switzerland, but cancelled due to a heavy cold. Thus his next important appointment was Friday 12 February, and the launch of the new de Tomaso Grand Prix car. It was a hectic time for Alessandro de Tomaso; just a few weeks earlier his prototype Pantera road car had appeared on Ford's stand at the New York Motor Show.

The still unpainted F1 car was unveiled outside the factory in Modena. Dubbed the 505, it looked a little bulky, but closer inspection revealed that it was extremely well made, much like the F2 machine that Gianpaulo Dallara had also been responsible for. And like its predecessor, it featured front and rear bulkheads

Above left Piers *made the cover of the first issue of* Motor Racing *of the new decade, the picture showing him in the previous year's Brabham BT26.*

Above right Piers *and Andrea de Adamich celebrate victory at Buenos Aires in January.*

Opposite top Piers *sits aboard the de Tomaso 505 prototype in Modena on 14 February. A proud Alessandro de Tomaso stands behind the car.*

Opposite bottom First time out for the de Tomaso in the South African GP at Kyalami. Piers had a difficult time in the overweight machine.

made from cast magnesium – a material that most manufacturers had avoided since Jo Schlesser's fiery crash at Rouen in 1968, although it was also used on the new March. It had been something of a rush job, as the project had only got the go-ahead some four months earlier. Dallara had used the Brabham BT26 as a study aid, and it was no secret that the suspension was derived from the older car.

"We took a lot of ideas," he admits. "We were completely new, and Frank had a Brabham, so we had a big look at it. But our chassis was much stiffer. We used magnesium because we considered that for machining everything, it would be more accurate when it came to fitting the suspension and engine on."

Frank Williams was optimistic that this deal would take the team to a new level. In some ways he was ahead of his time. In later years teams like his would prosper by joining forces with works engine suppliers, and the association with de Tomaso was a pioneering effort, with a twist – it involved not works engines but a works chassis. The main advantage was the sort of factory support he could never have with a second-hand Brabham or McLaren. As the off-the-shelf Cosworth DFV engine was perfectly capable of winning races, it made perfect sense to focus on getting an advantage from the car.

However, as Frank's carefully thought out 1969 proposal showed (see Chapter 8), the actual cost of a car was only a small percentage of the team's overall budget. He still had to supply the engines, mechanics, Hewland gearboxes, transport and pay Piers. There was a little support from Dunlop, and Ward Machine Tools, but Frank was still living on the edge. He explained his concerns to Doug Nye in *Autosport* in the week of the launch: "I'm going to be in for about three times as much as de Tomaso for the season, 61 grand at least."

There was very little time for any meaningful testing with the new car, and the weather didn't help, as Dallara recalls: "I remember in the morning Vallelunga was covered in ice and Piers and everybody was trying to take the ice out of the circuit!"

The season kicked off in South Africa on 7 March, and Sally accompanied Piers on the trip to Kyalami. All talk was of Robin Herd's new March 701, with no fewer than five cars split between the STP-backed works and Tyrrell teams. Stewart put his blue machine on pole, showing that it was possible for a complete newcomer to F1 to build a chassis, bolt on a DFV, and set the pace. A new era of Grand Prix racing was beginning.

In contrast it was soon apparent that the de Tomaso required a lot of work. It was massively overweight – to the tune of 120lb – and on the track Piers found it a real handful. Electrical gremlins didn't help, and he

Another promotional chore for Piers in London, although the job was not without its compensations. 'It's Austin Powers!' said son Amos when he saw this shot…

qualified only 20th in a field of 23, some 2.7sec off Stewart's pole time. In the race he was running 15th when he locked his brakes and clouted a kerb, retiring with damaged suspension on lap 39. It was not an auspicious start.

After the race Frank and Piers had a lengthy debrief with Dallara in the hotel – an unusual occurrence for the times. Piers had learned a lot from his brief association with Herd the previous year, and he had a fair idea of what sort of input the designer required.

"I remember the debrief after the race," says Frank, "It was at the Sleepy Hollow, with Piers and Dallara and me listening in as well. The car had very bad brakes, and they had a serious attitude to the problem. Piers knew what he was talking about; above all he was an intelligent person."

"We decided what to do and what changes to make," says Dallara. "It was very easy working with him, because he gave proper information. Of course he was concentrated on winning, but he also understood the problems. He was positive, always positive. We could immediately understand what was needed."

The company had six weeks to make changes before the next Grand Prix in Spain, and Frank waited to see what Dallara and his men would come up with. While the 505 had a long way to go, the de Tomaso Mangusta road car that Piers and Frank shared in England provided both men with a lot of fun.

"Tomato loaned us a Mangusta," says Williams. "It was a dangerous beast, but Piers was quick in that car. He came back stinking from the brakes. He had come from Essex – 104 miles in 88 minutes or something – and there were no motorways in those days. It was something quite extraordinary. Young men had big egos for cars!"

"He used to come up and stay with me in Huntingdon," says Charles Lucas. "He had a de Tomaso, and the police were always pulling him over. Piers tried to persuade them to be taken for a ride in it instead of booking him…"

Luke says that, despite his growing status, Piers hadn't changed: "Not at all. He'd just got a lot more self-respect. He missed the laughs we used to have in the old days, because it was actually very serious now. I remember him indicating that he was rather sorry that he'd gone on, and we'd all been left behind, doing rather mundane, dreary jobs. But I really don't think he changed at all. He got on so well with Frank. It was a terrific relationship they had, and they both built each other up."

"He didn't change," says Bubbles Horsley. "But obviously he grew up a bit. He definitely matured, no question."

While work progressed at Modena the Williams team missed the Race of Champions at Brands Hatch, but

that suited Piers, as he had to travel to Florida to contest the Sebring 12 Hours classic. Alfa was up to full strength for this World Championship event, with additional cars for Rolf Stommelen/Nanni Galli and Toine Hezemans/Masten Gregory.

Dutchman Hezemans recalls a pre-season test at Vallelunga where Piers made his mark: "Normally Rolf was our fastest driver, but when Piers went out for half an hour, he opened up new targets. He was so incredibly quick that everybody had to think very deeply whether we were good racing drivers at all! He really showed everybody what speed was, and I must say after three days of testing, the whole team was upgraded. Even Stommelen was surprised. If somebody is all of a sudden quicker, and by a lot, then everybody wakes up. I had a lot of respect for people like that. I drove with so many people, and some just cruised around. I have never met a faster driver in my life than Piers, let's put it that way."

It wasn't just the speed that mattered. Piers's enthusiastic and cheerful approach had quickly won the hearts of the whole Alfa team, especially that of eccentric team boss Carlo Chiti.

"Chiti was a fantastic man," says Hezemans. "He was really a sweetheart! A real nice guy, but completely chaotic. He had dogs and cats in his office. I came in one day, and I saw all these dogs and cats on the chair. There were piles of files, left and right, an unbelievable mess…"

"Chiti was a very good man," says his assistant Pierluigi Corbari. "He liked Piers. Sometimes Chiti had a problem with drivers because he didn't understand their mentality. Piers was different. He was a very fast driver, and a very good character. He was a real good guy. He was a driver who never created any problems – this I remember very, very well. He never made polemics. Different from the Italians sometimes! And he had a good instinct for the car."

"They were appreciating for sure a character like Piers Courage," says de Adamich. "Chiti was very happy when the drivers were nice and relaxed, because he was like that. It was very easy to criticise him, and how he was working, but he was really doing a lot with the money he had. The company was owned by the nation, and you can imagine the decisions on the budget. The only way to keep Alfa in races was to do things with the money available. Of course any good result, like Argentina, was important for political reasons."

In Buenos Aires there had been no works Ferrari 512s or Porsche 917s, but at Sebring they were out in force. These 4.5 and 5.0-litre machines had much more power than the 3-litre Alfas, and from now on good overall results would be hard to come by. Piers and de Adamich were the quickest Alfa qualifier in ninth, but the T33/3 was not at all suited to the bumpy airfield track.

"In this kind of circuit with lots of bumps and ups and

downs, the suspension was not very good," de Adamich recalls. "The car was not easy to drive, generally speaking. We didn't enjoy it, let's put it like that!"

After a difficult race that included much time spent in the pits the Alfa finished a humble eighth, 17 laps behind the winning Ferrari. Second place went to a private Porsche 908 shared by Piers's sometime F3 rival Peter Revson and movie star Steve McQueen, who was planning to make a film about Le Mans.

Piers had two weekends off before his next Alfa outing in the BOAC 1,000kms at Brands Hatch, held at the same time that the aborted Apollo 13 mission grabbed the headlines – and the official break-up of the Beatles somehow signalled the end of the sixties.

There was a single car for himself and de Adamich, and Piers qualified it eighth in one of the best fields assembled outside Le Mans, the varied entry including old comrades Jonathan, Luke and Roy Pike. On Sunday the heavens opened and rain soaked every inch of the Kent circuit. It was a day for heroes, and in the soggy early laps Piers made good progress to get up to fifth place behind Vic Elford, Jacky Ickx, Jo Siffert and Chris Amon – drivers with far more sports car experience than he had. He then took the Kiwi's Ferrari for fourth. However, his visor misted up as he arrived at Clearways, and lifting it up in an attempt to clear it, he lost control coming on to the pit straight.

Due to a clash with the Monza 1000kms, Piers missed practice for the International Trophy at Silverstone, and had to start from the back. He's seen here with the oddball USAF helmet that several drivers tried during 1970, as Sally wishes him luck.

A spectacular spin ensued, and using nothing but pure instinct Piers did his very best to steer the red car away from disaster. He almost made it, just clipping the pit wall with the tail. He resumed without too much trouble, and recovered to fifth. However, he was then delayed further by a puncture, and later de Adamich finished a bad day for the team by crashing terminally exactly where Piers had spun earlier.

By now the Anglo-Italian pair had become good friends: "I was putting the Alfa Romeo engine in the F1 McLaren," says Andrea, "So I was spending a lot of my time in England, and there was lot of opportunity to meet each other. I remember I went to his house, in the Chelsea area, and he had a small room over the flat. He had very big books everywhere, and he was writing already the history of his life. I thought what could you have to write? You're very young and you didn't do anything yet! But I was impressed with this room where a young person was already working to write a book."

In fact Piers was working with motoring writer Patrick Macnaghten on this new project. Aged 53, Macnaghten was not a Grand Prix specialist, but had an intriguing CV, and had even written a novel with a motor racing theme.

Macnaghten would turn Piers's thoughts into printed words, and then return them for approval.

"Patrick was this enormously elegant and sophisticated person," Barrie Gill recalled. "You really thought he should have been the chairman of Jaguar and not a writer! He wrote for the *Daily Sketch*. He'd written a book about a woman who'd slept with the Gestapo chief to get secrets for the British. But I can't remember him ever actually being at a Grand Prix."

After a long break since Kyalami the Grand Prix season resumed at Jarama on 23 April. The de Tomaso had reworked suspension, including a wider track in an effort to improve stability. It had also shed a little weight, although it was still well above the limit. However, since the fruitful debrief at Kyalami Dallara had addressed many of the problems Piers had outlined.

"For example, we changed the track because he was saying he had not enough roll stiffness," says Dallara. "He went off the road at Kyalami because we had a lot of 'anti-dive'. The car was not sensitive to braking, meaning the driver could not feel what was the level of braking, because the nose went down very little. So in the second version we changed the front suspension, and the car went better."

There were only 16 starting slots available for the 22 entrants, and there was much controversy over how the organisers were going to keep the big names in the race at the expense of the quicker 'non-seeded' teams. The meeting got off to a dramatic start on Thursday when Rindt suffered a brake failure, and had a huge spin at the first corner. He stopped short of the barrier, but it did little to endear him to the new Lotus 72, a car in which as yet he had no confidence.

On Friday Piers set a time that looked likely to guarantee him a start, and he improved on Saturday, until he had a huge accident at the uphill section behind the pits. In his biography of Jochen Rindt, Heinz Pruller recalled a conversation in Madrid's Luz Palacio hotel the previous night:

"Piers talked about the de Tomaso which 'oversteered like a pig.' Admittedly he had never seen a pig which oversteered, 'but you understand what I mean.' Jochen grinned and Piers had another complaint. 'Going up to that corner on top of the hill in fourth, I was headed directly into the sun and I couldn't see anything.'

"On Saturday during qualification trials, the de Tomaso hit the guardrail at precisely this point. It bounced back and impaled itself on a wooden post. Piers returned on foot. 'I only saw your second impact,' Stewart told him, 'but even that was pretty spectacular.' Jochen and Nina rushed over: 'Did anything break?' Jochen asked suspiciously. Piers shook his head; I asked him if it could have been oil. 'I hope so, otherwise I have no excuse at all; the car suddenly became so light'."

'Bruce bought it at Goodwood today.' And we never mentioned Surrey again."

The same sense of loss was felt in the Courage household. Their tenant Arabella von Westenholz remembers that day well: "That evening I got back from work, and I remember sitting in my room on my bed and Piers came in. I looked at him, and I knew he hated discussing all these things. I may have said something, I don't remember, but he couldn't say anything – he just squeezed my hand and said goodnight and left. We all knew what the dangers were, and he did more than anybody, but he was not about to face them or discuss them."

"He was very upset about that," says Frank. "He was a good friend of Bruce. It really got to him."

There was a familiar routine in such circumstances, as Bette Hill recalls: "I just packed a bag and went over to Pat McLaren's and stayed with her for a couple of days – the girls were doing shift work, caring for her. We'd just stay there the night."

"Piers and Sally were two of the first people to come to my house after Bruce died," says Pat. "We were great, great friends."

Sally admits that the tragedy hit home hard: "When Bruce was killed, it really did start sinking in. I thought that won't happen to me. My Piers is going to be OK. But a chink appeared in my armour. It shook Piers horribly, actually. It really did shake him up. Bruce and Patty were very good friends."

Although McLaren and Laine were the most high profile victims, in the first few months of 1970 there had been an awful roll call of fatalities in motor racing worldwide. Drivers had died in F3 in Europe, in NASCAR in America, and in British club racing. A fierce debate raged in the correspondence pages of the racing magazines, between folk who agreed with Jackie Stewart's crusade for change, and those who felt that unprotected trees at the trackside were all part of the game. Even before McLaren's accident Jackie Stewart's team-mate Johnny Servoz-Gavin had suddenly announced his retirement, admitting that he had been beaten by fear. That set a lot of people thinking.

Sally says that the dangers of her husband's chosen profession was not a subject that easily came up in conversation: "Not really. He was aware of the danger, he was aware of what could happen. The danger was always there. I knew it, and he knew it. You just hope it won't happen to you. I never thought about it. I know it sounds flippant, but I really didn't. I just knew I had a husband who was very good at what he was doing, and had total faith in what he was doing. If you thought about the danger, you would have gone potty.

"Anyway, what's the point of thinking about the danger? You married a man who was doing the job he was doing before you got married, and he wasn't going to change. What could be nicer than a man doing what he loved, so he's happy – and you're happy. You don't sit there thinking, 'Oh my god, he could be killed.' Otherwise you wouldn't have been there, he wouldn't want you around. It would be totally negative, wouldn't it? You're there to support, not be a drag. And if you sat there whinging and whining about the danger then you might as well not have got married or started going out with somebody like that.

"Because your husband was still racing, you had to let a shutter come down. If you didn't, you would have gone barking mad. And you would have been no help to your husband, you would have sat there and cried and whinged. What's the point? The whole point is to be a help, and be a strength, and be a support. It sounds too good to be true, but that's what you did, just put a shutter down. But it was that ghastly year 1970, it was like dominoes, it really did start to hit, it really did."

Just a few days after McLaren's accident the Grand Prix circus reconvened at Spa, where 150mph average lap speeds meant that any mistake could have devastating consequences. In the course of the weekend Piers joined the rest of the Grand Prix Drivers Association members for an emotional debate on matters of safety, and in particular what would happen if it rained on race day, as it had in 1966. Ironically some of those present had been part of a similar fictional debate in John Frankenheimer's *Grand Prix*, filmed that same year. Tensions ran high, and local hero Jacky Ickx refused to support his colleagues when they said they wouldn't race in the wet.

Fabulous overview of the de Tomaso at Spa. It was to be the last time that Grand Prix cars appeared on the original circuit, because safety measures could not cope with rising speeds.

"Jacky was against in principle doing anything that related to safety," says Stewart. "It was a very strong stance he took. It was in Belgium, it was his own country. He said it was a very poor country, and they couldn't afford to do things like that. I was very stuffy about it, and said if they can't afford it, they shouldn't have a race. We were losing a lot of people. At that time, to be frank with you, anything could have happened."

Fortunately the weather stayed good for the duration of the weekend. Piers used his regular car on Friday, and finished the day in an encouraging fourth place. A new car arrived from Italy in time for the final session on Saturday afternoon. Based on the chassis he had crashed in qualifying at Jarama seven weeks earlier, it was the lightest version yet. However, without time to sort it properly, and heavy steering again proving a problem, he made only a small improvement over his Friday time. He slipped to 12th on the final grid, although over the long 3min 30sec Spa lap he was only a second off seventh position.

"I remember the first day we were faster than Ferrari, believe it or not," says Dallara. "But then we had twice

a stupid problem with the steering. The car was not going to be a winning car, but it was probably at the medium level."

As usual Piers made a good start and finished the first lap in ninth place, but he retired at the end of the fourth lap with a loss of oil pressure. Before he hit trouble he was running ahead of the cars that eventually finished fourth, fifth and sixth, so it was clear that another potential points finish had been lost.

The problems in the race were frustrating, but at least the speed was encouraging. Sheridan Thynne recalls chatting to Piers on the phone at around this time: "He was never, even from the first race, downhearted about the Tomato. He was sure it was going to come good. They were confident that they were going to get on top of it. He did say that they were close to moving up a level, and then of course it would be down to him to prove that it was a different level altogether. So he was thinking whereas there hadn't been pressure in the first half of the year, because the car was so bad, they were approaching a stage where he had really got to push."

From Belgium Piers travelled to Le Mans for his fourth appearance in the round-the-clock classic. This year's race had special significance, for Steve McQueen was filming it as the basis for his forthcoming motor racing epic. Jonathan Williams had been hired to drive a Porsche 908, complete with front and rear facing cameras, in the actual event, while Piers was one of many top drivers who had been invited to take part in shooting extra sequences in the weeks after the race.

"It was Andrew Ferguson who went round," says Jonathan. "He had the job of roping people in. He'd gone down the list; everybody had a go. And I was driving this truck round with cameras on!"

Alfa was very much a supporting act to what was sure to be a hard fought battle between the more powerful Porsches and Ferraris. As usual Piers was teamed with de Adamich, and running in the lightweight spec debuted at the 'Ring, the T33s looked pretty competitive. It was hoped that a reliable run would pay dividends, but the car was in trouble almost from the start.

"I started the race," says Andrea, "For the second turn immediately after mine, Piers was driving. And we had the engine going onto seven cylinders. I was thinking to retire, but they took off the plug and said, 'You go.' And we went for another 18 or 19 hours, and by then we were thinking of finishing! We were not very fast, but were keeping on and keeping on, plus we were not using so much of the car, because there was no power, so we had no other problems. That was something we lived together. Each time we were changing seats we were a little bit laughing

Opposite Piers and Frank in the pits at Spa. The new chassis arrived late from Italy, and it was not a good weekend for the team.

Above Piers caught in the afternoon sun at Spa.

GRAND PRIX
ZANDVOORT 1970

GP70/PD/28

FASTEST TIMES FORMULA I, OVER ALL PRACTICING

1.	Rindt	x	(10)	1.18.50
2.	Stewart	x	(5)	1.18.73
3.	Ickx	x	(25)	1.18.93.
4.	Amon	x	(8)	1.19.25
5.	Oliver		(2)	1.19.30·
6.	Reggazoni		(26)	1.19.48
7)	Rodrigues	x	(1)	1.20.07
8.	Miles		(12)	1.20.24
9.	Courage		(4)	1.20.32
10.	Beltoise	x	(23)	1.20.38
11.	Gethin		(20)	1.20.41
12.	Brabham	x	(18)	1.20.76
13.	Pescarolo		(24)	1.20.89
14.	Cevert		(6)	1.21.18
15.	Peterson		(22)	1.21.24
16.	Siffert		(9)	1.21.28
17.	de Adamich		(21)	1.21.36
18.	Gurney	x	(32)	1.21.36
19.	Surtees	x	(16)	1.21.50
20.	Eaton		(3)	1.21.63
21.	Hill	x	(15)	1.21.75
22.	Stommelen		(19)	1.22.21
23.	Lovely		(31)	1.23.37
24.	Moser		(29)	1.24.29

GRAND PRIX
ZANDVOORT 1970

OFFICIAL STARTING GRID FORMULA I Sunday June 21, 1970

MODIFIED

25.
Jackie Ickx GB
Ferrari
1.18.93

5.
Jackie Stewart GB
March Ford
1.18.73

10.
Jochen Rindt A
Lotus 72-Ford
1.18.50

2.
Jacky Oliver GB
BRM
1.19.30

8.
Chris Amon NZ
STP-March-Ford
1.19.25

12.
John Miles GB
Lotus 72-Ford
1.20.24

1.
Pedro Rodriguez M
B.R.M.
1.20.07

26.
Clay Reggazzoni I
Ferrari
1.19.48

23.
J.P. Beltoise F
Matra Simca
1.20.38

4.
Piers Courage GB
De Tomaso Ford
1.20.32

24.
H. Pescarolo F
Matra Simca
1.20.89

18.
Jack Brabham Aus.
Brabham Ford
1.20.76

20.
Peter Gethin GB
McLaren Ford
1.20.41

6.
Francois Cevert F
March Ford
1.21.18

16.
John Surtees GB
McLaren Ford
1.21.18

3.
George Eaton
B.R.M.
1.21.35

9.
Jo Siffert CH
STP March-Ford
1.21.27

22.
Ronnie Peterson S
March Ford
1.21.24

15.
Graham Hill GB
Lotus 72 Ford
1.21.63

32.
Dan Gurney
McLaren Ford
1.21.56

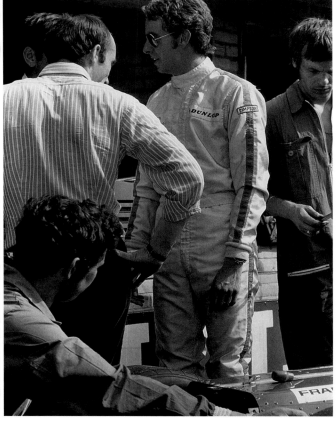

at the beginning, but we became to be very serious, thinking that we'd finish."

Through the night the pair soldiered on. Piers damaged the tail in a brush with a barrier, and then did it again, this time after spinning on his own leaking fuel. Eventually the engine had enough.

"There was very heavy rain, and there was fog," says de Adamich. "It would probably have been a record, running on seven cylinders since the second hour of the race. Then everything broke down at 19 hours, and we were very disappointed. It would be better to break everything immediately."

Piers brought the terminally crippled car into the pits at 10.30am, having run in the top ten despite its problems. It had been a long, hard slog for no reward, and in fact only seven cars finished the race. Still running at the end was Jonathan's Porsche camera car, albeit many laps down.

"Le Mans was the last time I saw him," recalls Jonathan. "He was coming back to be part of the film; they dragged in anybody who was free between races to do a stint. I was going to see him in a week, and we were going to be back doing our number."

Piers flew back to London from Paris on the Monday after the race, but experienced some sort of delay. He was due to meet Patrick Macnaghten that afternoon, but rang from France to postpone their meeting to Tuesday. When they met up at Drayton Gardens they ran through the 1968 season. Inevitably Jim Clark's accident at Hockenheim came up (as recounted in Chapter 8), and Piers was in a generally reflective mood.

Macnaghten recalled the conversation in a *Sunday Mirror* article published some 12 days later. They touched upon what drove him on: "I don't think it's ambition, really,' Piers said reflectively. 'I think it's just there's a tremendous satisfaction in finding something you're good at. And then trying to do it better. And it's all such enormous fun. What was it the poet said – something about one crowded hour of glorious life being worth an age without a name.

"Of course there are times when one feels very down. In the early morning of last Sunday, for instance. I was at Le Mans and very tired. It was pouring and I could hardly see through the windscreen. I suddenly wondered whether it was all worthwhile. I thought of my young wife and my two children, and I wondered.' He paused for a moment, and then looked up and grinned. 'But the race finished, the sun came out and it all looked different.'"

On the Wednesday Piers and Sally went to see Loti Irwin, who was expecting her second child and was in Westminster Hospital. With the Dutch GP weekend fast approaching, and the baby due any minute, they wanted to wish her well as they would be away for the birth.

"They popped in to the hospital to see me just before going off to Zandvoort," she recalls. "It was fraught and tense because Chris had already moved out, he'd already left me. Piers said, 'How are you fixed?' I said, 'I'm alright I'm alright, have fun.'"

Sally has another memory of that week: "The terrible thing was we went out to Annabel's just before we went to Zandvoort. There were 13 at the table, and Piers, who was not really superstitious, said 'I don't want to sit down.' I said, 'Please Piers, don't make a fuss, come on, it'll be alright.'"

Although she says Piers was not superstitious, it wasn't the first time that something odd had occurred: "I remember Nina reading his hand in a car once, and I think she saw something. I remember him snatching his hand away. I don't want to hear any more..."

Thursday was General Election day, and after six years of Labour government it was clear that Ted Heath's Conservatives would emerge victorious. In 1971 Arabella von Westenholz wrote of Piers acknowledging the news that morning: "He had an impish grin on his face. 'They're in – the Conservatives have won!,' he said. The look on his face was so wicked that I thought he was teasing. He stood there at the door, his feet turned out like Charlie Chaplin. He ran his hand though his hair and suddenly realised he had to leave – he had an airplane to catch. With a fair amount of overweight – Sally could never travel light – they got into the car and I waved to them from the front door as they drove away. It was a typical beginning to a weekend during the motor racing season. It was the last time I saw Piers."

Along with most of the other leading drivers, Piers and Sally were staying in an apartment at the Hotel Bouwes in Zandvoort. As folk arrived at the track the talk of the paddock was the accident that had befallen Jack Brabham in private testing on the previous Wednesday. The triple World Champion had suffered a puncture at the fast right-hander before the East Tunnel, and his BT33 had speared off the road into the wire mesh fencing that now protected the angled grass bank.

"We were tyre testing – I had a tyre go down," he recalls. "I was driving Rolf Stommelen's car. He was supposed to be there for the test and he didn't turn up, and Ron Tauranac said you'd better take his car out and give it a run. A rear tyre went, and I went off sideways into the sand, and of course when the wheel hit the sand it was just like a shovel going in and it rolled three or four times through a wire fence. When I came to rest I was upside down and I couldn't get out, as the wire was

Top left Piers talks to Gianpaulo Dallara at Zandvoort. The Italian engineer soon formed a good relationship with his driver.

Top right and bottom left The starting grid for the 1970 Dutch GP. The de Tomaso had begun to improve, and Piers was getting closer to the front-running pace.

Bottom right Piers and Frank at Zandvoort.

wrapped around the car. I was sitting there hanging in the seatbelts, I had the fuel running out of the car, although luckily it was disappearing into the sand. Being a test day it took forever for somebody to come over. I had my finger on the fire extinguisher in case there was any sign of fire. Eventually someone came along and started pushing the car up. I thought I'd better undo my seatbelts so I can get out in a hurry, and I fell out of the seat and ricked my neck!"

It was obvious that Jack had enjoyed a lucky escape. There were mixed views of Zandvoort's fencing, for while it had slowed the car, every driver's worst fear was being trapped in a situation that potentially involved fire.

"They had chain link fencing, and it was a big breakthrough at that time," says Jackie Stewart. "We all thought it was the thing to have."

The entry included three promising rookies. Clay Regazzoni made his Grand Prix debut at Ferrari, while François Cevert replaced the recently retired Servoz-Gavin in the second Tyrrell March. In addition Peter Gethin, Piers's Lucas F3 team-mate back in 1965, was at McLaren. The team was back after missing Spa, although a brave Denny Hulme was present only in the role of spectator, his hands still bandaged after a recent incident at Indianapolis.

Williams was one of several teams to be compromised by recent problems at Cosworth, a problem with a batch of crankshafts creating a shortage of serviceable engines. Thus the team faced the unusual situation of having two chassis, but just one DFV. Piers started out with the newer wide track car, as raced at Spa. The steering had been revised, following the problems at Monaco, and there were modifications to the fuel system.

Not long after Friday's action got underway there was another huge accident not far from the point where Brabham had crashed two days earlier. The victim this time was Pedro Rodriguez, who wrote off his BRM, fortunately without doing any harm to himself. Once again it was thought that a puncture was to blame, and there was some concern about debris on the circuit. The following day he had a tyre come completely off the rim, which gave Dunlop food for thought.

Piers finished the Friday session in 20th place, having found the revised steering too heavy. Gianpaulo Dallara decided to try the narrow track rear suspension for Saturday, so it was duly borrowed from the spare chassis. Piers was immediately quicker on Saturday morning, but ended his session in the sand after hitting oil at Tarzan, the hairpin at the end of the straight. The mechanics retrieved the car and cleaned out the sand, and Piers was able to get out for the final session in the afternoon. As at Monaco, he qualified in ninth place. He was 1.8sec off Rindt's pole winning Lotus 72, which was now going well in revised form, but nevertheless it was an encouraging position in a field of 24. Zandvoort had

been kind to Piers in 1964, when he first made his mark in F3, and in 1967, when he did the same in F2. With a reliable run on Sunday the Dutch track could this time provide a breakthrough for the de Tomaso.

"Piers and Dallara worked well together," says Frank. "By the time we got to Zandvoort, the end of the road, the car was much better, and quite different. Each one was better. That's what the deal would have been, just a lot of development. Dallara was competent, a good engineer, de Tomaso was a very ambitious man, and had a fair amount of wealth and money available to spend on the project."

As ever Piers was a popular man in the paddock, sought out by friends for a quick chat about this and that.

"It's funny what sticks in your mind," says Chris Amon, "But I do remember talking to Piers about the British election, which had just happened a couple of days before Zandvoort."

"We spoke directly at Zandvoort during practice," says de Adamich. "I admired Frank Williams, and I was watching the de Tomaso project closely, because originally de Tomaso was interested to be supported by Alfa Romeo on his project, and I was involved."

Zandvoort also allowed Piers and Sally to catch up with Sally Swart, who as Sally Stokes had previously

Left Piers in the de Tomaso in the pit lane during practice at Zandvoort with mechanic Pat Kay.

Above Piers captured in relaxed mood in the pits at Zandvoort.

been Jim Clark's girlfriend. In 1967 she married Dutch sports car racer Ed Swart, who also happened to be assistant clerk of the course for the Grand Prix.

"I first met Piers when he turned up with that F3 gang, who were so full of joie de vivre," says the 'other' Sally. "I admired them – they took life by the horns and lived it at full throttle. Piers was always a very kind person, and he was gentler than most racing drivers. We all had dinner together the night before the race, and I've never forgotten that. Jochen and Nina were there too, and maybe Frank. We went to Bloemendaal, which is a little village north of Zandvoort. It was just a merry dinner, lots of laughter. I don't remember anyone saying anything memorable – we were just having a jolly time."

That weekend there was also a GPDA party, an event that usually saw the presentation of the Wolfgang von Trips prize to the most promising newcomer. Stewart, Mike Parkes, Chris Irwin and Jackie Oliver were previous winners, but this time it wasn't awarded.

Zandvoort was noted for its changeable weather, and Saturday night was pretty miserable, as Denis Jenkinson noted in *Motor Sport*: "The North Sea mist had covered everything, and any building more than three storeys high was fast disappearing. It was an evil looking mist and obviously did not bode well for Sunday, and the whole of Zandvoort took on a heavy and gloomy atmosphere."

The mist was still in the air on the morning of 21 June. Piers and Sally planned to stay on for the usual prize giving and party after the race, so they didn't check out of the Hotel Bouwes before setting off for the track. Meanwhile Dallara, preferring to watch the race at home on TV, headed back to Italy. "I remember before leaving I wished Sally, 'Good day,'" he recalls. "But it was a terrible day."

For a while, there was some threat of rain, but otherwise it was a routine morning. A large crowd began to fill up the dunes around the circuit, confident that with the race starting early they could beat the traffic and get home in time to watch Pele's Brazil play Italy in the evening's World Cup Final.

Heinz Pruller described the scene in his Rindt biography: "Frank Williams, as always on race day, activated himself and his mechanics into a slight excitement. Piers and Sally arrived in the paddock and Piers immediately took up the question of tyres. He was one of the last to roll down to the start. Piers handed Frank his spare goggles and his wristwatch. Piers was no longer nervous but he didn't talk much. Frank gave him a casual thumbs up: 'Cheerio, see you later.'"

Sally has very clear memories of that morning: "Piers was very funny. He always came to say goodbye, but there

Fraught early battle for seventh place in Holland. The Lotus 72 of John Miles heads Piers, Jean-Pierre Beltoise, Peter Gethin (hidden behind the de Tomaso) and Henri Pescarolo.

FERODO LAP CHART

Date 2/6/70 **Event** Dutch Grand Prix **Circuit** Zanvoort

Driver P. Courage **Car** De Tomaso **Axle Ratio**

No.	CAR TYPE	DRIVER	LAPS TO GO / LAPS GONE	79/1	78/2	77/3	76/4	75/5	74/6	73/7	72/8	71/9	70/10	69/11	68/12	67/13	66/14	65/15	64/16	63/17	62/18	61/19	60/20	59/21	58/22	57/23	56/24	55/25
25	Jackie Ickx		1	25	25	co	co	co	co	co	co	co	co	co	co	co	co	co	co	co	co	co	co					
26	Clay Regazzoni		2	co	co	25	25	25	25	25	25	25	25	25	25	25	25	25	25	25	25	25	25	25	25			
10	Jochen Rindt		3	2	2	2	5	5	5	5	5	5	5	5	5	5	5	5	5	5	5	5	5	5	5	5		
12	John Miles		4	5	5	5	2	2	2	2	2	2	2	2	2	2	2	2	2	2	2	2	2	1	1	1		
2	Jackie Oliver		5	12	12	1	1	12	1	1	1	1	1	1	1	1	1	1	1	1	1	1	1	2	2	2		
1	Pedro Rodriguez		6	1	1	12	12	26	26	26	26	26	26	26	26	26	26	26	26	26	26	26	26	26	26			
5	Jackie Stewart		7	4	4	4	4	23	12	12	12	12	12	12	4	4	4	4	4	4	4	4	4	4	12			
6	Francois Cevert		8	23	23	26	26	4	4	4	4	4	4	12	12	12	12	12	12	12	12	12	12	12	23			
8	Chris Amon		9	6	26	22	23	24	23	22	23	8	23	23	23	23	23	23	23	23	23	23	23	22				
9	Jo Siffert		10	26	24	24	20	32	20	20	20	20	20	20	20	20	20	20	20	20	16	16	16					
22	Ronnie Peterson		11	2	20	18	24	18	26	24	26	24	24	18	18	18	18	18	18	18	18	18	18					
23	J.P. Beltoise		12		18			23	18		18	18	24	24	24	6	16	16	16	9	9	9	9					
24	H. Pescarolo		13			5			0	co	6	16	16	16	16	16	16	2	9	9	9	24	24	24	24			
18	Jack Brabham		14						9	9	9	9	9	9	9	9	9	9	26	24	24	15	15	15	22			
20	Peter Gethin		15						22	22	22	22	22	22	15	22	25	13	15	15	15	22	22	22	6			
32	Dan Gurney		16						6	22	6	6	6	22	8	22	22	22	22	22	6	6	6	15				
3	George Eaton		17						15		15	15	15	3	5	6	6	6	6	6	3	3	3					
15	Graham Hill		18						3		3	3	3		3	3	3	3	3	3								
4	Piers Courage		19																									
16	John Surtees		20																									

was something very wrong, like he sensed something ghastly was going to happen. He was really weird that day, and there was something very, very unusual about his behaviour. Not being able to talk to even Jochen, things like that, which was very strange for him.

"Normally he would always sort of give one a kiss, or pat one's head, 'see you later', give you his watch, things like that. 'Don't you go off and start talking to Nina. Try and do some lap times, try and get it right'. Before that race, he was uncommunicative, he wouldn't talk. He just gave me his watch and his ring, and he went off. And not a word. Just a funny look, a very funny look. A look like 'I don't think I'll see you again'. But I didn't recognise it as such then."

Sally joined the other wives and girlfriends on the crowded roof of the pits. However, she was not able to sit with her best mate: "I was talking to Nina, and then we had to go back to our respective pits."

Nina recalls it well: "We were always trying to sit together on top of the pits, chairs next to each other, and do these lap chart things. We were always being told off by Piers and Jochen, you can't do that, you've got to go and sit over your pit, and you go there, you can't sit together. So I had to leave her."

Sally settled down in a folding camping chair with her pad of blank Ferodo-supplied lap charts and a pencil. At races she usually carried a book with her in order to fill in any spare time, and to help calm the nerves, and on this weekend she was working on a Nevil Shute paperback.

The cars left the pit area one by one, some of them performing dragster starts, before making their way round to the grid, where Rindt, Stewart and Ickx

Race Result

1st ....

2nd ....

3rd ....

Average Speed ....

Fastest Lap ....

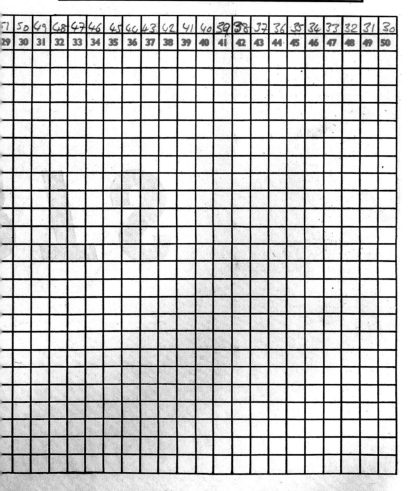

7	50	49	48	47	46	45	44	43	42	41	40	39	38	37	36	35	34	33	32	31	30
29	30	31	32	33	34	35	36	37	38	39	40	41	42	43	44	45	46	47	48	49	50

comprised the front row. The starter seemed determined to make a meal of his job, standing in front of the field until the last second, before dashing to the pit wall and scrambling onto his rostrum. Distracted by his antics, some drivers crept forward and dabbed their brakes just as he finally decided to wave the flag. Ickx surged ahead and claimed the line into the first corner, while on the second row a cooked clutch caused Amon to stagger away, giving those immediately behind, including Piers, some anxious moments.

From his ninth place on the grid Piers made a good getaway. He ducked past Amon, and as Regazzoni struggled to get off the line in his first Grand Prix start, slotted into seventh. He held that position for three laps until Regazzoni got back past. A lap after that Beltoise demoted the de Tomaso to ninth, but Piers immediately fought back to reclaim eighth next time round.

Piers was in the thick of a superb midfield dice, harrying Lotus number two John Miles, and confidently holding off Beltoise, Gethin and Pescarolo. On lap 12 he moved ahead of Miles to claim seventh. With some 68 laps still to run, it appeared that he now had a good chance of earning his first points of the season. Gethin then disappeared from the chasing bunch: "It was slippery in the race, because of the sand. I fell off and ended up on top of a dune somewhere."

Meanwhile Piers began to pull away from Miles, and with Regazzoni some way up the road, he was now circulating on his own. But on lap 23, he didn't come round.

"I remember running with Piers for the first 15 laps or so, and then he overtook me," says Miles. "He was flying. There were some fast sweeping corners at the back of the circuit, which were almost all flat out, or nearly flat out. He gained a couple of corners on me. Then I just saw this plume of smoke, and passed a burning car. You go past so fast you're not absolutely sure who's crashed. You're so busy, and that part of the circuit was not somewhere where you just drifted past and had time to look."

It was Piers. The de Tomaso had plunged off the road at the fast right-hander before the East Tunnel, close to where Brabham had crashed five days earlier in testing. The red car went through the single layer of catch fencing, rolled along the sharply sloping bank, and tumbled back into the fencing from the other side, coming to rest right at the edge of the circuit. Even before it stopped moving, the car burst into flames, and within seconds a thick pall of smoke hung over the sand dunes, as spilled fuel ignited the parched grass.

Fifteen-year-old spectator Rob Petersen was watching with his father from the dunes above: "What exactly happened, nobody could tell, including the people who were surrounding us. But there was immediately fire, before the car really stopped. I assumed that as soon as he went through the fence one of the fuel tanks was broken or whatever. Because it was dry, it was summer, the grass caught fire, so it was very difficult to see anything. It was such a heavy fire, because of this magnesium. It was coming out of the car like burning sparks, and it was immensely hot. We were about 20–25 metres higher on the dunes, and it was such a big fire, we had to move. He couldn't have known anything about it."

In fact in the initial impact a front wheel had been torn from the car, and struck the driver with sufficient force to dislodge his distinctive USAF helmet from his head. Piers was almost certainly dead even before the fire started.

Sally Courage undertook lap charting duties at the Dutch GP, just as she did at every race. This poignant document shows how her work came to an abrupt stop on lap 23.

Let it be

It took several minutes for a fire engine to arrive at the scene, but it was already too late to save Piers. Here Ronnie Peterson's March passes the accident.

In her folding chair on top of the pits Sally automatically noted the numbers of the next cars through – Miles and Beltoise – before realising that Piers was missing. Abandoning her lap chart, she looked back down the long pit straight. And like everyone else, she saw the smoke rising from behind the dunes.

Missing at the same time was Jo Siffert, who had been running in 12th place. There was anxiety in the March pits, but it soon emerged that the Swiss driver had stopped with an engine failure just after the accident scene, and was returning to the pits on foot. The smoke was indeed from the de Tomaso.

"Piers was going well at Zandvoort," Frank recalls. "He went missing, and I just remember seeing the pall of smoke. I remember thinking it could be him, then it was, yes it's him, but he's out of the car, no problem at all."

Reacting to a report from the trackside, circuit commentator Philip Keller made an announcement over the public address to the effect that Piers was out of the car. Word went round a relieved pit area, and Ken Tyrrell showed Jackie Stewart a signal reading, 'Piers OK.' At some point a Citroën ambulance drove onto the circuit.

Fashion photographer Justin de Villeneuve, a close friend and guest of Jochen Rindt and Bernie Ecclestone, was on the pit roof: "I was standing with Sally, and we were having a giggle. Then we saw the smoke rise from the other side of the track. The announcer said that Piers had crashed, but it seemed to be under control."

"We came down off the roof of the pits," Sally recalls. "I can just remember the accident, and seeing this ghastly fire. Nobody knew quite who it was for a couple of laps. I knew something had happened to Piers, because he had disappeared. But I think Siffert had disappeared at the same time... so there was a bit of confusion. Then people came and said, 'It's alright, he's gone to hospital.' That was the most awful thing.

"I was with Sally Swart. We'd heard this announcement that he was OK, they'd announced that he was all right. Frank had already come and said, 'He's OK, and I'll take you to the hospital.' So we went together and we sat in our car. Sally said, 'I'll get you a drink,' and I said, 'Could you get me a vodka and tonic?' I just felt rather shaky. She went off and got me a gin and tonic, and I can't drink gin, so I didn't really drink it. Someone wrote that we drank champagne. It's such a lie."

"I do remember getting her a drink," says Sally Swart. "I can't remember what it was – I don't know where I would have got hard alcohol. She asked for my help, because I lived in Holland and was a local girl by then, and she knew that."

Gradually the grim truth filtered back to race control. Later it was suggested that the crashing de Tomaso had cut the cable that fed the ancient army field telephone at the marshal's post closest to the accident. The report that Piers was safe came from an official at the next corner, who had seen a figure dashing around the car. It was a marshal in a fire suit.

The Citroën ambulance returned to the pits with no occupant. Frank was desperate to get confirmation of Piers's condition from Clerk of the Course, John Corsmit.

"Then they were not so sure he was out of the car," says Williams. "I waited around a bit, and then they confirmed a bit later on that he was in the car and had been burned to death. I remember saying to John, 'You must tell me three times definitely, is Piers dead, before I can go and tell his wife.' I asked him three times, and each time he said, 'Yes.'"

Heinz Pruller recalls the scene: "I remember Frank Williams, a very shaken guy, but still British, standing up. He said, 'Can you officially tell me what happened?,' they said, 'Yes, Piers Courage is dead.' Frank said, 'Can you repeat clearly, Piers Courage of England is dead...' Those were his words."

Frank now had the awful task of breaking the news to Sally, who was still sitting in a car behind the pits.

"And that's when Frank did this sort of dance to the car," she says, "He didn't come straight towards me; he went round all the different cars, so I knew something was wrong. He obviously now had to come and tell me the complete opposite. It's a helluva thing to come to say to someone, isn't it? He couldn't go round the houses – he had to say, 'I'm sorry, he's dead.' I'll never forget it. Can you imagine having to tell somebody that, after being told he's alive? It was wicked, absolutely ghastly. I remember getting out of the car and saying, 'Let's go to the hospital.' Then we couldn't get out of there. I remember going from one motorhome to

The first indication of trouble as smoke rises from behind the sand dunes at Zandvoort. At first it wasn't clear if the car of Piers or Jo Siffert was involved.

another. I wanted to go back to the hotel and for people to go away."

"She told me later she saw me coming," says Frank, "And she knew what I was going to tell her. She didn't know if he was dead or not, but when she saw me coming towards her, she knew what I was going to say. Somebody took care of her, fortunately."

"They asked me immediately to rush off to see Sally," says Nina. "She was sitting in the car with Frank Williams. You knew immediately. Sally was very, very upset. She said, 'Say it's not true, say it's not true.' But I knew, I think Frank told me."

Also stepping in to help was the oft-maligned BRM boss Louis Stanley, who came into his own in such circumstances, and knew exactly what needed to be done: "Sally was distraught. She thought if we could get him to the mobile hospital all would be well, but sadly it couldn't be. It was really heartbreaking when she got the news."

Frank's next task was to contact Piers's parents at Fitzwalters, before they heard the news from the media. He went to the press office and dialled Brentwood 191, the number he'd called Piers on so many times in the past. Pruller heard the call: "He called the parents and said, 'I would like you to know that Piers was dead instantly.'"

"I'd been at a dance with some friends quite a long way from home," says Piers's younger brother Andrew. "Holland was one hour ahead of England. I didn't realise that, and I'd assumed that the race was just about to begin. I rang home, and they told me. It was a terrible shock. Someone drove me home from there in my car – it took a long time to sink in."

Meanwhile the sad news quickly went around the paddock.

"We were on the roof," says Bette Hill. "We were all sitting up there in little camping seats doing all the timing, and I will never, ever forget that horrendous pall of smoke. We had been told he was all right, but gloom fell upon the place. Denny came up to me, with his hands still bandaged, and said, 'Not another.' And we realised then that Piers had gone – in the most horrendous way."

As always in those days, the race ran to its conclusion. For lap after lap, the drivers passed the smouldering wreckage of the de Tomaso, the magnesium parts making it almost impossible to extinguish. At some point marshals and firemen covered it with a tarpaulin, and then covered that with sand. Piers was still in the cockpit.

"There was a smell of burning," says Jackie. "You don't lose that. We had to go right through the smoke when we were racing, and there was a stench. The fire was very real. But you never stopped in cases like that. You never stopped, it was part and parcel of the job. Racing drivers were made of different stuff in those days.

"I remember Piers was wearing an unusual helmet. It was one we'd got from America, and I had raced it as well. It was a fighter pilot's helmet, and it was considered safer because it was crushable, more deformable. That was the awful thing about the accident. I remember seeing the helmet lying on the ground."

Rindt dominated the race, and Jackie followed home in second. Jochen stopped at the scene of the accident on the slowing down lap, asking for news. Back in the pits, he handed his own helmet to Bernie Ecclestone, who confirmed the worst.

"I remember talking with Jochen," says Pruller. "He was really in tears, you know. He saw the helmet in the fire, and he knew what happened."

Stewart had seen Piers's helmet, but he'd also seen Tyrrell's positive signal, and thus had assumed that he was all right. He described the aftermath of the race in *Faster*, his diary of that tragic season: "As I was stepping out of the car, Ken motioned me to remove my helmet so I could hear what he had to say, and it was then, I think, that I knew Piers was dead. Someone had given me a Coke and I remember smashing the bottle on the ground as I went off to the transporter. Yet, despite it all, my mind was cold. Absolutely cold. In neutral. All my concentration had been exhausted and I felt empty, as I always do at the end of the race. Piers's death had come as a shock, but there was no way left for me to show it. I was drained. There was nothing left inside of me."

After a solemn podium ceremony at the track, it was announced that the prize giving and other planned festivities were cancelled. Jochen climbed onto the pit roof and bravely gave Pruller an interview for Austrian TV, saying, "That somebody is lost in this sport is nothing new. But it is bitter indeed when it happens to be your friend."

Other friends of Piers, with whom he had shared so much over the past decade, were to hear the news second-hand.

"I just heard it on the radio," recalls Charles Lucas. "I was driving down the A1 at the time with my wife, and I had to stop. Chris Irwin had had a horrendous accident at the Nürburgring a couple of years before… It was in a horrendous patch for us. I simply couldn't believe it."

"My brother-in-law telephoned me," says Sheridan Thynne. "I suppose he'd heard on the radio. The race was an hour earlier than I thought it was, so I wasn't really thinking about it much. Four or five years earlier we thought Piers took enormous risks, and by the time he was racing seriously in F1 we didn't expect him to have an accident, so I was deeply shocked by it."

Meanwhile Nina, Helen and Sally Swart took Sally to the Bouwes Hotel.

"The four of us went back together," says Sally Swart. "The boys were still driving, and Ed was doing his organising. I remember Sally saying in the car, 'Why

Above *Officials place a tarpaulin on the smouldering wreck of the de Tomaso. The magnesium chassis bulkheads and wheels kept the fire going.*

Opposite *A distraught Jochen Rindt on the podium. All other ceremonies were cancelled, and the Austrian headed to the hotel to find his wife, Nina.*

Piers? He never harmed anyone.' We were all devastated. Then we all went up to the room. She just wanted us to hold her hand. I remember trying to think of something to say, and I couldn't think of anything to comfort her."

"I remember after the accident Sally went completely to pieces," says Helen. "I went back to the hotel with her and Nina, and we went into the room and packed all his things. The impression of his head was still on the pillow… We packed the things and put everything together."

"I had left and I didn't even know Jochen had won," says Nina. "Someone said, 'You know Jochen won,' I thought, 'Oh my God, how can he win?' Not that he won because of what happened, but he won. It was a very weird situation. I've seen film when he gets the wreath. He's not happy at all."

"We were in the sitting room," Helen recalls, "and I remember thinking, 'I've got to keep all this together,' because Nina was all upset because of Sally. I can't remember what I did, but I acted very positively, anyway. Then Jackie came on the scene, and he organised getting Sally back to England."

Stewart described the scene in *Faster*: "Sally was quiet

from a sedative Helen had given her on the way over, and Helen herself had been crying. But she managed to stay strong – how, I don't know. Frank Williams was there too. He had been Piers's best friend for years, and was taking it hard. He needed to be with somebody now and he stayed with me all the while. There were people to be called and arrangements had to be made to get Sally back to England. Frank called Piers's mother, but he was in no condition to do anything else."

"Frank was in tears, I was very touched by that," says Sally Swart. "I think Ed came and got me, because I realised I couldn't do much more for her at that point. Then Jochen and Jackie came back and they kind of took over."

In fact Bernie Ecclestone found space for Sally on his private plane, and together with the Rindts and Justin de Villeneuve, they made their way to the airport. On the journey, an emotional Rindt spoke of retirement. Heinz Pruller would later hear the details of the conversation: "There was the famous ride in the taxi, when he told Bernie he was going to stop; I got it independently later from Jochen, from Nina and from Bernie. Jochen said he wanted to retire at the end of the year, and Bernie said, 'If you feel like retiring, stop now.'"

"I remember Jochen talking about throwing the towel in," says de Villeneuve, "but that's a natural reaction.

Sally sobbed all the way, but she was heavily sedated. It was a nightmare. Bernard organised the plane, getting her home – he organised everything. He was marvellous at that, and always kept a cool head."

On arrival in England the group went first to Ecclestone's country house in Farnborough to pick up Justin's girlfriend Twiggy, who had spent the weekend there. Then they headed to London and 70 Drayton Gardens, the house Piers had left just four days earlier. Friends and family had already rallied round and were waiting for Sally's arrival.

Daphne Thorne, who had been Sally's daily help for several years, did her best to get things organised: "Their nanny rang me and said, 'Will you come over?,' and I heard the news from her. It was terrible. The telephone was ringing, and friends began arriving, and we just had to wait until Lady Sarah got back. You can imagine what it was like, the hustle and bustle, trying to find things for people to drink or get them something to eat. Everything happened at once."

Arabella von Westenholz also found herself in the middle of the storm: "I had been out and I was walking back along Drayton Gardens when I saw Mrs T, the housekeeper cum daily. She did everything – a bit of cooking, looking after us all. I didn't know why she was there, because it was a Sunday, and we weren't expecting her. I said, 'What are you doing?' Her face was absolutely bright red. She said something terrible had happened…"

"I heard it in the country and came up to meet Sally in London," says her sister Frances Denman. "It was one long ghastliness."

It was late when Sally finally arrived, as Nina recalls: "It was such a scene. For some reason I remember that Twiggy and Justin de Villeneuve were with us. We took Sally straight home. Her mother and everyone was there to greet her. Her mother wasn't a big fan of racing drivers, so she wouldn't even say hello to us. She just snubbed us. We continued and stayed with Bernie, and Justin and Twiggy were there for dinner. It was such a weird scene…"

Meanwhile the devastated Frank stayed behind in Holland.

"I had dinner that night in the Bouwes with Frank and Jackie," says Louis Stanley. "He really felt it very deeply. At that time it wasn't a question of trying to place blame. When there's genuine grief, that sort of thing is put at the back. It was just taking stock of what had happened."

Sadly, some of Piers's closest friends didn't hear the news until Monday.

"I was in France, flying a plane at an air show near Cannes," says Jonathan Williams. "I went to the airport and said, 'What are we doing today, how's everybody?' I thought people were looking at me funny. Gianni Bulgari, from the jewellers in Rome, was a partner in this aeroplane outfit. He took me on one side and said, 'You haven't heard then?' 'Heard what?' 'Piers has been killed.' So I was out of the airport and on a Nice to London plane that afternoon. It was very, very miserable."

"I was in Brussels," Charlie Crichton-Stuart recalled. "I picked up the paper and it said the typical thing – Grand Prix driver killed in fireball. And that was Porridge. That was the first I knew about it. It was a shock, because it's always the nice people who get killed, isn't it?"

That morning Frank, Jackie and Louis Stanley returned to the circuit. Stewart described what happened in *Faster*: "There was a horrible, tragic smell in the area and it was absolutely quiet, only the wind coming in off the sea, rustling the dune grass, and the three of us there on that empty road. We drove our small road car into the corner at an angle corresponding to the traces of tyre marks left by Piers's de Tomaso, and determined the point of initial impact and where the car finally stopped. The accident seemed to have been set off by a particular bump in the circuit which must have upset the balance of Piers's car as it went into the corner. It hit a fence post

and the impact ripped off a wheel and part of the front suspension; the wheel had spun back and taken off Piers's helmet."

Frank remembers that grim day: "I had to go to the police station to identify the remains of the car. It took them a long time to put the fire out, because the bulkheads were magnesium. What was left of the car was in something like a little porter's barrow from a station, a wire grill caged thing, all the bits were in there. There was nothing left of the monocoque.

"Piers, I never saw. But his helmet turned up. It had a big black smudge on the front, from a tyre, and a little bit of hair and scalp on the inside as far as I remember. I thought about it later and I wondered if the front suspension tore away, and that caused the accident, and the wheel came back. I just don't know. No one ever stood up and said I definitely I saw him doing this, or the car went wrong, or whatever. Dunlop at the time didn't say, 'Oh shit, sorry.' A tyre could have lost pressure. It could have been anything. It could have been a mistake, or it could have been a car control problem."

The wreck provided no clues, but the front wheel that had been torn off survived the fire. Stewart noted that he had it returned to Dunlop for inspection, although company engineer Alec Meskell can't recall it coming back, or any serious discussion about the possibility of a

tyre failure, despite the incidents involving Brabham and Rodriguez earlier that week.

No definite cause for the accident was ever determined, but teenage spectator Rob Petersen – who would later become part of the Zandvoort organisation – remains convinced it wasn't a driver error: "Everyone around me said it happened so suddenly that something was not right with the car. If it was a driver error, I think he wouldn't have crashed there. If you made a mistake you'd crash further around the corner. That's the reason why the fences were so close to the track, because normally the crash would be further away. So something went wrong before the corner. I'm certain it was a technical problem."

However, today Stewart still suggests that Piers probably lost control on a bump while running on the absolute limit – a scenario that he also suspects claimed his close friend François Cevert at Watkins Glen three years later. Had Piers paid the price for his acknowledged bravery through the fastest corners? At the time Jackie tried to take an analytical approach at the accident scene.

"In my case I became very detached from things like that," he says. "It sounds hard and unfeeling, but there was a compartmentalisation of emotion. The mind was able to block things off. You just had to do that, because we were there for a reason. Why would it not happen

Every race wife's moment of dread

PHOTONEWS

Lady Sarah keeps calm with a book before race starts ... then tragedy comes in a pall of smoke

Across the Dutch countryside a pall of smoke rises after Piers Courage's car crashes and explodes

A PALL of smoke ... and for a young wife and mother who sits in the sunshine the ever-present dread of a woman who lives with danger becomes a tragic reality.

This yesterday was the moment that made beautiful 25-year-old Sarah Courage a racing driver's widow on a Sunday afternoon in Holland.

For her the dangers of the car racing which her husband knew, loved, have been with her since childhood.

Her father was Earl Howe, the great driver of the pre-war days, when the racing car was safer.

CONFIDENT

Pictures by VICTOR BLACKMAN

FATAL LURE OF THE CHEQUERED FLAG...

by **MICHAEL KEMP**

SKETCH MOTORING CORRESPONDENT

A NOTHER racing driver died yesterday. And if anyone asks why he took the inherent, fearsome risks of the game, the answer is probably the same as to that other old question of why people climb Everest: because the chequered flag, like the mountain peak, is there.

Jim Clark, the world's leading racer when he died in 1968 in a still unexplained circuit crash, put it neatly to me once.

"I just enjoy," he said, "proving to myself that I can do something, like taking a corner, better, faster than it's ever been done before."

Piers Courage, rich, handsome, 28-year-old Etonian, who was killed in the Dutch Grand Prix at Zandvoort yesterday, knew the dangers of his trade as well as anyone who reached the starting grid.

He came second in the race in which that other world champion, Graham Hill was nearly killed last October in America.

Ambitions

Afterwards he was asked about his ambitions. He said these were "to get as far as I can, and to go on racing for as long as I can."

He approached the risks calmly ... "When you're driving you're never frightened. I used to scare myself quite a lot because I did not know what I was doing. But now I have things under control."

He added: "One never tries to drive over one's head. That's a big mistake."

Like all the racing professionals, Courage raced coldly and calculatingly. But yesterday the incalculable happened.

His De Tomaso car spun off the circuit into the trees and exploded. He was rich enough not to need to race for money. He probably made only a tenth of the £100,000 that the current world champion Jackie Stewart pulls in.

Many others race for much, much less.

So why take odds that few bookmakers would offer against a possible fatal accident?

Briefly ... a love of speed, an in-built urge to win, and as Jim Clark said, an urge to go on winning and proving yourself faster than anyone else

It is a demand that tremendous toll ... C—— brewery chief, h—— months. He —— two chil——

in a 180 m.p.h. crash at Goodwood in a test run. Just before 37-year-old Martin Brain died at Silverstone in his Cooper BRM.

And ex-world champion Denny Hulme is still recovering from the severe burns he suffered in a crash at Indianapolis.

Burns. That, if there is one thing to scare a racing driver, is the fear.

Fire disfigures. And the thought is terrifying. And against it drivers take the most stringent precautions including new fire-proof clothing which will give them something like a second start on escaping a blazing car.

Changing

But fear or not it does not stop them racing, or the racing wives thinking that their —— lucky one to whom the —— happen.

"——I was injured, his —— the only person ——outwardly—to ——"I want what ——er try changing —— be happy." ——ace driving is ——rt—you can't

Piers Courage dies as car crashes in flames

Firemen work on the still-smouldering wreckage of the racing car in which Piers Courage died when it rolled over and exploded in flames at Zandvoort yesterday.

The British racing driver Piers Courage was killed when his car crashed and caught fire during the Dutch Grand Prix at Zandvoort yesterday. He was driving an Italian-built De Tomaso.

The crash occurred on the 23rd lap at the east tunnel of the Zandvoort circuit. Mr Courage's car rolled over, exploding almost immediately. The fire was so fierce that the adjoining woodland was set ablaze.

Firemen tried to release Mr Courage but were driven back by the tremendous heat.

Rated one of the most improved drivers of 1968, Mr Courage rose to Formula One prominence when he finished second in last year's Monaco and American Grand Prix.

He had been racing for about eight years. On leaving school he was articled to a firm of accountants but left after two years to devote all his time to motor racing.

Mr Courage (28) was heir to one of Britain's biggest brewery businesses. He said that his ambition was "to get as far as I can and to go on racing for as long as I can."

He felt that the dangers of motor racing were exaggerated. "When you are driving, you're never frightened," he once said. "I used to scare myself quite a lot because I didn't know what I was doing."

He also said: "Now I have things under control. One tries never to drive over one's head. That's a big mistake."

Mr Courage married Lady Sarah Curzon, a half-sister of the Earl of Howe, in 1966. They have two sons, Jason (2) and Amos, who was born in February.

An official race statement later said that Mr Courage's car rolled over several times before it exploded in the woods. Trackside firemen were unable to put out the flames and the accident service and the fire brigade were called.

First reports said that Mr Courage had escaped unhurt. This was because of the remote area where the crash occurred. Race officials began an immediate inquiry.

Because of the crash there was no victory lap of honour for the winner and all festivities in connection with the race were cancelled.

In April, Mr Courage walked from the track unhurt after his car crashed during qualifying trials for the Spanish Grand Prix in Madrid.

Mr Courage was the second Formula One driver killed recently. On June 2 Bruce McLaren, of New Zealand, died when he crashed during a test drive at Goodwood.

Mr Wilfrid Andrews, chairman of the RAC said last night: "All in motor racing will be shattered by this news, coming as it does so soon after the loss of Bruce McLaren.

"Piers Courage was not at the very top of the Grand Prix tree, but after several seasons of great endeavour he had at last established himself as a regular in Formula One racing. There were indications that much more success awaited"

Piers Courage

Car blaze kills Piers Courage

Piers Courage

From **BRIAN GROVES** in Zandvoort, Ho——

OLD Etonian Piers Courage, —— old member of the brewery fam—— in the blazing wreckage of h—— car in the Dutch Grand Prix —— voort yesterday.

His wife, Lady Sarah Courage, 25-year-old model, was timekeeping for him in the pits when the crash happened.

She was one out of thousands of spectators who saw a pall of black smoke and flames rise over the sand dunes at the far side of the circuit.

At first officials broadcast that her husband was safe. Lady Sarah, daughter of the late racing veteran Earl Howe, went for a drink.

Then she was told that her husband had died. She collapsed and was taken away by friends.

The couple were married just over four years ago. Their two sons, Jason, three, and Amos, one, were being looked af——

AR ACE DIES IN BLAZE

By SUN REPORTER

THE shocked wife of racing driver Piers Courage was under sedation last night after her husband was burned to death in the Dutch Grand Prix.

Courage's car was hurtled off the Zandvoort track at more than 100 mph, overturned in a wood and was enveloped in flames.

Firemen fought vainly to quell the blaze...

Sarah is comforted by other race-goers after the tragedy.

Continued on P.2

COURAGE HEIR DIES IN CRASH

By PATRICK MENNEM in Zandvoort, Holland and MARGARET HALL in London

RACING driver Piers Courage, heir to the Courage brewery fortune, died in a blazing Grand Prix car in Holland yesterday.

The Dutch Grand Prix was nearing the half-way stage when his car careered out of control on the fastest section of the circuit.

The car somersaulted at 160 miles per hour, spun into a wooded section beside the track and exploded in a fierce blaze.

Rescuers who raced to the scene were driven back by the intense heat and were unable to reach the trapped driver.

Courage's beautiful wife, the former Lady Sarah Curzon, was in the pits, keeping a lap-chart.

She was later led sobbing from the circuit at Zandvoort by race officials.

Cancelled

The couple, married in 1966, have two children, aged three and one. Their home is in Pimlico, London.

Courage was lying seventh in his De Tomaso Ford when he crashed.

The race was won by Austrian Jochen Rindt in a Lotus. The traditional lap of honour and prize-giving party were cancelled because of the tragedy.

Piers Courage was the 28-year-old son of Mr. Richard Courage, chairman of the giant brewery group.

His was the story-book image of a racing driver.

With his dashing good looks and wealth he could have been the romantic hero of the international racing set.

Instead, he chose to be a dedicated driver.

Mistake

It was his prowess behind the wheel that swiftly rid him of his "playboy" tag.

It made him a respected driver — recognised throughout the world as a champion in the making.

He is on record as saying: "When you're driving, you're never frightened."

"I used to scare myself quite a lot because I didn't know what I was doing."

"But now I have the car under control. One tries never to drive over one's head. That's a mistake."

In 1966, he set out on the track to stardom. He was named by the Guild of Motoring Writers as the young driver most likely to succeed.

Last year he was second in the United States Grand Prix.

THE BRIDE A wedding-day picture of Piers Courage and his wife in 1966.

THE WIDOW A distraught Mrs. Courage being helped away after the crash.

RACE CRASH KILLS HEIR TO COURAGE

LONDON, Sun., AAP. — British racing driver Piers Courage, 28, was killed when he crashed in the Dutch Grand Prix today.

Courage, a handsome ex-Etonian, was one of the millionaire Courage Brewery family, and an heir to the family fortune.

Courage's wife, former fashion model Lady Sarah Curzon, 25, daughter of the fifth Earl Howe, a famous racing driver, was watching the race.

She was keeping a lap chart, as she always did, for Courage from the pits.

His De Tomaso car spun into a wooded section of the Zandvoort circuit and exploded into a fierce blaze.

Courage, known to his friends as "Porridge," was one of the gentlemen of motor racing.

He started his career as an accountant but later took up motor racing with Jonathan Williams. He took part in events all over Europe.

Courage crashed in the first half of the Grand Prix.

When Courage crashed in flames a track announcer first said he was unhurt.

But later an official announcement said: "We regret to announce that Piers Courage died in his burning car after his accident."

About 50,000 people saw the Dutch Grand Prix.

The race was over 80 laps of the 2.6 miles Zandvoort circuit — a total of 208.43 miles.

The winner was Jochen Rindt, of Austria, in a Lotus 72 Ford.

Jackie Stewart, of Britain, in a March Ford, was second. Jackie Ickx, of Belgium, in a Ferrari, was third.

Courage raced in the Tasman series in Australia and New Zealand last year. He won the Teretonga Park International at Invercargill, New Zealand.

He won the South Pacific championship at Longford, Tasmania, in...

Piers Courage

Lady Sara

DUTCH GRAND PRIX

Moment of truth on lap 3 as Rindt dives up the inside at the end of the start-finish straight to take the lead from Ickx's Ferrari.

Rindt dominates race in new Lotus 72 — Piers Courage dies in tragic crash

Story by PATRICK McNALLY
Photography by DAVID PHIPPS
Race data by ALAN PHILLIPS

Jochen Rindt won his second Grand Prix brought him little joy, for the race cost the life of his close friend Piers Courage, who was killed when his de Tomaso crashed and exploded in flames just after quarter distance. This was the first lap and never looked anything but a winner, covering the race distance at a new record average speed. Jacky Ickx's Ferrari, which took the second place after a race-long third place, lying just one point ahead of his great rival Rindt.

As well as the two Ferraris, both Matras also took the flag, Beltoise finishing fifth and placed eighth, John Miles drove the second works Lotus 72 very well, only losing Amon's car having a clutch breakage on the line. Marches suffered mechanical failure, BRMs went well but were out of luck, Rodriguez holding fourth place until loose body work forced him in, while his team-mate Oliver after an excellent start blew his engine after 24 laps. Tyres played a significant role, Firestone's latest equipment proving ideal for the circuit, while Dunlops were a very good second, but Goodyears for a change were right out of the running.

ENTRY

After all the talk that financial trouble might lead to the cancellation of the Dutch Grand Prix the organisers managed to get sponsorship from 33 different companies and even some financial support from the Dutch Ministry of Culture and Recreation. Backed by this support they accepted entries for 26 cars and were prepared to run a 20-car field.

As usual most of the works teams had been testing at Zandvoort prior to the race, and this tight, sinuous course. The Owen Racing Organisation still flushed with success after Spa arrived with four of the Yardley coloured BRM type 153s. Pedro Rodriguez had his usual car (153-02), with a brand new car (153-05) as a spare while Jackie Oliver was in his usual car (153-04). The engine failures at Spa had turned out to be less serious than was first thought, and the engines were now giving a reliable 437 bhp at 10,600 rpm, with excellent torque.

(242 lbs-ft at 8750 rpm). Their Marelli ignition had cured the oiled plug problem and Aubrey Woods seemed quietly confident. As usual a third car was entered for Canadian George Eaton, and this was identical to the works cars except that it didn't have titanium springs and Koni shock absorbers.

That very professional team Frank Williams Racing arrived with two de Tomasos usual for Piers Courage but, this time the short of engines due to recent drama at Cosworth, they were desperately crankshafts had been discovered that a batch after being nitrided. Cosworth had recalled all the engines fitted with the dodgy cranks, but as they only had ten spares in the store there were an awful lot of people short of spare mills. Due to this Frank Williams only had one complete car while the wide-track engine they raced at Spa. The steering rack which had given trouble at Monaco now had a longer casing and ran on roller bearings, and the fuel system had also been revised. They had hoped to fit a lighter aluminium

radiator, but the local firm who were doing the rest of the plumbing took so long that they inverted original copper radiator for this race.

The Tyrrell Racing Organisation were once again a two-car team, the young Freeman François Cevert replacing the retired Servoz-Gavin as Jackie Stewart's Number 2 in the blue March 701s. The World Champion had his usual car as well as a lightweight spare. They had tested here immediately prior to the car and there were no radical changes the spare as so far it was no quicker.

The March Engineering 701 for Chris Amon and Jo Siffert were also virtually unchanged. Chris Amon and Robin Herd had left for the States immediately after Spa to test at Watkins Glen. Siffert having tested earlier at St Jovite. They had taken their special cars with alternate pick-up points and learnt a lot, but for the moment Amon's and Siffert's cars were running in normal trim, although lots of detail changes had been made in the interests of reliability. Siffert's car now had most of the lightweight features to be found on the Amon machine, which weighed in at 1235 lbs. Testing in the USA

F1 World Championship/round 5

AUTOSPORT, JUNE 25, 1970

POST OFFICE TELEGRAM

Charges to pay
£ s. d.
RECEIVED

Prefix. Time handed in. Office of Origin and Service Instructions. Words.

No.
OFFICE STAMP
22 JUN.70

At _____ m

At _____ m

To

By

Ŧ=ŦHD 84 PRIORITY 1.20

27 July

By

BUCKINGHAM PALACE OHMS 32 PRIORITY

MR RICHARD COURAGE FITZWALTERS SHENFIELD ESSEX

= I WAS SO SORRY TO HEAR OF THE DEATH OF YOUR

SON PIERS MY HUSBAND JOINS ME IN SENDING YOU OUR

SINCERE SYMPATHY = ELIZABETH R

For free repeti... at office of deli...

with this form, ...e, the envelope B or C

OFFICE

No.
OFFICE STAMP
23 JUN.70

Service Instructions. Words. 23 JUN.70

At _____ m

ANO 40900 31 22 1945

DRAYTON GARDENS

LONDONSW10

WE ARE VERY CLOSE TO YOU ON THIS SAD OCCASION

STOP WE ALL MISS ABOVE A FRIEND AND ALSO A

VALUABLE COLLABORATOR ALFAROMEO

For free repetition of doubtful words telephone "TELEGRAMS ENQUIRY"...

COL 70 10 OSEAGM SP12 LN¥

...his form ...envelope. B or C

RECEIVED

Prefix. Time handed in. Offic...

TE

At _____ m

1220 DO010 GTX182 BOL...

24 1807FAMIGLIA COURAGE

TO

PROFONDAMENTE COLPITO DAL GRAVE LUTTO CHE CI PRIV...

DEL CARO PIERS PARTECIPO VS DOLORE E PREGO ACCOGLIERE

SENSI MIO COMMOSSO CORDOGLIO = ENZO FERRARI +¥

RG O

For free repetition of doubtful words telephone "TELEGRAMS ENQUIRY" or c... at office of delivery. Other enquiries should be accompanied by this form and, if possible, the envelope B or C

again? It has happened, it was Piers, that's terrible, but this is why it happened. Was it mechanical failure, Frank thought? I said 'No, I think it was an accident of a racing track. You were going in there very fast, probably fourth, if not fifth, but it was very fast. There was no margin for error, nowhere to go.

"I always tried not to drive like that, because once you're right on the limit, and you know there's a bump there, if that bump catches you out the wrong way, then you're exposing yourself to an unmanageable set of circumstances. There's no space capable of accommodating what needed to happen for you to bring it back. That's why I never liked the Nürburgring. There were so many places where you knew if X was to happen, then Y would definitely have followed. That's why I was so sure and told Frank that I did not think it was a mechanical failure. Obviously for Frank that would have

been the worst thing of all, to think that one of his best friends had died, that it could have happened in his car."

Jackie and Frank both say that they were not involved in formally identifying Piers's body, so that job was done by Stanley, although he prefers not to comment on whether he undertook that sad task.

Stewart wrote in *Faster* that he arranged for disposal of what was left of the car: "I thought about a scrap yard but then realised people might take bits of it for souvenirs and that sort of thing, so I knew this was out of the question. Frank just said, 'Get rid of it… I don't ever want to see it again. Get it away,' and I had it hauled to Amsterdam or Rotterdam maybe, I can't remember, where it was melted in an incinerator and the remaining bits chopped up after they cooled."

On Monday evening Jackie finally returned to

Geneva, while Frank went back to London and straight to Drayton Gardens to see Sally.

"All the girls were supporting her," says Bette Hill. "We went to Camden Town when Piers was brought back, and waited for her to come out. We were there for her. We just switched around, whoever happened to be near or in London, so I was trailing up and down. There were other friends who weren't so closely involved in motor racing. It was like shift work. He was so young, and she was so young and beautiful, and it was just so sad. There they were, the glamour of motor racing... they had two babies, which made it even worse and more difficult."

Peggy Taylor, the wife of former F1 driver and Ford motor sport boss Henry Taylor, found herself involved almost by default. It was the start of a lasting friendship: "I met Bette Hill for lunch, and she was going to see Sally. She said, 'Why don't you come too?' I said 'She wouldn't know me from a bar of soap,' although I had actually first met her when she was 15, when she was with Earl Howe. The funny thing is she sort of fell on me, and we have been amazingly good friends ever since. If I hadn't been with Bette I wouldn't have thought of interfering at a time like that."

Loti Irwin, who had given birth to her second child days before, was among those to help out: "I left Alexander in the Westminster Hospital. I levered myself out of bed and went round and said, 'What can I do?' It was most peculiar, sort of surreal. Everyone was just sitting there looking completely stunned, and Frank was being wonderful, sort of organising everything. You couldn't believe that it had happened. And someone said, 'For God's sake, get some food,' because the house didn't have any food in it all, so I went off and did an enormous shop, and thought, 'What on earth am I doing? I've just had a baby and I'm carting around crates of wine.' They kept ringing me up and saying, 'When are you going to pick this thing up?' And I said, 'Can you hang on to it for another day?'"

"Sally would come to meet people who came to see her," says her sister Frances. "There were lots and lots of people who were very sweet. And every night when she went to sleep she put all the photographs of Piers all around the bed."

"I was in London with Sally, and mainly stuck around her place," says Jonathan Williams. "When I arrived she started crying and said, 'I know it's true now because you've turned up.' And an hour later Jochen came in. He looked like a ghost."

Sally and Piers's parents Richard and Jean received hundreds of telegrams and letters of condolence. There were messages from Her Majesty the Queen, from Enzo Ferrari, from a devastated Alfa Romeo team, and from all over the world of motor racing. Bruce McLaren's grieving parents took the trouble to write from New Zealand.

There were also many letters from people who had nothing to do with the sport but who had been part of Piers's short life. They included Patrick Knox-Shaw, headmaster of St Peter's Preparatory School, Nigel Wykes, the housemaster he'd argued with at Eton, and even Madame Wolkonsky Mortimer Mannier, in whose Parisian apartment Piers had rented a room during his unhappy time with WHSmith back in 1961. Actress Joanna Lumley, who had only recently met Piers and Sally, captured the mood: "He will always be remembered as the kindest, grooviest, gentlest man."

Wednesday was an emotionally charged day for those close to Grand Prix racing. Arranged some weeks earlier, a memorial service for Bruce McLaren took place at noon at St Paul's Cathedral. It now carried an extra resonance for everyone, including his widow Pat. She had been in New Zealand for her husband's funeral, and had returned on Sunday – only to learn that Piers had died that afternoon. Sally was brave enough to accompany the Rindts and the Stewarts to St Paul's, despite her own grief, and the preparations for Piers's funeral the following day.

Immediately after the service the drivers headed to the Dorchester Hotel for a meeting of the GPDA. A few weeks earlier they had been vilified for saying they wouldn't race at Spa in the rain, and now their priority was to get the upcoming German GP switched from the Nürburgring to Hockenheim. Emotions ran at fever pitch.

After the accident Sally and Piers's parents Richard and Jean received hundreds of messages, including telegrams from Her Majesty the Queen, the Alfa Romeo team, and Enzo Ferrari.

"Jack Brabham came along as well," says Stewart. "I didn't think Jack would give us support to the stopping of the Nürburgring, but he did. We all agreed on it. It was an unusual quorum, if you know what I mean. At that time there was so many things going on, and safety was such a controversial issue. Nobody was prepared to listen or pay any attention when you tried to do something. The resistance, the interference, was extraordinary. That's what was more frustrating when you're involved in something like that. The hypocrisy of some people...They're not involved, they're not the sufferers, they don't see the family close up, and they don't have to go to the funerals other than to say they've been to the funeral. Pathetic. They won't stand up and do things."

Jackie kept his deepest feelings to himself, as Helen recalls: "I don't know what he was thinking. I remember that following week we all went out like nothing had happened, because what do you do? I remember Nina being upset because we were going to restaurants and laughing and joking. But that's not what you feel inside."

Nina remembers it well: "I remember that Jackie and Jochen had plans to go to Annabel's for dinner, the day before Piers's funeral. I said, 'There's no way you're going to Annabel's for dinner, like nothing happened. We just cannot go.' I was so angry, I was just crying, saying I'm not going to Annabel's with you. I don't remember what we did…"

Thursday was a beautiful June day. The funeral took place at 12.15pm at St Mary the Virgin Church in Shenfield, just a few minutes from the Courage home, where members of the family had been buried for several generations. The tiny church, reached by a small lane, was packed with hundreds of Piers's closest friends, and most of the biggest names in Grand Prix racing. The service included a reading of Psalm 23, and a rousing chorus of Jerusalem. Both of which had featured at his wedding a little over four years earlier. Afterwards everyone was invited to Fitzwalters, where Richard Courage proved to be a tower of strength. The day made a lasting impression on all who were there.

Loti Irwin: "It sounds dreadful to say, but the funeral was just perfect. It was a wonderful summer's day, and everything looked lovely, and there were roses everywhere."

Frank Williams: "The ceremony was very moving. Lots of drivers were there, all wearing dark glasses to hide the tears. It was Old England, not far from his house. I adored the guy. It was my first direct exposure to death of any sort, and I was very moved by the whole thing."

Charles Lucas: "I wept, and I was rather ashamed of that at the time. In the church I was sitting beside Lady Watson, Piers's grandmother. I was amazed that she was just standing there singing along. And there was a box with Piers inside it. I asked her, 'How can you do this?' She said, 'After the first and second wars, do you realise how many times I've done this?'"

Frances Denman: "It was awful. We were leaving the grave and Sally sank onto her knees and just sort of collapsed. All those young people were just sort of shattered. And poor Mrs Courage. It was awful for her. She just adored Piers, and it was shattering for her."

Helen Stewart: "I remember thinking, 'My God, Piers is in there. I didn't want to think what had happened in the aftermath of the accident. It was seeing the devastation of Sally. Would this ever happen to me, and how would I cope? I was living in a foreign country – would I go home? You think all these things."

Bubbles Horsley: "It was pretty grim and emotional. I think it broke his mother, completely."

Sheridan Thynne: "It was a deeply traumatic funeral. It was a lovely summer's day, and that made it more difficult to get through, I seem to recall. In the garden at Fitzwalters his father was going up to people of Piers's generation who he felt might have found it difficult to

The biggest names in the sport struggled to keep their emotions in check at the funeral. After Bruce McLaren, it was too much to take in.

talk to him, which was very courageous."

Jackie Stewart: "It was really British. 'Thank you so much for coming, thank you for looking after Piers so well, I really can't believe you've come all the way from Geneva.' It was the real salt of British aristocracy. You weren't allowed to show any grief."

Heinz Pruller: "I remember Jochen was shaking at the funeral. And Sally said to Gianpaulo Dallara, 'Thank you very much for building such a beautiful car."

"I remember going up there with Bubbles," says Sally. "I took Piers's Alfa coat, because I couldn't be parted from it. It was an unbelievably hot day, and it was packed, overflowing. We'd just seen *2001: A Space Odyssey*, and I wanted them to play that music on the organ. And they did. It wasn't very good, but it was Piers. And I do remember collapsing at the grave. And then everybody leaves, that's the worst part. Everybody thinks that someone else is taking care of her, so she'll be all right. That's the loneliest time. Before that it's so jam packed with people, you don't know where to turn, and you want some time to yourself."

For the drivers at least, it was soon back to business as usual. Jochen had an F2 race to go to in France, and practice started that very afternoon.

"From Piers's funeral we went straight into the aeroplane of Jack Brabham to the circuit for the F2 race at Rouen," says Nina. "We were all dressed in black, and I went into the motorhome and changed into jeans. And off they went practising. I was sick to my stomach. I was just sitting in the car reading my book. I didn't want to move, I didn't want to go anywhere. It was terrible."

Jochen finished a subdued ninth in the race. In the supporting F3 event promising young Frenchman Jean-Luc Salomon – who was due to rent a third works Lotus for the French GP – lost his life. A second driver, Denis Dayan, died later from injuries received in a separate accident. Meanwhile that weekend Stewart went to Silverstone to honour a commitment to Ford.

"Racing drivers are made of funny stuff," says Jackie. "I remember going to drive at the TT with Chris Craft in an Escort. It was just like a breath of fresh air, because it was an easy car to drive by comparison. It was an escape.

"There was no chance that you were ever going to stop racing because of an accident, that's the point. That's because we had become, in a funny sort of way, soldiers of the time. People were killed in the trenches, people still had to fight on. Motor racing had a peculiar ability for that to happen. It was amazing, really."

Keen to get away from London, a few days later Sally travelled to the Rindts in Switzerland. Bubbles Horsley volunteered to accompany her: "I could spare the time. We went there for about a week, and then came back to England. It was awful, absolutely awful, but Nina was very good, she was brilliant."

During that bleak summer Sally and Nina would

Race aces mourn

Piers Courage

Lady Sarah Courage leaning on the arm of her father-in-law, Mr. Richard Courage.

Jackie Stewart and his wife.

GRAHAM HILL.

spend a lot of time together.

"She came to stay with Jochen and me in Switzerland, with Bubbles," says Nina. "Later on in August we went to a lake in Austria, and Sally came with her son, Jason, to stay with us again. All I can remember is that Jochen was very, very irritated by Sally and me, because we were most of the time crying. It was heavy for him."

Nina says that Jochen didn't talk much about Piers: "He had enough with Sally and me around to remind him! You just didn't. It was just too new. I think maybe later on you could talk about nice memories, but at the time it was too soon."

Ecclestone remembers that Rindt really was affected: "The worst one was Piers, really and truly. That was the one that shook him up more than anything."

"Jochen thought about stopping at this point," says Nina, "But weeks went by, and towards the end of the season he said, 'I can't stop now.' I said, 'Servoz-Gavin, he stopped, he's much braver than you.' He said, 'No, no, I can't, it's just a few races, I have to see the contract

out, I may stop after the season.' He thought Servoz-Gavin was irresponsible, because he didn't keep his contract! It's a thing you have to do. I can see that today, but then I was so panicking."

After Zandvoort Jochen won the French GP at Clermont-Ferrand, the British GP at Brands Hatch, and the German GP, which had been successfully moved from the Nürburgring to Hockenheim. It seemed that he could do no wrong.

"It was dreadful," says Nina. "Before I had Sally there, and now she wasn't at the races, so it was very strange. Plus Jochen kept winning, which I thought was even worse. It was like I was having a bad conscience. How can you just win when Piers dies? Plus he won Zandvoort. I was angry at him for winning Zandvoort.

"He kept saying, 'Things are going too well, something will happen.' He hated that car. I knew about the discussions he had with Colin [Chapman], trying to make the parts stronger, and Colin refused.

"I was a nervous wreck after the accident, completely.

I was very unhappy about him driving after that. I must say though that Sally has a lot more humour than I do. She was very good at making people laugh, and saying stupid things. 'Silly old cow, stop crying, don't be stupid,' stuff like that."

Rindt continued to send out contradictory messages as to whether he was going to carry on. "Jochen was beginning to have second thoughts," says Stewart. "He had been very affected by all of those things. And Jochen was a tough guy. We talked a lot about it, because he lived close by. I don't know whether he would have continued or not."

"I wanted him to stop," says Nina. "I said that I'd take Natascha and go home to Finland, and once you've decided to stop racing I'll come back! It was a bit of blackmail. 'If you do that, it means you do not love me.' I said, 'OK, I'll stay.' We did have these discussions, yes."

Bernie admits that Jochen thought he was riding his luck: "It never happened that he thought, 'I'm going to get killed' or something like that, but you always think when you've had two or three wins… You think, 'Thank Christ I was lucky, maybe I'm not going to continue to be lucky like that.' But he didn't consider himself to be in a position where he was going to get hurt."

Above Flowers at St Mary the Virgin *after the funeral. The church itself was packed to overflowing.*

Opposite Piers's *grave at St Mary the Virgin, as it looks today. The headstone features the Courage family crest, in the form of a cockerel.*

"When somebody's close to you like Piers was close, obviously it makes you think a little bit. But it doesn't change people, because you think that was unfortunate, but it won't happen to me."

Meanwhile Frank had taken the only decision he could. The team missed the French GP, but returned at Brands with Brian Redman at the wheel of the surviving de Tomaso. Giving up was never an option.

"No, no, no question about that," Frank insists. "I don't mean I thought it through and said, 'Fuck it, why should I stop?' It just never really entered my mind. It was just a very unfortunate event."

"Frank picked himself up and carried on," says Bubbles Horsley, "but he was obviously very cut-up about it. We'd all been boys together, lads fighting a war together, in a funny sort of way, with all that gypsy living, going round Europe. When you grow up and take yourself more seriously things change, and I think relationships with drivers do change. They sort of climbed the ladder together. Frank wanted to climb it as a driver as well, he had switched roles and put a different hat on."

In filling Piers's shoes, Redman had a difficult task, and inevitably it was a very businesslike relationship: "Even in those days Frank was a very intense person, but I don't have any recollection of anything being peculiar in any way. It was obviously extremely upsetting for him, but racing in those days was extraordinarily dangerous."

The de Tomaso didn't actually start at Brands Hatch. Although little was said at the time, today Redman makes an interesting suggestion: "They withdrew because they found something on the point of breaking which they thought might have broken in Piers's accident – a front suspension part. They said very little about it, but they inspected it, and said, 'We're not running.' They were a bit reticent."

Alessandro de Tomaso was known for his short attention span, and by now it was obvious to Frank that he'd lost interest in the F1 project. For the balance of the season, Frank received only minimal assistance, and after a while designer Gianpaulo Dallara was not allowed to go to races.

"Straight away it was finished," recalls Dallara. "I remember I was supposed to go to America, but he did not allow me. I went to Monza as a personal trip, but not with de Tomaso. He delivered some parts, but he was not interested in the car any more."

"That year would be a washout," says Frank. "He made it clear that he wouldn't carry on the following year."

Meanwhile Sally was trying to adjust to life without Piers: "I worked a lot, and I went to America. Mary Quant and her husband were wonderful to me. It was very empty and lonely, and I just didn't understand. I was only 25, and I had two children. The whole of one's world had totally imploded. Suddenly there were debts and bills, and cars were repossessed. Almost the day after he died, someone came asking for keys. It was terrible, quite frankly."

A second visit to see Nina and Jochen provided some comfort.

Sally recalls a strange experience at the end of her trip: "When I said goodbye to Jochen, I looked at him, and he looked so sad. He could hardly say goodbye. And I thought, 'I'm never going to see you again.' Then I thought I was just being silly, stop thinking these thoughts."

That month the new Österreichring hosted a Grand Prix for the first time. Just a few miles from his hometown of Graz, Jochen was under massive pressure, but he was not too disappointed when the engine failed.

"I met him after the race and he was resting in this small motorhome," says Pruller. "He was almost relived because he thought this was the bad luck that was due to come, because you cannot win four races in a row and never have bad luck... So he was really relieved, that was the strange thing."

Later Rindt became concerned when he found out that team-mate John Miles had retired when the right front brake shaft, which connected the wheel to the

inboard disc, had failed. Miles had a huge fright when the car lunged to the right, but a vibration had at least given him some warning, and he was able to trundle back to the pits.

The end of the winning streak seemed to take a weight off Jochen's shoulders, and before the Italian GP, he was in good spirits. He now led Brabham by 20 points, and with only 27 up for grabs after Monza, a victory could clinch the title.

"This time between the Austrian GP and Monza was very, very hectic for Jochen," says Pruller. "He was full of activities. It was, 'I'd like to buy this forest, this old house is nice, and we'll make a tennis court there.' He had so many ideas. Piers had obviously shown him how quickly it can go."

Bernie Ecclestone confirms that Rindt was in a good mood: "I stayed with him on the way to Monza. He was in good shape, and happy with life in general."

In fact the pair, who already ran an F2 team together, were considering working together in Grand Prix racing: "It was much easier in those days to do something. But whether it would have been a sensible thing to do, I don't know. We would have had to have a look at it. We'd have to have done a deal to buy cars – it may well be that we could have done something with Lotus. It was really seeing what was available, more or less, rather than any particular plan to do something different."

The qualifying schedule in Italy was fairly relaxed, and Jochen didn't leave Switzerland until Friday morning, Bernie and Nina joining him in his BMW 2800. As they drove to Milan the subject of retirement came up once again, as Nina recalls: "Going to Monza, Jochen said, 'I can't stop, I want to go on. If I win the World Championship I want to go on; this is the time I can make the big money.'"

Ecclestone agrees that stopping was no longer a possibility: "No, that's not what he had in mind – his blood was racing."

Towards the end of the Friday afternoon session Rindt decided to run without front and rear wings. He'd done that with the 49B the previous year, and Tyrrell and McLaren were already wingless. He was delighted to find that the DFV was revving 800rpm higher, and the car was potentially much quicker. There was no time to fit new ratios to take full advantage, so the real test would come on Saturday.

Practice that day didn't start until 3pm, so Jochen had a lazy morning at the Hotel de Ville, before heading to the track. The car now had new ratios, good for a top speed of 205mph in wingless spec. The previous year Jochen and Piers had agreed to tow each other round, and that had helped the Austrian onto pole. Pruller remembers reminding Jochen of that fact: "I said something to him in practice, like 'Now you could use Piers for the slipstreaming.' He agreed, and said, 'Yes, yes, I'm missing Piers.'"

In fact Jochen felt that it wasn't worth chasing pole, and that a position somewhere near the sharp end would be good enough. Of more importance was getting the car primed for the slipstreaming contest that was sure to come on Sunday. Jochen immediately picked up a tow from the wingless Denny Hulme. He followed the McLaren for three laps, before passing it just after Lesmo. Hulme was still behind the Lotus as the pair rushed towards Parabolica. When Jochen got on the brakes, teetering on the edge of adhesion without its wings, the car snapped to the left, almost certainly after a failure of the front left shaft. The 72 struck the barrier, and its wedge nose forced a gap under the bottom layer, and slammed into a solid supporting post. The impact was horrific, and unsurvivable. Jochen's luck had finally run out.

"It was one disaster after the other," says Ecclestone. "I rushed up to the corner where the accident happened, and he was coming back. By the time I ran back to the ambulance they were banging on his chest, because they thought that was the right thing to do. There wasn't any one who was super professional, and it was a bloody VW ambulance. Then the ambulance went to the wrong hospital and had to come back and come into Milan. By

the time I got there I couldn't have done much anyway, but I'm quite sure he would have been in a much, much better position if it all happened today."

"It's weird to say this, but I wasn't in the same way shocked as I was when Piers died," says Nina. "It was like I wasn't surprised any more. The first time it was really, 'My God, it can actually happen.' You're so young, and you're so stupid, you have a certain defence, and you don't think about it. And I don't think Sally did either."

Sally now found herself in the extraordinary position of comforting Nina, only 11 weeks after she had lost Piers.

"Frank had leant me the de Tomaso, and I was driving to see the Courages at Fitzwalters. Andrew came out of the front door, and I thought something ghastly's happened. And he told me. I said, 'I must get over there to be with Nina.' We tried to find out some information, and she was trying to get hold of me, she said later. I managed to get myself on a plane, and Charlie Courage came with me. He was very sweet, because I wouldn't have managed on my own. We knew that Nina was being brought back by private plane, so we waited at the airport in Switzerland, just sitting on a bench, and then went home with her."

After Monza Lotus mechanic Herbie Blash, then aged just 21, drove Jochen's BMW 2800 back to Switzerland.

"There I was as a boy sitting with two widows who were crying their eyes out," he recalls. "You basically grew up very quickly. What could you do apart from try to comfort two very, very distraught ladies?"

"He gave me Jochen's bag," says Sally, "and said, 'this needs sorting out.' And boy, did it need sorting out. It was his overalls and helmet. I had to wash it all before Nina saw it…"

Nina's neighbour Helen Stewart also found herself in a strange situation: "I felt bad that I was the only one left out of this group, because so many of them didn't come back to racing. I would see them from time to time, and I really felt guilty. And they'd say, 'We feel happy for you.' But I never knew that I'd be all right, I never had that security of knowing."

"After Jochen's death Sally came again, to look after me," says Nina. "And Helen came up and looked after both of us! That was terrible. We were saying, 'I wonder if there's a race up there. I'm sure they're having good fun.' We were trying to make fun; you see what I'm saying? Between the crying we were trying to joke as well, thinking about them, and what they must think of us now. You sort of try and put some humour with it all, and think maybe they are having a good time up there. It was quite sweet, but what can you do? You can't just sit and cry…"

Postscript

Happier times, as a youthful Piers enjoys a trip to France on his father's boat, Barleycorn. *Alongside is his step-cousin Julian Reynolds, a descendent of the painter Sir Joshua Reynolds.*

For those close to Piers, there were to be many more tears. Most people who knew Jean Courage say that she never got over the death of her beloved eldest son. Richard found it much harder to express his sorrow.

"My dad had his boating," says youngest brother Andrew. "He was a very, very reserved person, but my mother was much more emotional, and in a way they really weren't able to communicate about her grief, I suppose. That's something I just guess at really, so I don't know if it's true. Not long after Piers died we went off, my mum and myself and a cousin of ours, and drove round France to try and get away from it all. She was terribly depressed. I wouldn't say she ever recovered from it. Even before he was killed she was in some way searching for some deeper meaning in her life, and she converted to Catholicism."

"My mother was behind Piers hook, line and sinker, but it did her no good when he was killed," says Charlie Courage. "She blamed herself then for the whole thing. Everybody had said, 'Look this is daft, he's going to kill himself,' and all the rest of it, and I think she basically sealed it off, put it to the back of her brain. Here was her number one son doing what he wanted to do. She held him up as hard and as far as she could. I know that at times father used to blow his top, but on the whole she was very supportive, and he became more so. Piers's death did no favours to my mother at all. She changed her faith. She found it very, very difficult."

Jean Courage was killed in August 1977 when she was struck by a car on the A12, the main road at the end of the Fitzwalters driveway. By tragic coincidence, it was the weekend of that year's Dutch GP at Zandvoort.

Richard later remarried, and lived at Fitzwalters until his death in 1994. Like Jean he is buried at St Mary the Virgin. She was laid to rest next to Piers, while Richard is just behind.

Charlie now lives at Fitzwalters, running the family farming business. The house has hardly changed since Piers's childhood, and the shed where his Lotus Seven was put together is still there. Any connections with Courage Breweries ended long ago. Like Piers, Charles never worked for the company, although youngest brother Andrew did. After Eton he spent two years as a management trainee, and then stayed on for a further three years, although he acknowledges he was "a square peg in a round hole."

Sally made her racing debut in a Talbot Sunbeam in a celebrity race at Brands Hatch, at the behest of Loti Irwin. She wore the full-face Bell helmet that Piers had used in early 1970, before he switched to the special USAF model.

Andrew says that the loss of his oldest brother had a profound effect on the direction his life has taken.

"Piers's death left a huge gap in my life," he says. "His personality, his friends and not least the excitement of following along in his races provided me with a kind of shield behind which I could now and then escape from the realities of life. The emptiness after his death haunted me, and although I had many good friends and few financial worries, it began to dawn on me that now my life was fairly empty.

"I began to search for a meaning in life and looked to God, in whom I had had a fundamental faith right from my childhood. After a time the realisation came that the only way to fill the emptiness was to live wholeheartedly for God and devote all my time, money and energy to do His will and not my own. My wife Jane and I had just before this become involved in a youth club in Berkshire. We then met a Christian church that had its roots in Norway. The message they brought was one of discipleship and victory over sin. This gave me what I needed so that my life could have a meaning.

"In the meantime the Courage family continued to be stalked by tragedy. In August 1977 Jane gave birth to a baby girl, Jessica. However, a few hours later my mother was run over and killed. Five months later Jessica died suddenly of a crib death. These events, on top of Piers's death, were almost inhuman blows for all of us."

Andrew and Jane subsequently started a new life in Norway. After obtaining a degree he worked as a business studies teacher, and together they now run a successful translation company, and remain closely involved with the church.

After 1970 Jonathan Williams stayed in contact with the Courages, and became very friendly with Richard: "I used to see him fairly regularly, and we became great chums. He had this sailboat in the Med, and he used to go off. He always liked to have young people around him. He was a very nice man."

Jonathan's own racing career ended in the early seventies. He subsequently made a living as a pilot to wealthy businessmen, but by the early nineties he'd had enough of waiting around at airports.

Today Jonathan lives in a motorhome, travelling around the continent and seeking the sunshine, just as he did when he and Piers towed their little Lotus F3 cars from race to race. He keeps in touch with the rest of the world via the internet and his mobile phone and says, only half jokingly, that his ambition is to distil his life into a rucksack he can carry on his back. Having seen everything there is to see in Europe, he is looking for "an upmarket third world country" to move to! He occasionally writes articles on his own racing history, and in 1999 co-authored a book about the making of the Le Mans movie, in which he was so closely involved.

"After I stopped racing, I went cold turkey," he says. "For ten years I didn't look at a motor race, I didn't look at a car magazine. It's only now that I'm learning stuff from magazines like *Motor Sport*!"

Piers's other pals followed disparate paths. Charles Lucas continued to run racing car constructor Titan Engineering until 1972, when he sold his half of the business to partner Roy Thomas, with whom he remained close friends. The company was very successful, and over 360 Formula Ford cars were sold to the USA, where an enthusiastic Titan Registry keeps the marque alive.

A couple of years ago Luke and Tom the Weld attended one of their meetings in Michigan, where they were delighted to meet current owners of the cars. Tom was already ill at the time, and he died on 5 November 2001, at the age of 66. His widow Diana was better known in the sixties as 'Seccy', for she was secretary of the Lucas F3 team, taking care of paperwork for Piers and Roy Pike. She now runs Titan Motorsport, a successful racing fabrication business. And nearly 40 years after Tom built that ersatz F3 car for Piers, the company he founded supplies Lotus with steering racks for the Elise road car!

After ending his involvement with Titan, Luke continued to compete in historic racing, contesting his last event in 1983 at, of all places, Zandvoort. For several years he ran the family farm in Yorkshire, where he still lives. Like Jonathan, he's done a bit of writing, and used to have a column in *The Field*, although his most ambitious project

failed to find a publisher: "It was a novel about a transsexual racing driver. A brilliant idea, much better than Dick Francis. But I never figured out the end of it..."

On the aforementioned trip to America, Luke and Tom spotted amongst the many Titans an Ausper, a car that Roy had helped to build at Cliff Davis's yard. Its green livery made it instantly recognisable as the very machine once owned by Bubbles Horsley – the two-seater F3 car!

Today Horsley and March founder Robin Herd run a successful business making waste management machinery – where's there's muck, there's brass. But in the early seventies, just as Jonathan and Luke were drifting away from a direct involvement in motor sport, Bubbles was getting even more involved.

After taking a sabbatical from the sport ("I went off to India for a year") he found his way back into F3, this time with the support of the young Lord Alexander Hesketh, who he had met through Luke. In 1972 Hesketh agreed to run a second car for a driver with a little more pace than Bubbles, and the name of James Hunt emerged. Known as a crasher, Hunt had just about run out of options when Horsley invited him to join the *équipe*, although the patron was initially a little sceptical.

But the new partnership gelled. In 1973 Hesketh decided that both he and James were ready for F1. He bought a March and, with Bubbles in the role of team manager, Hesketh Racing made its F1 debut at the Monaco GP. At the end of 1973 Hunt finished second in the US GP, just as Piers had four years earlier.

It was a flashy operation which reminded some of the arrival of the Charles Lucas team on the F3 scene back in 1965, but lacking perhaps the innocent sense of fun that Luke, Piers and Jonathan brought to the show. By coincidence, in 1974 Luke volunteered to join his pals and drove the team motorhome around for the European Grand Prix season, and raced a Hesketh-owned Maserati 'Birdcage' in historic events.

That year the team built its own car, and in 1975 Hunt won the Dutch GP. However, by the end of the year, Hesketh had run out of funds. Hunt went to McLaren, and became World Champion. Without Horsley's support, he wouldn't have made it.

You might think that Hunt had little in common with Piers other than their use of their old school colours on their crash helmets, but there were some similarities: "I think there were," says Bubbles, "similar background, slight playboy image, although less in Piers's case – he wasn't the *enfant terrible* that James was! But they could both have flown in the same wing years earlier..."

After Alexander Hesketh withdrew Horsley managed to find some money to keep the F1 operation going for another three years, but it was not the force it had been. The team closed for good at the end of 1978. Ironically that was just as Frank Williams finally started to put the pieces in place, after enduring years of struggle since losing Piers. The full story of Frank's amazing career is beyond the scope of this book, but the essentials are worth recording in brief.

Having parted company with de Tomaso, Frank had to start afresh in 1971, and his only option was to buy a customer March from his former driver Max Mosley. He knew he had to become a constructor in his own right, but his first attempt in 1972 – with backing from toy company Politoys – was a failure. He tried again in 1973 with the support of Marlboro and Italian car company called Iso.

(It's worth noting here that the man who would later be responsible for the cigarette brand's budget was John Hogan, who in autumn 1960 had been on the same Cambridge crammer course as Piers. Like Piers, Hogan failed the exams, and went instead into marketing. In his role as Grand Prix racing's biggest sponsor, he would play a significant part in the sport through his dealings with McLaren and Ferrari, and was very close to drivers like Hunt and Niki Lauda. In 2003 he became boss of the Jaguar team, where he works with Jackie Stewart.)

As the costs of running a team increased, Frank had to go to extraordinary lengths to keep the team alive, at some stages running it from a telephone box when his own line had been cut off. Then at the end of 1975, he appeared to have found someone with de Tomaso's enthusiasm and wealth. He linked up with Canadian millionaire Walter Wolf for 1976, under the Wolf-

Williams banner. As a short cut to a competitive car Frank bought the abandoned Hesketh 308C project. When he went to collect the cars he found them sitting on stands, without wheels. It was an in-joke on the part of Bubbles, a payback for an incident when they were both dealing in F3 cars a decade earlier...

During 1976 Wolf gradually took over, and a despondent Frank found himself levered out of his own team. Rather than become Wolf's lackey, he left, and vowed to start again. The only thing he took away from Frank Williams (Racing Cars), the company he'd spent ten years building, was the friendship of a talented young engineer called Patrick Head.

In early 1977 Frank bought a second-hand March from Max Mosley, and Head agreed to join him. With sponsorship from Belgian driver Patrick Neve, they set about creating Williams Grand Prix Engineering. Frank needed serious finance to do the job properly, and looked to the Middle East, landing sponsorship from Saudia Airlines. Keen to find more money from the region, he turned to his old friend Charlie Crichton-Stuart, who had a priceless royal contact. Charlie brought in more names, and was directly responsible for introducing TAG to the sport. "I was just a guy with a briefcase selling motor racing," he told me. Eventually he joined full time to manage the commercial side of WGPE.

Sheridan Thynne and Frank Williams in the pits at Detroit in 1984.

For 1978 Head designed a new car, the FW06. It was a neat little machine, and new signing Alan Jones became a regular points scorer; for the first time some of his rivals began to take Frank seriously. In the middle of 1979 Head's latest FW07 became the pacesetter, and in July Clay Regazzoni – the man Piers was chasing when he crashed at Zandvoort – scored the team's first Grand Prix victory at Silverstone.

At the end of that season Frank added another old friend to his management team, Sheridan Thynne, who gave up his career as a stockbroker. In 1980, ten years after Piers's death, Alan Jones gave Frank Williams his first World Championship. Sherry and Charlie Stu both played a part, and thus shared in the success.

Since then Williams has been firmly established at the forefront of Grand Prix racing, winning further titles with Keke Rosberg (1982), Nelson Piquet (1987), Nigel Mansell (1992), Alain Prost (1993), Damon Hill (1996) and Jacques Villeneuve (1997). And most of this was achieved after Frank was paralysed in a road accident in France in March 1986, while dashing back to the airport after a test session at Paul Ricard. He was lucky to survive, but his life would never be the same again. His refusal to allow his injury to stop him running his business is a reflection of the determination that kept him going through the sixties, when Piers was one of the few who really believed that his friend would ever make it. In 1999, he became Sir Frank Williams.

But what would have happened had Piers not been killed? Frank is not the sort of guy to waste time on speculation: "I don't indulge in that very much. It would have been so unpredictable, but it was a terrible shame, the death of Piers. It was a shame that a good act, which was visibly getting better, was terminated. But clearly I saw myself and Piers as something like the Tyrrell/Stewart partnership. I wanted it to work as successfully as that."

It seems unlikely that we would have seen Piers struggling around in the cars that the cash-strapped Williams provided to the likes of Henri Pescarolo and Arturo Merzario in the early seventies. Even Frank is happy to admit that, had Piers lived, his team could have made faster progress.

"He was a well-known name, and he was going to be a premier British sportsman, and he was socially very acceptable. So there could have been a lot of money following him, not more than a few months down the road. I had a few little strings going along."

Many observers accuse Frank of being rather harsh on his drivers, the infamous sacking of Damon Hill – while he was on the way to the 1996 World Championship – being a case in point. You don't need a psychology degree to speculate that the loss of Piers caused Williams to change his approach.

"It's part of the reason for Frank's attitude to drivers, why some drivers say that he's insufficiently supportive," says Sheridan Thynne. "I'm not sure if he's conscious of this, but I'm sure that he doesn't try and get on the terms with them in the way that some people get on with their drivers, because he doesn't want to go through that again. I've seen him with drivers; he doesn't try and get very close to them."

Sheridan stayed on board until the end of 1992, latterly as commercial director. During that time he became very close to Nigel Mansell, and often played a key role in smoothing the sometimes rocky relationship between the team and its fiery driver. He helped to smooth the path for Nigel's return for his second stint with the team in 1991, which led to Mansell's World Championship in 1992.

When Mansell left at the end of that year and joined the CART series, Thynne left his role at Williams and went with him as advisor and all-round helper. He remained with Nigel until the end of his racing career in 1995. Today Sheridan is involved in the organisation of hillclimbing and historic racing: "It's terrific fun, and the best drivers have some of the attitude and banter of the old days."

Crichton-Stuart left Williams in 1983, and worked briefly for McLaren – he was close to TAG boss Mansour Ojjeh, who had switched teams. In 1985 he helped to start the short-lived Beatrice/Haas F1 team. He also kept an eye on the career of his titled young cousin, who raced under the name of Johnny Dumfries. Charlie subsequently drifted away from motor sport, and began searching for profitable shipwrecks in the Pacific and Indian oceans. He was on the

verge of striking it big when he suffered a fatal heart attack in the Philippines in July 2001.

His funeral in Scotland proved to be a reunion for the old Pinner Road brigade. Over the years they have kept in touch with each other to varying degrees, and all have taken care to maintain a close interest in Piers's sons, Jason and Amos. After losing Piers at just 25 Sally started a new life with John Aspinall, the zookeeper and casino owner, who had known and liked Piers. They married in 1972, and had a son, Bassa.

"Aspers was very impressed with Piers," she says. "I knew his second wife very well, so we went and stayed with them down at Howletts. We went to a couple of their parties. He always thought Piers was one of the most remarkable young men that he'd met. Piers was a very impressive character, and he in turn appreciated what John was doing with animals even in those early days. He could see greatness in other people."

Sadly Sally was widowed for a second time when John died of cancer in June 2000. Obviously for a while after 1970 she found it hard to look back on her life with Piers, but time has enabled her to put things into perspective.

"It's important to get on and cope with life," she says, "and not think about the negative side, especially if you've got children. I actually wanted to curl up in a ball and just let the world go by, but if you have responsibilities, you have to get on. I was brought up to believe there's no point

in dwelling on the past too much, but you never forget.

"Sad things have happened in my life, but if I think about my time with Piers, we had four wonderful years together. I'm immensely privileged to have had two such remarkable husbands, a wonderfully interesting life, and three marvellous sons, and I'm a very lucky woman in that respect.

"Jason and Amos are very like their father, although they never knew him. Talk about genes coming through! It's uncanny. Their manner, behaviour, way of thinking, determination, and Amos is very like him to look at as well. They are both very, very different, but the bond there is very strong. They're immensely proud of their father and what he achieved. From what they've read or what they've heard from my family, from Luke, from all the people that surround and love them, they've built up a picture of what he was like."

Sally stayed away from racing for a long time, but in 1980 she took the kids to the British GP at Brands Hatch, at Frank's invitation. They were a little disappointed when their seats proved to be in the back row of the grandstand, but were delighted to see Alan Jones win for Williams. At around that time Sally was invited by Loti Irwin to take part in a Talbot Sunbeam celebrity race, also at Brands. She even dug out one of Piers's two surviving crash helmets for the event: "In retrospect it wasn't such a sensible move. It didn't achieve anything, and I thought afterwards it was a mistake, because you can't go back. But there was a definite adrenaline rush. And it did open my eyes to what they did, even if I was only piddling around!"

She has not been back to a Grand Prix for many years, and says she sees no reason to do so.

"I still enjoy watching races on the television, and I find it an exciting sport. Because of the influence of my father and my husband, I've never lost my admiration for the skill of the drivers, and their bravery. But I'd rather not go to a motor race now, because my reason for being there was Piers.

"I made some wonderful friends through motor racing, and a lot of people helped tremendously after Piers was killed. I've always felt trust and friendship with many of the women, because you have that bond. We've all gone our separate ways now, but if we met up again, it would be like yesterday. Two of the people I still see a lot of are Nina Rindt and Peggy Taylor, both of whom are Bassa's godmothers. They've been a wonderful influence and guiding force to the boys and myself, as has Peggy's husband, Henry. Many of the people who still influence motor racing these days have kept in contact, and Bernie and Frank have both been very helpful and supportive to myself and the boys all these years."

Right Jason early in his racing career. He contested the British Formula Renault championship in 1990, but was forced to stop the following year when he ran out of cash.

Opposite Jason in action at Donington with his Martini. His helmet design paid homage to his father.

From early childhood Jason was a huge fan of the sport, in contrast to brother Amos, who was never interested. Jason was just three years and four months old when his father was killed, and inevitably has only the vaguest first hand memories.

"I sort of remember doing that photo shoot at Drayton Gardens, when we were playing with the toy cars. Otherwise I don't remember that much. My mum was really, really good. We always looked forward, and we were never in any situation where there was any sort of retrospective view on things, on what might have been. There was never any sadness about daddy not being around.

"But when I went to St Peter's School in Sussex, where my father went, I do remember being sad on occasions. I was in the lower bunk bed, and I remember crying myself to sleep sometimes with a photo of him next to me. I did actually miss him quite a lot. I'm very proud to have been his son. Everyone who knew him has always spoken so fondly about him."

As he grew older his enthusiasm for motor sport developed, with the encouragement of Frank Williams.

"When I went to Malvern College I was a real racing fan. I used to go to Frank's factory and fool around, and sometimes I stayed with him and Ginny. I travelled by coach and he used to pick me up at the Oxford services in his smart Jaguar XJS! I've got the nosecone off the car Carlos Reutemann won the 1981 Brazilian GP in…"

After leaving school Jason worked in Australia for two years, and on his return he decided it was time to have a go at motor racing.

"I was always terrified of discussing it with my mother! It was a touchy subject. I would have liked to have had encouragement, but she used to say, 'You're too tall to be a racing driver. I've spoken to Frank, and we both agree!'"

It's hardly surprising that someone who lost their first husband to motor racing didn't want their son to follow the same career. In fact Sally says her objections were not based on any concern that Jason might hurt himself.

"It was nothing to do with safety," she says. "I just wanted him to know the difficulties of making a living at it. Look at his father. I'd seen what we'd gone through, and you don't really want that to happen to your children, do you? The money, the anxiety, things like that. I didn't want him to be hurt by rejection and everything else. It's like modelling – you have to have a very thick hide to get through it. Anyway, he was determined. But Aspers was absolutely brilliant. He said, 'Even if he uses all his money, you've got to let him do it. If he doesn't do it, he'll resent you. You've got to let him go.'"

As a first step Jason went to a racing school run by Mike Knight, a sometime F3 rival of his father. His fellow pupils included future touring car star Jason Plato.

"I can't remember how it happened, but I heard about the Winfield Racing School at Magny-Cours, and I went

there in 1989. I was 22 by then, and I was old enough to do it myself. I wanted to be good at racing, and I was always conscious that I never wanted to damage my father's memory by doing badly. So I didn't want to fail."

With the help of Charlie Crichton-Stuart, Jason managed to extract a little unaccredited sponsorship from Frank. He bought a Martini Formula Renault car from Mike Knight, and competed in the British championship in 1990: "My best result was 10th at Snetterton, so it was never really that successful. But I didn't have any experience at all." Sally never came to a race, but did help him financially.

Towards the end of 1990 Jason heard of an opportunity for two young British drivers to compete in that winter's Formula Ford series in New Zealand. He applied, and got the job. The team bore the name of none other than Nigel Mansell, who had just left Ferrari to rejoin Williams.

"I met up with Nigel and Rosanne at the Conrad Hotel in November. He said, 'Oh yeah, I spoke to Frank about you.' The funny thing was he was wearing a tux with all these sparkly bits, and I thought he'd been out in the rain! And then I headed off to New Zealand."

Jason and his team-mate Jonathan Harmer travelled around together, and had the time of their lives. It was just like Piers and another Jonathan nearly three decades earlier.

"We did 12 races, two at each of six circuits. I met a lot of people who knew my father from the Tasman days, and we had a really great time. It was a very, very useful experience for me, because we were constantly either testing or racing. We took it very seriously. I didn't have any money for the following year, and the prize for winning the championship was a paid drive in Formula Renault. I was hoping to win, but I came fourth. I won one race at Bay Park, after protests were flying around and two guys got thrown out. But I really enjoyed it. When you're young it's the whole world to you, and it means more to you than anything else."

Despite his best efforts, Jason ran out of funds, and the racing career fizzled out.

"I put most of the money I inherited into racing. I was brought up by my stepfather, who had no value for money in itself, and threw everything he earned into what he loved doing. I grew up with that ethos. I had a test with Jackie and Paul Stewart with a view to driving their Vauxhall/Lotus in 1991, but I didn't have any money. I suppose I was always scared to approach my stepfather's friends for sponsorship, so I just did it by writing to companies.

"Eventually I had to go back and work in property, because I needed money just to live on a day to day basis. I could only afford a bike, so I bought a Suzuki GSXR750. I had three of those, and they were all stolen! I always had a special exhaust on them, which went almost straight through, so it was very loud. Initially it was to show off, but it was also to let people know that

I was coming, because they would just pull out and turn and didn't pay attention. I got my thrills for speed out of my bikes. I used to have a lot of frustration at not being able to race. I didn't drive dangerously on the road, just fast. In September 1995 my third one was stolen, so I bought a Honda 900CBR-R, and that was super quick, but it also had the best brakes of the time."

Jason's life was to change for ever on the evening of 15 October, just a few weeks after he bought the new machine.

"It was 8pm on a Monday night, and I'd just been to the gym. I was on the way to pick up my girlfriend in South Kensington, so I was going west where the Brompton Road becomes the Cromwell Road, doing about 35mph. Then a guy coming towards me did an illegal right turn in front of me to go south, just before I crossed Exhibition Road. I remember thinking, 'Christ, where did this guy come from?' And I don't remember anything else after that."

The driver was not from London, and unfamiliar with the local traffic rules. Jason had no chance to avoid him.

"I was pretty badly injured. I had a thoracic transection, which means I basically tore myself in half. My surgeon said I was one of two people to survive, in his recollection. I broke both shoulders, both collarbones, ten ribs, punctured both lungs. And I broke my spine. They had to put me into an induced coma, because otherwise it would have been too much of a shock to have me wake up immediately."

"I'll never forget it," Sally recalls. "John and I were at Mrs Thatcher's birthday party at Claridges. The Queen was there, and a lot of luminaries. A policeman went to our house, and Helena, who's worked for me since 1971, told him where we were. So they knew I was in there, and they even knew where I was sitting. But they didn't come and get me out, because they thought it might upset the party! So they waited outside until the end. Jason could have died during those two or three hours – I'll never forgive them for that. Before the coffee, John and I decided to sneak out by a side entrance, and we went home and went to bed. The telephone rang, and it was Helena, saying 'Where are you? I'm at the hospital. You must come here quickly – Jason's had an accident.' That's how we found out…

"It reminded me of Piers's accident, because at first there was no mention of the catastrophic situation I was going to find. I just thought he'd come off and bumped his head, or maybe had a broken arm or something. I didn't expect to find that my son was so near death. I could hardly comprehend it when I arrived there, and the doctor took me aside and told me what had happened."

Suddenly the newspapers were full of the Courage name, just as they had been in March 1966, when Piers and Sally got married, and in June 1970, after Zandvoort. As well as the obvious family connections, now boosted by the Aspinall name, the media made much of the fact that Jason was 28, the age his father was when he died.

"It was the most devastating thing that could have

Opposite top *Jason chats with Clay Regazzoni at Vallelunga. The Swiss driver made his Grand Prix debut in the race in which Piers was killed. Twenty seven years later he helped give Jason a chance to race again.*

Opposite bottom *Many who knew Piers comment on the resemblance between younger son Amos and his father. Amos is pictured here in 1998 with Massisa, one of the gorillas he worked with in the Congo.*

Above *Jason's accident attracted coverage in the national press.*

happened," says Sally. "I couldn't believe this could start up all over again, especially when we didn't know if he was going to live or die. Life never prepares you for this sort of thing, and it doesn't matter whether you've been through it before. In order to keep going, the shutter comes down, and then gradually you have a look and realise the enormity of what's happened."

As the weeks went by, so Jason came off the critical list. After over five months in hospital he was able to leave and begin the adjustment to a new life in a wheelchair. He spent some of his early recuperation in South Africa, before returning to a job in England some ten months after the accident. He refused to allow his injury to hold him back, and he was soon behind the wheel of a road car. Racing was the next logical step. He was inspired by Clay Regazzoni, paralysed in a crash at Long Beach in 1980, and long a pioneer of hand controls in motor sport.

"I thought, 'Wouldn't it be great to race with hand controls?' Clay had written to me in hospital, and in the summer of 1997 I went down to do a school that he was running at Vallelunga. We raced BMW 316s, or did time trials, and there were about 12 of us. It was like the Winfield School for wheelchair users! I actually won the championship. That was no great accolade, but I was the fastest of all the guys."

Jason was determined to get back to mainstream racing. He got his RAC licence, worked hard at raising sponsorship and generating media coverage, and carefully planned the budget he needed to contest the Renault Spider series. Everything was done with the thoroughness and attention to detail that was a trade mark of his father.

"We had the car converted by Clay's company in Italy. Unfortunately the controls were a pretty crappy design. Clay tested the car at Brands Hatch, when Tiff Needell also drove it for *Top Gear*, and said, 'How can you race with this?' My best result was a sixth at Donington. I didn't have enough money for the following year. I was 30 then, and I asked myself where I was going, really. Someone said to me, 'Shouldn't you be doing something about your career?' so I sort of stopped. But I would love to do it again."

In recent years Jason has completed a business degree in California, but he's still trying to find a career that gives him the sort of satisfaction he got from racing. He's had a couple of jobs with an F1 connection. For a while he attended Grands Prix working behind the scenes at Bernie Ecclestone's digital TV service, where his colleagues included Natascha Rindt, Jochen's daughter. In 2002 he attended several races on behalf of an aviation firm, trying to persuade Grand Prix drivers to buy flying time in private jets.

The previous year Jason visited Zandvoort for the first time, accompanying some friends who were competing in an historic event. In the pits he met the circuit commentator. It was Rob Petersen, who as a teenager had witnessed Piers's accident, and whose passion for motor sport history has, inevitably, included a special interest in Piers. He took Jason to the scene of the crash, long by-passed when the track was shortened. It was a moving experience for both men.

Despite his injury, Jason remains fiercely independent, living on his own and getting around with almost as much energy as he did before the accident. His south London flat is decorated with pictures of his father and

grandfather Earl Howe, including some of the prints that once hung in Piers's study.

"I'm immensely proud of my sons," says Sally. "Jason could have become an embittered old man, but he hasn't. He's a vibrant young man. What he has achieved since the accident is amazing."

His younger brother Amos followed his stepfather's love of animals. He grew up around Howletts and Port Lympne, Aspinall's two zoos in Kent.

"I guess I'm evidence of nurture over nature, whereas Jason is probably the opposite!" he says. "He's always been racing mad, although it never clicked with me at all. I've been working in Africa pretty much since I left university. That's where my heart lies. I grew up with animals around me, and I was lucky enough to travel and go abroad a lot with John, and it grew out of that. I worked for a documentary maker in Zaire, and spent four years in Congo. We have projects in Central Africa, which I run, and now I'm based out of Port Lympne, so I manage that as well. It's not just the wildlife, because I do like to travel. Maybe I inherited that from my dad!"

He modestly declines to point out that he was involved in some hair-raising situations while in Africa. He ran a gorilla orphanage in a Congo war zone, and before that, was in Rwanda.

"He went to hell and back," says Sally. "That was very much like his father, his determination to succeed and keep going. He was shot at, he was beaten up. Many people would have cracked and come home, but he didn't, and stayed for five years."

1966

Date	Event	Venue	Entrant	Car	Result and notes
23/1/66	Temporada F3	Buenos Aires	Charles Lucas Team Lotus	Lotus 35	Did not start, practice accident
02/4/66	Oulton Park F3	Oulton Park	Charles Lucas Team Lotus	Lotus 41	Race cancelled, qual 2nd
08/4/66	Les Leston Trophy F3	Snetterton	Charles Lucas Team Lotus	Lotus 41	Retired, overheating when 6th
11/4/66	Chichester Cup F3	Goodwood	Charles Lucas Team Lotus	Lotus 41	7th
17/4/66	Pau F3	Pau	Charles Lucas Team Lotus	Lotus 41	1st
24/4/66	Trofeo Juan Jover F3, Heat	Montjuich Park	Charles Lucas Team Lotus	Lotus 41	4th
24/4/66	Trofeo Juan Jover F3, Final	Montjuich Park	Charles Lucas Team Lotus	Lotus 41	5th, clutch failure
1/5/66	Vigorelli Trophy F3, Heat	Monza	Charles Lucas Team Lotus	Lotus 41	2nd to Irwin
1/5/66	Vigorelli Trophy F3, Final	Monza	Charles Lucas Team Lotus	Lotus 41	6th, misfire due to fuel vaporisation
08/5/66	Les Leston Trophy F3	Brands Hatch	Charles Lucas Team Lotus	Lotus 41	1st, PP, FL
14/5/66	Radio London Trophy F3	Silverstone	Charles Lucas Team Lotus	Lotus 41	Retired, oil pipe while leading
21/5/66	Monaco F3, Heat 2	Monte Carlo	Charles Lucas Team Lotus	Lotus 41	2nd to Irwin
21/5/66	Monaco F3, Final	Monte Carlo	Charles Lucas Team Lotus	Lotus 41	Retired, accident on lap 3 while leading
29/5/66	Les Leston Cup	Brands Hatch	Charles Lucas Team Lotus	Lotus 41	1st, FL (new record)
30/5/66	Bromley Bowl F3	Crystal Palace	Charles Lucas Team Lotus	Lotus 41	2nd to Irwin, shared FL (new record)
30/5/66	London Trophy F2, Heat 1	Crystal Palace	Ron Harris Team Lotus	Lotus 44	Retired, accident with Attwood
30/5/66	London Trophy F2, Heat 2	Crystal Palace	Ron Harris Team Lotus	Lotus 44	Did not start
18–19/6/66	Le Mans 24 Hours	Le Mans	Maranello Concessionaires	Ferrari 275GTB	8th, 1st GT class (w/Pike)
03/7/66	Coupe de Vitesse F3	Rheims	Charles Lucas Team Lotus	Lotus 41	3rd, GP support
10/7/66	Coupe de L'AC Normand F3	Rouen	Charles Lucas Team Lotus	Lotus 41	1st, FL (new record)
07/8/66	**German GP (F2)**	**Nürburgring**	**Ron Harris Team Lotus**	**Lotus 44**	**Retired, accident on lap 4**
13/8/66	Danish GP F3, Q/Heat 1	Roskildering	Charles Lucas Team Lotus	Lotus 41	Retired, spin
13/8/66	Danish GP F3, Q/Heat 2	Roskildering	Charles Lucas Team Lotus	Lotus 41	6th
14/8/66	Danish GP F3, Heat 1	Roskildering	Charles Lucas Team Lotus	Lotus 41	4th
14/8/66	Danish GP F3, Heat 2	Roskildering	Charles Lucas Team Lotus	Lotus 41	14th
14/8/66	Danish GP F3, Heat 3	Roskildering	Charles Lucas Team Lotus	Lotus 41	9th after spin (8th on aggregate)
21/8/66	Kanonloppet F3	Karlskoga	Charles Lucas Team Lotus	Lotus 41	2nd to Irwin, collided with Pike after flag
29/8/66	Brands Hatch F3	Brands Hatch	Charles Lucas Team Lotus	Lotus 41	1st, FL, wet race
04/9/66	Zandvoort F3	Zandvoort	Charles Lucas Team Lotus	Lotus 41	6th, second until rain
11/9/66	Coppa del Campioni F3, Heat	Enna	Charles Lucas Team Lotus	Lotus 41	6th
11/9/66	Coppa del Campioni F3, Final	Enna	Charles Lucas Team Lotus	Lotus 41	4th
18/9/66	Coupe de Vitesse F3	Le Mans Bugatti	Charles Lucas Team Lotus	Lotus 41	Retired, throttle cable
25/9/66	Coupe de Vitesse F3, Heat 1	Albi	Charles Lucas Team Lotus	Lotus 41	1st
25/9/66	Coupe de Vitesse F3, Heat 2	Albi	Charles Lucas Team Lotus	Lotus 41	1st , FL, (1st on aggregate)
02/10/66	European F3 Challenge, Heat 2	Brands Hatch	RAC (CLTL)	Lotus 41	Retired, oil leak
02/10/66	European F3 Challenge, Final	Brands Hatch	RAC (CLTL)	Lotus 41	2nd to Irwin

Notes: The Lotus 35 crashed in Argentina was 35-F-19. The Lotus 44 Piers used on 30/5 and 07/8 was chassis 44-F-2, with 1.6-litre Cosworth SCA engine. World Championship Grand Prix entries are in bold.

1967

Date	Event	Venue	Entrant	Car	Result and notes
02/1/67	**South African GP**	**Kyalami**	**Reg Parnell (Racing)**	**Lotus-BRM 25-R13**	**Retired, fuel leak lap 52**
28/1/67	Teretonga Intl Tasman, Heat 2	Teretonga	Owen Racing Organisation	BRM P261-6	4th
28/1/67	Teretonga Intl Tasman, Final	Teretonga	Owen Racing Organisation	BRM P261-6	Retired, engine, spin first lap
12/2/67	Lakeside Intl Tasman	Lakeside	Owen Racing Organisation	BRM P261-4	Retired, gearbox
12/3/67	Race of Champions F1	Brands Hatch	Charles Lucas Engineering	Lotus-Martin 35	Did not start, engine
24/3/67	Guards 100 F2, Heat 1	Snetterton	John Coombs	McLaren M4A-2	7th
24/3/67	Guards 100 F2, Heat 2	Snetterton	John Coombs	McLaren M4A-2	Retired, misfire, classified 11th
24/3/67	Guards 100 F2, Final	Snetterton	John Coombs	McLaren M4A-2	7th
27/3/67	BARC 200 F2, Heat 1	Silverstone	John Coombs	McLaren M4A-2	7th, collision with Hulme
27/3/67	BARC 200 F2, Heat 2	Silverstone	John Coombs	McLaren M4A-2	Retired, metering unit
02/4/67	Pau GP F2	Pau	John Coombs	McLaren M4A-2	Did not start, practice accident
15/4/67	Spring Trophy F1, Heat 1	Oulton Park	Reg Parnell (Racing)	Lotus-BRM 25-R13	7th
15/4/67	Spring Trophy F1, Heat 2	Oulton Park	Reg Parnell (Racing)	Lotus-BRM 25-R13	Retired, oil leak, classified 8th
15/4/67	Spring Trophy F1, Final	Oulton Park	Reg Parnell (Racing)	Lotus-BRM 25-R13	Retired, engine
23/4/67	ADAC Eifelrennen F2	Nürburgring Sud	John Coombs	McLaren M4A-2	5th
07/5/67	**Monaco GP**	**Monte Carlo**	**Reg Parnell (Racing)**	**BRM P261-6**	**Retired, spun and stalled lap 65**
29/5/67	London Trophy F2, Heat 2	Crystal Palace	John Coombs	McLaren M4A-2	3rd
29/5/67	London Trophy F2, Final	Crystal Palace	John Coombs	McLaren M4A-2	5th
10–11/6/67	Le Mans 24 Hours	Le Mans	Maranello Concessionaires	Ferrari 412P	Retired, engine (w/Attwood)
25/6/67	Rheims GP F2	Rheims	John Coombs	McLaren M4A-2	Retired, engine seized
09/7/67	Deutschland Trophy F2, Heat 1	Hockenheim	John Coombs	McLaren M4A-2	3rd
09/7/67	Deutschland Trophy F2, Heat 2	Hockenheim	John Coombs	McLaren M4A-2	4th after spin (3rd on aggregate)
15/7/67	**British GP**	**Silverstone**	**Reg Parnell (Racing)**	**BRM P261-6**	**Did not start, car given to Irwin**
16/7/67	OAMTC Flugplatzrennen F2	Tulln-Langenlebarn	John Coombs	McLaren M4A-2	9th
23/7/67	Madrid GP F2	Jarama	John Coombs	McLaren M4A-2	8th, lost clutch
30/7/67	Zandvoort GP F2, Heat	Zandvoort	John Coombs	McLaren M4A-2	5th, slow puncture
30/7/67	Zandvoort GP F2, Final	Zandvoort	John Coombs	McLaren M4A-2	2nd to Ickx
20/8/67	Mediterranean GP F2, Heat 1	Enna	John Coombs	McLaren M4A-2	Retired, accident
20/8/67	Mediterranean GP F2, Heat 2	Enna	John Coombs	McLaren M4A-2	Retired, misfire
28/8/67	Guards Trophy F2, Heat 2	Brands Hatch	John Coombs	McLaren M4A-2	3rd
28/8/67	Guards Trophy F2, Final	Brands Hatch	John Coombs	McLaren M4A-2	Retired, accident
24/9/67	Albi GP F2	Albi	John Coombs	McLaren M4A-2	10th, five laps down, pit stop battery
08/10/67	Rome GP F2, Heat 1	Vallelunga	John Coombs	McLaren M4A-2	Retired, engine when sixth
08/10/67	Rome GP F2, Heat 2	Vallelunga	John Coombs	McLaren M4A-2	Did not start, engine
29/10/67	Motor Show 200 F3, Heat	Brands Hatch	Frank Williams	Brabham BT21B	1st
29/10/67	Motor Show 200 F3, Final	Brands Hatch	Frank Williams	Brabham BT21B	Did not start, electrics on warm-up lap

World Championship: No points
Tasman Championship: No points
European F2 Championship: 4th, 24 points

Notes: 2.0 and 2.5-litre BRM V8 used in F1 and Tasman races. 3.0-litre Martin V8 used in Race of Champions. 1.6-litre Cosworth FVA used in F2 races. Although Piers's McLaren retained the chassis number M4A-2 throughout the season, it was substantially rebuilt after Pau, and certainly received a new tub after the crash at Brands Hatch on 28/8/67. The original lay in the McLaren factory for some time until Bruce McLaren gave it to Howden Ganley, who subsequently built it up as a 'Bitza'! The Lotus 25 chassis R13 that Piers drove early in the season is also sometimes recorded as a 33. The Lotus 35 he drove in practice at the Race of Champions was 35-F-19, rebuilt as an F1 car after its crash in Buenos Aires in January 1966.

1968

Date	Event	Venue	Entrant	Car	Result and notes
06/1/68	New Zealand GP Tasman	Pukehohe	Piers Courage	McLaren M4A-2	3rd
13/1/68	Rothmans Intl Tasman, Heat 1	Levin	Piers Courage	McLaren M4A-2	5th
13/1/68	Rothmans Intl Tasman, Final	Levin	Piers Courage	McLaren M4A-2	2nd to Amon
20/1/68	Lady Wigram Trophy Tasman, Heat 2	Lady Wigram	Piers Courage	McLaren M4A-2	5th
20/1/68	Lady Wigram Trophy Tasman, Final	Lady Wigram	Piers Courage	McLaren M4A-2	4th
27/1/68	Teretonga Tasman, Heat 1	Teretonga	Piers Courage	McLaren M4A-2	2nd
27/1/68	Teretonga Tasman, Final	Teretonga	Piers Courage	McLaren M4A-2	5th
11/2/68	Rothmans 100 Tasman, Heat	Surfers' Paradise	Piers Courage	McLaren M4A-2	4th
11/2/68	Rothmans 100 Tasman, Final	Surfers' Paradise	Piers Courage	McLaren M4A-2	3rd
18/2/68	Warwick Farm Tasman	Warwick Farm	Piers Courage	McLaren M4A-2	3rd
25/2/68	Australian GP Tasman	Sandown Park	Piers Courage	McLaren M4A-2	5th
02/3/68	South Pacific Trophy Tasman, Heat	Longford	Piers Courage	McLaren M4A-2	Retired, accident on oil
04/3/68	South Pacific Trophy Tasman	Longford	Piers Courage	McLaren M4A-2	1st
31/3/68	Barcelona GP F2	Montjuich Park	Frank Williams	Brabham BT23C-7	4th
07/4/68	Deutschland Trophy F2, Heat 1	Hockenheim	Frank Williams	Brabham BT23C-7	5th, Jim Clark killed
07/4/68	Deutschland Trophy F2, Heat 2	Hockenheim	Frank Williams	Brabham BT23C-7	2nd (3rd on aggregate
15/4/68	BARC 200 F2, Heat 2	Thruxton	Frank Williams	Brabham BT23C-7	2nd to Rindt
15/4/68	BARC 200 F2, Final	Thruxton	Frank Williams	Brabham BT23C-7	Retired, holed radiator, led race
21/4/68	ADAC Eifelrennen F2	Nürburgring Sud	Frank Williams	Brabham BT23C-7	Retired, stalled in pits after black flag, led race
27/4/68	International Trophy	Silverstone	Reg Parnell (Racing)	BRM P126-1	5th
28/4/68	Madrid GP F2	Jarama	Frank Williams	Brabham BT23C-7	Did not start, practice accident
05/5/68	Limbourg GP F2, Heat 1	Zolder	Frank Williams	Brabham BT23C-7	Retired, accident
05/5/68	Limbourg GP F2, Heat 2	Zolder	Frank Williams	Brabham BT23C-7	Did not start, damage
12/5/68	**Spanish GP**	**Jarama**	**Reg Parnell (Racing)**	**BRM P126-1**	**Retired, metering unit lap 53**
26/5/68	**Monaco GP**	**Monte Carlo**	**Reg Parnell (Racing)**	**BRM P126-1**	**Retired, broken chassis lap 13**
03/6/68	London Trophy F2, Heat 1	Crystal Palace	Frank Williams	Brabham BT23C-7	2nd to Rindt
03/6/68	London Trophy F2, Final	Crystal Palace	Frank Williams	Brabham BT23C-7	Retired, injection nozzle, classified 8th
09/6/68	**Belgian GP**	**Spa**	**Reg Parnell (Racing)**	**BRM P126-1**	**Retired, engine lap 23, while 4th**
16/6/68	Rhine Cup F2	Hockenheim	Frank Williams	BRM BT23C-7	7th
23/6/68	**Dutch GP**	**Zandvoort**	**Reg Parnell (Racing)**	**BRM P126-1**	**Retired, accident in rain lap 51**
07/7/68	**French GP**	**Rouen**	**Reg Parnell (Racing)**	**BRM P126-1**	**6th, pit stop loose fuel tank, tyre change**
14/7/68	OAMTC Flugplatzrennen F2, Heat 1	Tulln-Langenlebarn	Frank Williams	Brabham BT23C-7	Retired, overheating
14/7/68	OAMTC Flugplatzrennen F2, Heat 2	Tulln-Langenlebarn	Frank Williams	Brabham BT23C-7	Retired, overheating
20/7/68	**British GP**	**Brands Hatch**	**Reg Parnell (Racing)**	**BRM P126-1**	**8th, pit stops misfire**
28/7/68	Zandvoort GP F2, Heat 2	Zandvoort	Frank Williams	Brabham BT23C-7	1st
28/7/68	Zandvoort GP F2, Final	Zandvoort	Frank Williams	Brabham BT23C-7	Retired, accident/brakes
04/8/68	**German GP**	**Nürburgring**	**Reg Parnell (Racing)**	**BRM P126-1**	**8th**
17/8/68	Gold Cup F1	Oulton Park	Reg Parnell (Racing)	BRM P126-1	Retired, suspension
25/8/68	Mediterranean GP F2	Enna	Frank Williams	Brabham BT23C-7	2nd to Rindt
08/9/68	**Italian GP**	**Monza**	**Reg Parnell (Racing)**	**BRM P126-1**	**4th**

15/9/68	Trophees de France F2	Rheims	Frank Williams	Brabham BT23C-7	3rd
22/9/68	**Canadian GP**	**St Jovite**	**Reg Parnell (Racing)**	**BRM P126-1**	**Retired, transmission lap 23**
06/10/68	**US GP**	**Watkins Glen**	**Reg Parnell (Racing)**	**BRM P126-1**	**Retired, suspension lap 94, classified 7th**
20/10/68	Albi GP F2	Albi	Frank Williams	Brabham BT23C-1	3rd
03/11/68	**Mexican GP**	**Mexico City**	**Reg Parnell (Racing)**	**BRM P126-1**	**Retired, overheating lap 26**
01/12/68	Temporada F2	Buenos Aires	Frank Williams	Brabham BT23C-1	Retired, wing mount
08/12/68	Temporada F2	Cordoba	Frank Williams	Brabham BT23C-1	6th, FL
15/12/68	Temporada F2	San Juan	Frank Williams	Brabham BT23C-1	Retired, engine
22/12/68	Temporada F2, Heat 1	Buenos Aires	Frank Williams	Brabham BT23C-1	4th
22/12/68	Temporada F2, Heat 2	Buenos Aires	Frank Williams	Brabham BT23C-1	1st (1st overall)

World Championship: 19th, 4 points
Tasman Championship: 3rd, 34 points
European F2 Championship: 6th=, 13 points

Notes: 1.6-litre Cosworth FVA engine used in all Tasman and F2 races. 3-litre BRM V12 used in F1 races.

1969

Date	Event	Venue	Entrant	Car	Result and notes
04/1/69	New Zealand GP Tasman	Pukehohe	Frank Williams	Brabham BT24W-3	3rd
11/1/69	Rothmans Intl Tasman, Heat 1	Levin	Frank Williams	Brabham BT24W-3	Retired, oil leak
11/1/69	Rothmans Intl Tasman, Final	Levin	Frank Williams	Brabham BT24W-3	2nd
18/1/69	Lady Wigram Trophy Tasman, Heat 2	Lady Wigram	Frank Williams	Brabham BT24W-3	4th
18/1/69	Lady Wigram Trophy Tasman, Final	Lady Wigram	Frank Williams	Brabham BT24W-3	4th
26/1/69	Rothmans Intl Tasman, Heat 1	Teretonga	Frank Williams	Brabham BT24W-3	2nd
26/1/69	Rothmans Intl Tasman, Final	Teretonga	Frank Williams	Brabham BT24W-3	1st, FL
02/2/69	Australian GP Tasman	Lakeside	Frank Williams	Brabham BT24W-3	Retired, collision with Hill
09/2/69	Tasman International 100	Warwick Farm	Frank Williams	Brabham BT24W-3	Retired, collision with Amon in rain
16/2/69	Sandown Park Intl Tasman	Sandown Park	Frank Williams	Brabham BT24W-3	Retired, broken driveshaft
16/3/69	Race of Champions F1	Brands Hatch	Frank Williams	Brabham BT26-1	Retired, fuel leak lap 16
30/3/69	International Trophy F1	Silverstone	Frank Williams	Brabham BT26-1	5th
07/4/69	BARC 200 F2, Heat 2	Thruxton	Frank Williams	Brabham BT23C-16	1st
07/4/69	BARC 200 F2, Final	Thruxton	Frank Williams	Brabham BT23C-16	7th, pit stop puncture
13/4/69	Deutschland Trophy F2, Heat 1	Hockenheim	Frank Williams	Brabham BT23C-16	5th
13/4/69	Deutschland Trophy F2, Heat 2	Hockenheim	Frank Williams	Brabham BT23C-16	3rd (3rd on aggregate)
20/4/69	Pau GP F2	Pau	Frank Williams	Brabham BT23C-16	3rd
04/5/69	**Spanish GP**	**Montjuich Park**	**Frank Williams**	**Brabham BT26-1**	**Retired, engine lap 19, stalled on grid**
11/5/69	Madrid GP F2	Jarama	Frank Williams	Brabham BT23C-16	3rd, lost third gear
18/5/69	**Monaco GP**	**Monte Carlo**	**Frank Williams**	**Brabham BT26-1**	**2nd to Rindt, official 'FL'**
08/6/69	Limbourg GP F2	Zolder	Frank Williams	Brabham BT30-5	3rd
14–15/6/69	Le Mans 24 Hours	Le Mans	Equipe Matra Elf	Matra 650	4th (w/Beltoise)
21/6/69	**Dutch GP**	**Zandvoort**	**Frank Williams**	**Brabham BT26-1**	**Retired, clutch lap 13**
29/6/69	Rheims GP F2	Rheims	Frank Williams	Brabham BT30-5	3rd, FL (record), 0.2s behind winner
06/7/69	**French GP**	**Clermont-Ferrand**	**Frank Williams**	**Brabham BT26-1**	**Retired, broken nose mountings lap 22**
19/7/69	**British GP**	**Silverstone**	**Frank Williams**	**Brabham BT26-1**	**5th**
03/8/69	**German GP**	**Nürburgring**	**Frank Williams**	**Brabham BT26-1**	**Retired, accident lap 2**

Date	Event	Venue	Entrant	Car	Result and notes
24/8/69	Mediterranean GP F2, Heat 1	Enna	Frank Williams	Brabham BT30-5	1st
24/8/69	Mediterranean GP F2, Heat 2	Enna	Frank Williams	Brabham BT30-5	1st (1st on aggregate)
07/9/69	**Italian GP**	**Monza**	**Frank Williams**	**Brabham BT26-1**	**5th, led race, misfire**
14/9/69	Albi GP F2	Albi	Frank Williams	Brabham BT30-5	Retired, broken fuel line
20/9/69	**Canadian GP**	**Mosport**	**Frank Williams**	**Brabham BT26-1**	**Retired, fuel leak lap 14**
05/10/69	**US GP**	**Watkins Glen**	**Frank Williams**	**Brabham BT26-1**	**2nd to Rindt**
12/10/69	Rome GP F2, Heat 1	Vallelunga	Frank Williams	De Tomaso 103-101	3rd, cramped cockpit, spin
12/10/69	Rome GP F2, Heat 2	Vallelunga	Frank Williams	De Tomaso 103-101	Retired, ignition
19/10/69	**Mexican GP**	**Mexico City**	**Frank Williams**	**Brabham BT26-1**	**10th, handling problems**

World Championship: 8th, 16 points
Tasman Championship: 3rd, 22 points
European F2 Championship: Graded driver, not eligible for points

Notes: 2.5-litre Cosworth DFW used in Tasman Series. 3.0-litre Cosworth DFV used in F1 races. 1.6-litre Cosworth FVA used in F2 races. The Brabham BT26 was substantially reworked after Piers's crash in the German GP.

1970

Date	Event	Venue	Entrant	Car	Result and notes
11/1/70	Buenos Aires 1000kms	Buenos Aires	Autodelta	Alfa Romeo T33/3	6th, 11 laps down (w/de Adamich)
18/1/70	Buenos Aires 200, Heat 1	Buenos Aires	Autodelta	Alfa Romeo T33/3	1st, FL, PP (1st on aggregate, w/de Adamich)
07/3/70	**South African GP**	**Kyalami**	**Frank Williams**	**De Tomaso 505-381**	**Retired, suspension failure**
21/3/70	Sebring 12 Hours	Sebring	Autodelta	Alfa Romeo T33/3	8th, 17 laps down, distributor change (w/de Adamich)
12/4/70	BOAC 1000kms	Brands Hatch	Autodelta	Alfa Romeo T33/3	Retired, accident (w/de Adamich)
19/4/70	**Spanish GP**	**Jarama**	**Frank Williams**	**De Tomaso 505-381**	**Did not start, practice accident practice**
25/4/70	Monza 1000kms	Monza	Autodelta	Alfa Romeo T33/3	13th, 16 laps down, accident (w/de Adamich)
26/4/70	International Trophy, Heat 1	Silverstone	Frank Williams	De Tomaso 505	3rd, from back of grid
26/4/70	International Trophy, Heat 2	Silverstone	Frank Williams	De Tomaso 505	3rd, as above, (3rd on aggregate)
03/5/70	Targa Florio	Circuit Madonie	Autodelta	Alfa Romeo T33/3	Retired, accident (w/de Adamich)
10/5/70	**Monaco GP**	**Monte Carlo**	**Frank Williams**	**De Tomaso 505-382**	**Not classified, pit stop due to steering failure**
24/5/70	BEA Trophy	Brands Hatch	Ford Motor Co	Ford Capri 3000 GT	1st
31/5/70	ADAC Nürburgring 1000kms	Nürburgring	Autodelta	Alfa Romeo T33/3	Retired, suspension failure (w/Stommelen)
07/6/70	**Belgian GP**	**Spa**	**Frank Williams**	**De Tomaso 505-383**	**Retired, engine**
13–14/6/70	Le Mans 24 Hours	Le Mans	Autodelta	Alfa Romeo T33/3	Retired, engine (w/de Adamich)
21/6/70	**Dutch GP**	**Zandvoort**	**Frank Williams**	**De Tomaso 505-382**	**Retired, fatal accident on lap 23**

World Championship: No points

Notes: 3.0-litre Cosworth DFV used in F1 races. 3.0-litre Alfa V8 used in sportscar races. De Tomaso 505-38/2 also used in practice in Belgian GP. 38/3 was rebuilt version of 38/1. Piers did not drive in practice for the International Trophy, but the car was shaken down by both Roy Pike and Jackie Stewart. The Buenos Aires 200 was held over two heats, with Piers contesting the first and de Adamich the second.

Index